Revision Guide

Cambridge International AS and A Level

Computing

Tony Piper

CAMBRIDGE
UNIVERSITY PRESS

4381/4 Ansari Road, Daryaganj, Delhi 110002, India

Cambridge University Press is part of the University of Cambridge.

It furthers the University's mission by disseminating knowledge in the pursuit of education, learning and research at the highest international levels of excellence.

www.cambridge.org
Information on this title: www.cambridge.org/9781107690554

First published 2014

Printed in India by Shree Maitrey Printech Pvt. Ltd., Noida

A catalogue record for this publication is available from the British Library

ISBN 978-1-107-69055-4 Paperback

....

....

....

Every effort has been made to trace the owners of copyright material included in this book. The publishers would be grateful for any omissions brought to their notice for acknowledgement in future editions of the book.

Contents

iv   **Contents**

Revision Guidelines

Revision by the nature of the word implies that this is re-visiting the content and topics that you have studied throughout the year. What you already have in terms of resources to help you with your revision will largely determine the way in which you set about and plan your revision program.

Key issues include:

- ✓ Have you got a copy of the textbook you have followed throughout your course?
- ✓ Did you use it as your course progressed to make your own notes?
- ✓ Has your teacher provided you with notes as each topic has been covered?
- ✓ Have you worked through worksheets prepared by your teacher?

All of these are a good starting point and your first revision task is to gather together all the materials you have produced and accumulated throughout the course. Organise them in the same way as the syllabus you are revising for.

When should I start revising?

As early as possible. Examinations are generally a stressful time and so you need to do everything possible to make this a 'stress free' experience.

A trawl through all the materials you have should establish:

- ✓ What topics you have clear notes for and where you do not
- ✓ Topics where you can do lots of practice, for example, the number systems content in section 3.4
- ✓ Topics which you are definitely confident about and those that you are not.

All questions must be answered in the exam

You must not have large gaps in your understanding and skills to apply this knowledge. Both are important. The trend generally for all advanced level examinations is away from questions which only ask you to reproduce basic knowledge, for example reproducing a basic definition. For a question about database design this could be 'State what is meant by a primary key and a foreign key'. However, a much better assessment of your ability will be if you are able to apply this to a given simple practical scenario. The question you are more likely to face is – 'Which attribute would be the primary key for table X' – 'How is the relationship formed using a foreign key to table Y'.

Computing is a practical based subject – probably second only to engineering – and so it is reasonable that your computing examination papers should reflect this with questions that require answers which apply your knowledge in the context of practical scenarios.

Past examination paper questions

Looking at as many previous questions as possible can be a very valuable part of revision. Many examples from Cambridge past papers have been carefully selected and included at the end of each section in the course textbook.

> **Note**
>
> Cambridge International Examinations bears no responsibility for the example answers to questions taken from its past question papers which are contained in this publication.

Your teacher will be able to supply you with further past papers and specimen papers and guide you to relevant questions for the syllabus you are following.

So, you've trawled through and organised the materials you have produced throughout the course – what next?

Specific Revision Materials

Cambridge International AS and A Level Computing Revision Guide

This is a new book from Cambridge University Press. The organisation is identical to the course textbook and has frequent 'test yourself' questions as you work through each section.

Revision cards

These are a favourite with students and have the obvious advantage that you can carry them around with you and dip into them in any odd five minutes you can find. Cards are available in different colours and so you could easily develop a system to code cards on the same general topic in the same colour. See the example for Chapter 22 on Databases which follows.

How will you organise the cards?

✓   Separate sets for each section
✓   Separate sets for each topic

Database design

Attribute – Data item recorded as part of a database design.
Entity – In database design, something about which we record data, for example, a Customer. Entities are implemented as tables.
Primary key – An attribute (or combination of attributes) chosen to ensure that all the records in a table are unique.
Secondary key – An attribute for which an *index* has been created other than the primary key.
Relationship – A link between two tables.
Can be:

• One-to-one – which are uncommon
• One-to-many – the most common
• Many-to-many – which cannot be implemented with relational database software.

Foreign key – An attribute in a table which links back to the same primary key attribute in a second table.
See also cards:
• Normalisation
• Flat files versus Databases and Database Management Systems
• Data Definition Language (DDL) and Data Manipulation Language (DML)

Section 3 of the Cambridge syllabus requires that you are also familiar with related topics studied in Section 1. You could devise a system to quickly reference cards to each other where some of the cards have content which was first studied in Section 1 are referenced easily?

Mind mapping

Mind maps provide an effective way to break the content down into manageable amounts and if you are a person who 'thinks visually' then you will probably take to mind mapping. My experience is that students tend to be polarised into 'I like using them' or 'I hate them' but I have found that students do agree they are a useful revision tool. A simple example is shown for (some of) the database content for Chapter 22.

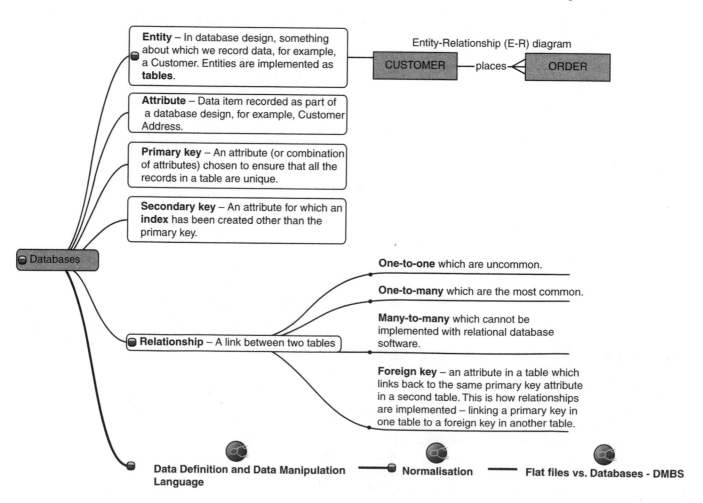

Also there is available on the World Wide Web free mind mapping software and this usually has features which are very appropriate for revision:

- ✓ The expansion (for the detail) and collapsing (to see the 'big picture') of branches
- ✓ The inclusion of graphics.

How do I revise?

What time of day?

There are all sorts of conflicting evidence about when your brain is at its most receptive! You will need to decide what time of day seems to work best for you and how long each session should be.

Shall I revise on my own?

Maybe, but it will be much less daunting if you team up with a fellow student – a 'revision buddy' – and revise together. This could include:

- ✓ Share the work of producing the revision cards and/or the mind maps
- ✓ Test each other on some basic definitions and the factual knowledge of a topic.

Do lots of past examination questions

But consider carefully what 'doing examination questions' actually means for you. It is tempting to look at a question then, talking to yourself recite the answer you would give – then move on to another question. That might be sufficient, but remember the examination is a *written* paper and so why not spend the extra time in writing out the answer on rough paper? That way when you read it back it may be clear that there are some points which you have omitted or some points where the meaning when reading it back is unclear.

Seek advice

You need to be confident with all the syllabus content (remember there is no choice of questions) so don't try to bury problems and topic areas where you are unsure. Your revision buddy may be confident about it and after five minutes of him/her talking it through, something about which you have been unclear for six months, becomes clear for the first time. Failing that, be honest that you are unsure and seek help from your teacher. Problems will not go away and solve themselves – you must be pro-active in plugging the gaps in your understanding.

On the day – Examination technique

Reading the paper

It is sensible to read the entire paper before you start to attempt any of the questions. This will give you a good idea as to the questions you are confident about and those which may need more time spent on them.

The number of marks is a good indicator of the time the examiner expects you to take. For example, if a paper has a total of 90 marks and 2 hours to complete every three marks should take 4 minutes – or a ten mark question should take around 13 minutes.

Layout of the paper

All papers have the questions displayed in the answer booklet so the amount of space provided is an indicator of the length of answer the examiner is expecting.

Is it important to answer the questions in a paper in order? You do not need to answer the questions in order. As a general rule questions which are considered less demanding will be at the start of the paper.

Question keywords

Some questions will have a short introduction and this will apply to all parts of the questions which follow. Specific questions will each have a keyword which is the indicator as to the style of answer expected.

'Define ...' – 'State ...' – 'Give ...' all require an answer of only one or only a few words giving a short and concise answer. For example: Give the attributes for the Loan table below, showing the primary key.

You should **not** create a LoanID for this table.
Loan (........., ..., ..., ...)

(2 marks)

'Describe ...' now wants more detail and the indicator of precisely how much is the number of marks for the question; a three mark question will usually require three different points to be made. For example 'Describe how an assembly language program is translated into machine code'.

'Explain ...' now wants not only a description but the answer will contain some reasoning. For example: 'Explain why an interpreter has better diagnostics features than compiler software'.

The following question – taken from a Cambridge past-paper illustrates many of these points.

Question from a Cambridge past-paper

1. (a) State what is meant by a real-time application.

   ....

   ....

   ....

> There is no introductory statement. The keyword is 'State' and what is wanted is the basis 'bookwork' definition of a real-time system.

   .... [1]

   (b) An air conditioning system is a real-time application.
   Explain how sensors and actuators are used to control an air conditioning system in an apartment.

   ....

   ....

   ....

   ....

> The introductory statement applies to part (b) only. The keyword is 'Explain' and there are four marks. The answer must make at least four clear points describing how temperature sensors send data values to the processor – how they are processed – when an actuator is involved.

   ....

   ....

   .... [4]

   (c) Give *one other* example of a real-time application. Justify why your choice is a real-time application.
   Example...

   Justification...

> Keyword is 'Give' but you are having to be more resourceful and come up with your own example of a real-time system. The key requirements are the example and its justification and the paper makes it clear how you are to present this. You can assume there will be one mark for the example and the second mark for the justification.

   ....

   ....

   .... [2]

Cambridge 9691 Paper 31 Q4 June 2011

Acknowledgement

The following is reproduced by permission of Cambridge International Examinations:

Syllabus Name and Code	Paper and Question Number	Month/Year	Chapter/Page in Book
Cambridge International AS and A Level Computing 9691	Paper 31 Q4	June 2011	Revision Guidelines, Page X
Cambridge International AS and A Level Computing 9691	Paper 11 Q1(a)	June 2011	Chapter 1 Page 6
Cambridge International AS and A Level Computing 9691	Paper 11 Q1(a) & (b)	November 2011	Chapter 1 Page 6
Cambridge International AS and A Level Computing 9691	Paper 11 Q1(b)	June 2012	Chapter 1 Page 6
Cambridge International AS and A Level Computing 9691	Specimen Paper 1 Q1		Chapter 2 Page 14
Cambridge International AS and A Level Computing 9691	Paper 1 Q5	June 2009	Chapter 2 Page 15
Cambridge International AS and A Level Computing 9691	Paper 11 Q3	June 2011	Chapter 3 Page 25
Cambridge International AS and A Level Computing 9691	Paper 11 Q5	November 2011	Chapter 3 Page 26
Cambridge International AS and A Level Computing 9691	Paper 11 Q7(b)(ii)	November 2011	Chapter 3 Page 26
Cambridge International AS and A Level Computing 9691	Paper 13 Q5	June 2011	Chapter 4 Page 36
Cambridge International AS and A Level Computing 9691	Paper 12 Q1(b)	November 2011	Chapter 4 Page 36
Cambridge International AS and A Level Computing 9691	Paper 12 Q6	November 2011	Chapter 4 Page 36
Cambridge International AS and A Level Computing 9691	Paper 12 Q7(b)	November 2011	Chapter 4 Page 36
Cambridge International AS and A Level Computing 9691	Specimen Paper 1 Q8		Chapter 5 Page 46
Cambridge International AS and A Level Computing 9691	Paper 11 Q8	June 2011	Chapter 5 Page 46
Cambridge International AS and A Level Computing 9691	Paper 11 Q8	November 2011	Chapter 5 Page 47
Cambridge International AS and A Level Computing 9691	Paper 11 Q1(b) & (c)	June 2011	Chapter 5 Page 47
Cambridge International AS and A Level Computing 9691	Paper 11 Q2	June 2011	Chapter 6 Page 57
Cambridge International AS and A Level Computing 9691	Paper 11 Q2	November 2011	Chapter 6 Page 58

(Continued)

Syllabus Name and Code	Paper and Question Number	Month/Year	Chapter/Page in Book
Cambridge International AS and A Level Computing 9691	Paper 11 Q5	June 2012	Chapter 6 Page 58
Cambridge International AS and A Level Computing 9691	Paper 11 Q8	November 2010	Chapter 6 Page 58
Cambridge International AS and A Level Computing 9691	Paper 11 Q1(d)	June 2011	Chapter 7 Page 66
Cambridge International AS and A Level Computing 9691	Paper 11 Q2(a) & (b)	June 2012	Chapter 7 Page 66
Cambridge International AS and A Level Computing 9691	Specimen Paper 1 Q5		Chapter 8 Page 73
Cambridge International AS and A Level Computing 9691	Paper 11 Q4	November 2011	Chapter 8 Page 73
Cambridge International AS and A Level Computing 9691	Paper 11 Q1(b) & (c)	June 2011	Chapter 8 Page 73
Cambridge International AS and A Level Computing 9691	Specimen Paper 1 Q4(c)		Chapter 9 Page 77
Cambridge International AS and A Level Computing 9691	Paper 11 Q7	June 2011	Chapter 9 Page 78
Cambridge International AS and A Level Computing 9691	Paper 11 Q3	November 2011	Chapter 9 Page 78
Cambridge International AS and A Level Computing 9691	Paper 11 Q7 (a)(i)	November 2011	Chapter 9 Page 78
Cambridge International AS and A Level Computing 9691	Specimen Paper 1 Q7		Chapter 10 Page 82
Cambridge International AS and A Level Computing 9691	Paper 11 Q9(b)	June 2012	Chapter 10 Page 82
Cambridge International AS and A Level Computing 9691	Paper 13 Q6	June 2011	Chapter 10 Page 82
Cambridge International AS and A Level Computing 9691	Paper 12 Q9	November 2011	Chapter 10 Page 83
Cambridge International AS and A Level Computing 9691	Specimen Paper 2 Q1(b) (c) & (d)		Chapter 13 Page 110
Cambridge International AS and A Level Computing 9691	Paper 13 Q9	June 2010	Chapter 13 Page 110
Cambridge International AS and A Level Computing 9691	Paper 21 Q1(a) (b) & (c)	June 2012	Section 2 Page 127
Cambridge International AS and A Level Computing 9691	Paper 21 Q2	November 2011	Section 2 Page 130
Cambridge International AS and A Level Computing 9691	Paper 23 Q4	June 2011	Section 2 Page 130
Cambridge International AS and A Level Computing 9691	Paper 22 Q2	November 2011	Section 2 Page 132
Cambridge International AS and A Level Computing 9691	Paper 23 Q3(a) (c) (d) (e) & (f)	November 2011	Section 2 Page 133
Cambridge International AS and A Level Computing 9691	Specimen Paper 2 Q3		Section 2 Page 135
Cambridge International AS and A Level Computing 9691	Paper 21 Q3	June 2012	Section 2 Page 136

Syllabus Name and Code	Paper and Question Number	Month/Year	Chapter/Page in Book
Cambridge International AS and A Level Computing 9691	Paper 31 Q1	November 2011	Chapter 17 Page 144
Cambridge International AS and A Level Computing 9691	Paper 31 Q5	June 2011	Chapter 17 Page 144
Cambridge International AS and A Level Computing 9691	Paper 33 Q8	November 2011	Chapter 17 Page 144
Cambridge International AS and A Level Computing 9691	Specimen Paper 3 Q3(a) & (b)		Chapter 18 Page 152
Cambridge International AS and A Level Computing 9691	Paper 31 Q4	November 2010	Chapter 18 Page 153
Cambridge International AS and A Level Computing 9691	Paper 33 Q2(a)	June 2011	Chapter 18 Page 153
Cambridge International AS and A Level Computing 9691	Paper 31 Q9	November 2011	Chapter 18 Page 153
Cambridge International AS and A Level Computing 9691	Paper 32 Q11(b)	June 2011	Chapter 19 Page 157
Cambridge International AS and A Level Computing 9691	Paper 32 Q3(b) (i) & (ii)	November 2010	Chapter 19 Page 158
Cambridge International AS and A Level Computing 9691	Paper 31 Q2	November 2011	Chapter 19 Page 158
Cambridge International AS and A Level Computing 9691	Specimen Paper 3 Q5		Chapter 20 Page 176
Cambridge International AS and A Level Computing 9691	Paper 32 Q2(a) (b) & (c)	June 2012	Chapter 20 Page 177
Cambridge International AS and A Level Computing 9691	Paper 31 Q7	June 2011	Chapter 20 Page 177
Cambridge International AS and A Level Computing 9691	Paper 33 Q3	November 2011	Chapter 20 Page 178
Cambridge International AS and A Level Computing 9691	Specimen Paper 3 Q4		Chapter 21 Page 194
Cambridge International AS and A Level Computing 9691	Paper 32 Q8	November 2011	Chapter 21 Page 195
Cambridge International AS and A Level Computing 9691	Specimen Paper 3 Q8(a)		Chapter 21 Page 195
Cambridge International AS and A Level Computing 9691	Specimen Paper 3 Q2		Chapter 22 Page 207
Cambridge International AS and A Level Computing 9691	Paper 31 Q8	November 2009	Chapter 22 Page 207
Cambridge International AS and A Level Computing 9691	Paper 31 Q4	June 2011	Chapter 23 Page 213
Cambridge International AS and A Level Computing 9691	Paper 33 Q5	November 2011	Chapter 23 Page 213
Cambridge International AS and A Level Computing 9691	Specimen Paper 3 Q9		Chapter 24 Page 221
Cambridge International AS and A Level Computing 9691	Paper 31 Q12	June 2011	Chapter 24 Page 221
Cambridge International AS and A Level Computing 9691	Paper 31 Q4	November 2011	Chapter 24 Page 221

Section 1 System Software

Components of a Computer System and Modes of Use

1

1.1 Hardware, software, input devices, storage devices and output devices

Hardware

Hardware is the physical – mostly electrical – components which make up the computer system. Examples of hardware would be the motherboard and a device controller circuit board.

Software

Software are the programs – made up of program instructions – which run on the hardware. Software makes the hardware useable.

Input devices

One of the fundamentals principles of any computer system is that its operation consists of a continuous cycle of input – processing – output.

Consider when a user keys in a search phrase to say Amazon (the input) – the computer system searches the database for that product (the processing) and then produces the search results (the output).

Consider the embedded computer system inside a washing machine. A user selects the wash programme to use on their washing machine (the input) – the computer system senses that the door is shut etc. (the processing) and an LED display shows the wash time remaining (the output).

The keyboard

The standard QWERTY keyboard is the widely used input device.

Sensors

Sensors are used to 'sense' physical attributes in the real-world.

Specialist input devices

These are often designed for the rapid input of large quantities of data such as optical character recognition (for billing applications) and high speed scanning devices (for the scanning of student examination scripts).

> 📖 **Later**
>
> Chapter 4 Peripheral devices

Storage

Temporary storage

Short term storage is required for the intermediate processing of data. The Amazon search example requires that the search results are temporarily stored immediately before being displayed to the user. This type of storage is called primary storage.

Permanent storage

Permanent storage is required for all files which are used by the computer system. A personal computer

(PC) which has the programs and user's data stored on the PC will all require permanent storage. This is done with an internal hard drive. Other devices used for permanent storage are discussed later. This type of storage is called secondary storage.

> 📖 **Later**
>
> Chapter 4 Secondary storage devices

Output devices

A monitor used as a display screen is the most popular output device. Other forms of output would be hard copy output using a printer or some form of sound using speakers/earphones such as speech output or simply a warning 'bleep' to the user.

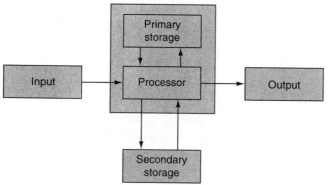

Central Processing Unit (CPU)

1.2 Different types of software

Software falls into two categories:

- ✓ *system software*
- ✓ *applications software*

> 📖 **Later**
>
> *Library programs* in Section 2
> *Programming language translators* in Chapter 18

Some of these are discussed here – other software are discussed in later sections.

Operating System

The one piece of software which will be provided when we purchase a computer is the operating system. The computer system is unusable without an operating system.

The role of the operating system is to manage the resources of the processor.

The operating system provides the interface between the hardware and the user and hides all the complexities of the hardware away from the user.

> **Progress Check 1.1**
>
> When the definition of the operating system describes the 'resources' of the computer – what are these?

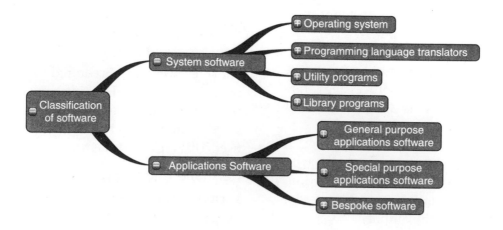

> 📖 **Later**
>
> A fuller discussion of the operating system follows in the next chapter.

Applications programs

Applications programs are generally mass marketed and so the user will have a choice to make.

Applications programs can be classified as either:

- ✓ *general purpose applications programs*
- ✓ *special purpose applications programs*

General purpose applications

Also known as *'generic' software*. A general purpose applications program can be used for a variety of tasks.

Word processor

A word processor can be used for a variety of task including:

- ✓ basic word processing
- ✓ producing a company report
- ✓ writing a textbook etc.

The software has features for the basic creation, saving, retrieval and editing of text.

Spreadsheet

A spreadsheet consists of a grid of columns and rows called *cells* into which text, numbers and formulae can be arranged.

A spreadsheet can be used for a variety of tasks:

- ✓ presenting a costing for an event such as a music concert
  - ➢ This allows for 'what-if' type use – what if we increase the cost of a ticket to $30? What effect will this have on the projected profit?
- ✓ maintaining a simple list of information.

Database

Early databases were little more that a computerised 'card file'. Modern relational databases and database management systems are the backbone of most large commercial applications.

Presentation software

There are now many different applications of presentation software, such as Microsoft PowerPoint, that it can be classified as general purpose. Applications include:

- ✓ a student presentation of some research work
- ✓ teaching a new topic to a class
- ✓ running a rolling display of slides advertising the school at a marketing event.

As the presentation is in electronic form it can be distributed on a magnetic medium or through a website to make it more widely available.

General points

Many of these general purpose software programs (for example, Microsoft Office) now come with a built-in programming language (for example, Visual Basic for Applications) and so this extends the scope of the software's usage and so fits even closer to our definition of being 'suitable for a variety of tasks').

Use of general purpose software is the 'starting point' to develop a computer solution which assumes that:

- ✓ an audit of the features available with (for example a spreadsheet) has been done and we are satisfied that the required software features are present from which the solution can be produced
- ✓ the user has sufficient skills with the software to do this.

Special purpose applications software

Special purpose software is software designed for one particular task. The list of applications and uses is almost endless!

For the purpose of the exam, learn (for example) two or three which are clearly special purpose and make sure you can justify each as such. Some suggestions are given here.

Route planner software

The software is designed for the user to key in the start and final destination (could be the name of the town or some form of postal code). The software calculates and displays the route, estimated time etc.

Tax calculator software

The only task for which this is appropriate is the calculation of the income tax a person will have to pay.

Bespoke software

We showed this on the classification of software diagram. It is really a description for the way in which the software was developed.

Bespoke software is written for a particular client following their program specification.

For example, the software needed for a Cambridge Examiner to upload all the marks from the scripts they have been allocated was written specifically for Cambridge International Examinations.

Exam-style Questions

1. Define the terms:
   (i) hardware

   ....

   ....

   (ii) software

   ....

   .... [2]

   Cambridge 9691 Paper 11 Q1(a) June 2011

2. (a) Describe the purpose of storage devices.

   ....

   .... [2]

   (b) A student has a computer at home as well as using computers at school. State **two** different storage devices that the student would use on her computer and explain what she would use each for.

   1. ....

   ....

   2. ....

   .... [4]

   Cambridge 9691 Paper 11 Q1(a)&(b) November 2011

3. Define what is meant by:
   (i) an input device

   ....

   ....[1]

   (ii) an output device

   ....

   ....[1]

   Cambridge 9691 Paper 11 Q1(b) June 2012

System Software

2

Revision Objectives

After you have studied this chapter, you should be able to:

☞ describe the purpose of operating systems
☞ describe the characteristics of different types of operating systems and their uses: batch, real-time (transaction processing and process control), single-user, multi-user, multiprogramming, multi-tasking and network
☞ identify a range of applications requiring batch processing, transaction processing and process control

☞ describe different types of user interface: forms, menus, GUI, natural language and command line, suggesting the characteristics of user interfaces which make them appropriate for use by different types of user
☞ describe the purpose of a range of utility software, for example, disk formatting, file handling, hardware drivers, file compression and virus checkers.

2.1 The Operating System (OS)

The computer hardware is unusable without an operating system. When we purchase a PC it is the one item of software we expect to be provided along with the hardware.

The OS is the software which makes the hardware usable. This is obvious but we need to appreciate what the computer system has to perform behind the screens.

⬅ Look Back

To Chapter 1 for a definition of the OS.

Consider the following example:

You load the word processing software and at the end of the session save the document.

You simply have to key in a document name and click the save button. Consider what the operating system is doing behind the screens.

The OS must:

✓ check that the document name is valid
✓ check that there is sufficient free disc space. If so, decide which sectors on the disc it will use for storage of the file

✓ mark these sectors as used
✓ remove these sectors from the list of 'free space' on the secondary storage
✓ make a new entry in the file directory for the device.

This suggests that the purpose of any operating system is to:

✓ hide the complexity of the computer hardware away from the user
✓ provide a user-friendly interface between the user and the computer hardware.

Progress Check 2.1

1. Is the operating system applications software or systems software?
2. Write two possible definitions for the operating system.

⬅ Look Back

To the previous chapter.

The discussions so far are points which would apply to any computer system. We shall now study computer systems which operate in a specific way.

Batch processing OS

Before the advent of the microcomputer the majority of computer usage was batch processing. A program would be loaded together with the data which the program would process and the printed output produced.

Key features

Characteristics of any batch processing system are given here.

- ✓ All aspects of the processing occur as a 'batch'
  - ➤ The data is collected and entered as a batch
  - ➤ The data is all processed at the same time (i.e. as a batch)
  - ➤ The output is also produced as a single 'batch' of documents.
- ✓ This may result in an acceptable time delay between the data entry stage and final production of the output
- ✓ The 'job' once started will run to completion without any interaction from the user.

Progress Check 2.2

A college operates a payroll program for the payment of all monthly paid staff. Staff must submit a form showing their hours worked before the 14th of each month. The data from these forms is keyed in and saved a batch. The payroll program is run on the 25th of each month and the payslips are posted to employees the following day.

Does this application meet all the key points bulleted above?

Real-time OS

Real-time processing is the exact opposite of batch processing. Whereas with batch the nature of the application means there is an acceptable time delay between inputs and outputs, for a real-time application the processing must occur almost instantaneously.

Applications which require a real-time OS therefore are process control type applications.

Key features

Characteristics of real-time processing are:

- ✓ there is a continuous cycle of input-processing-output called a *feedback loop*
- ✓ the inputs may not be sequential in nature
- ✓ the nature of the output(s) will affect the next input
- ✓ events (and so inputs) may occur in parallel and at intermittent intervals.

Progress Check 2.3

A large greenhouse is temperature controlled. The inputs come from a number of temperature sensors. Each sensor sends temperature readings back to the computer (for example) every 1/100 th of a second. The computer processes these readings and will, if required, send signals to a set of motors which control the opening and closing of the windows. This continuous cycle of input-processing-output maintains a constant temperature inside the greenhouse.

Does this application meet the bullet pointed requirements for a real-time operating system?

Transaction processing

Some computer applications require the processing and outputs to take place quickly but on a time scale of seconds (rather that fractions of a second as with our greenhouse application).

Consider purchasing concert tickets from a ticketing agency. Once a reservation is made for tickets, the reservation data must be brought up-to-date immediately as each new reservation transaction is completed. If not, the likely outcome will be a 'double booking'. Modern websites will often 'reserve' the selection made by the user for around two minutes, to give the user sufficient time to make payment for the tickets selected.

Single-user – Multi-user OS

A stand-alone microcomputer system will require a single-user operating system. This is clouded by the ability to create different user profiles for use on the same computer, but when the computer system is in use it is always a single-user system.

Multi-user means the computer system can be concurrently used by several users.

Network OS

Each computer on the network will have its resident operating system software. Communication across the network is provided for with another layer of software called the network operating system.

Tasks for the network OS include:

✓ control of access to the network (user IDs and passwords)
✓ management of all available resources (for example, a printer)
✓ management of all users' data files.

Multiprogramming

When using a stand-alone computer we almost take for granted that we can have several programs concurrently loaded. Strictly we should use the term *'process'*. For example, there may be two copies of the word processor program loaded and the OS will treat each of these as a separate process. However, remember that there is only one processor and so – although there are several programs loaded into the main memory – the processor is only ever actually processing one of the processes at any one time.

Multiprogramming is the ability to have more than one program concurrently loaded in main memory.

♦ For the Windows operating system we can see the loaded programs sitting on the taskbar.
♦ Running the 'Task Manager' utility will display the list of processes loaded.

Don't confuse

♦ Multi-tasking
♦ Multi-processing
♦ Multiprogramming

 Note

Some of the OS classification descriptions are not mutually exclusive.

A multi-user operating system is likely to be provided for by on a network; the operating system therefore provides both network and multi-user usage.

2.2 User interfaces

We have already stated that it is a key role of the operating system to provide the user of the computer system with an interface through which the computer hardware is made usable.

Forms based interface

Many applications are web-based and require the completion of a form for data capture. The screen shows the entry of the data for ordering a pair of spectacles on-line. The form will contain the usual 'widget' controls for data entry including:

✓ text boxes
✓ radio buttons
✓ check boxes
✓ drop-down lists.

♦ Why does drop-down list help with data validation?
♦ Note the fields marked with the star must be entered – a form of validation.

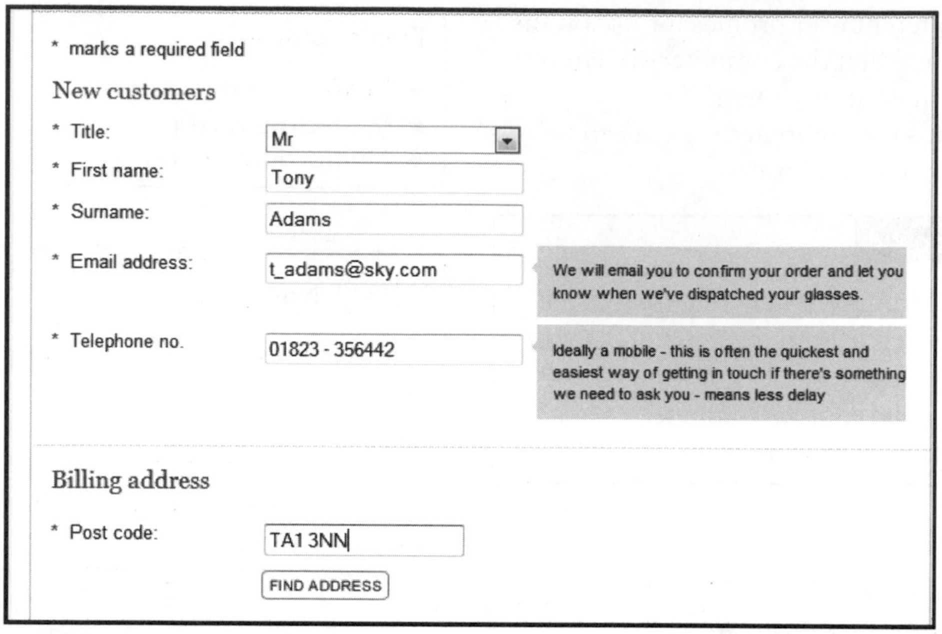

Figure 2.1

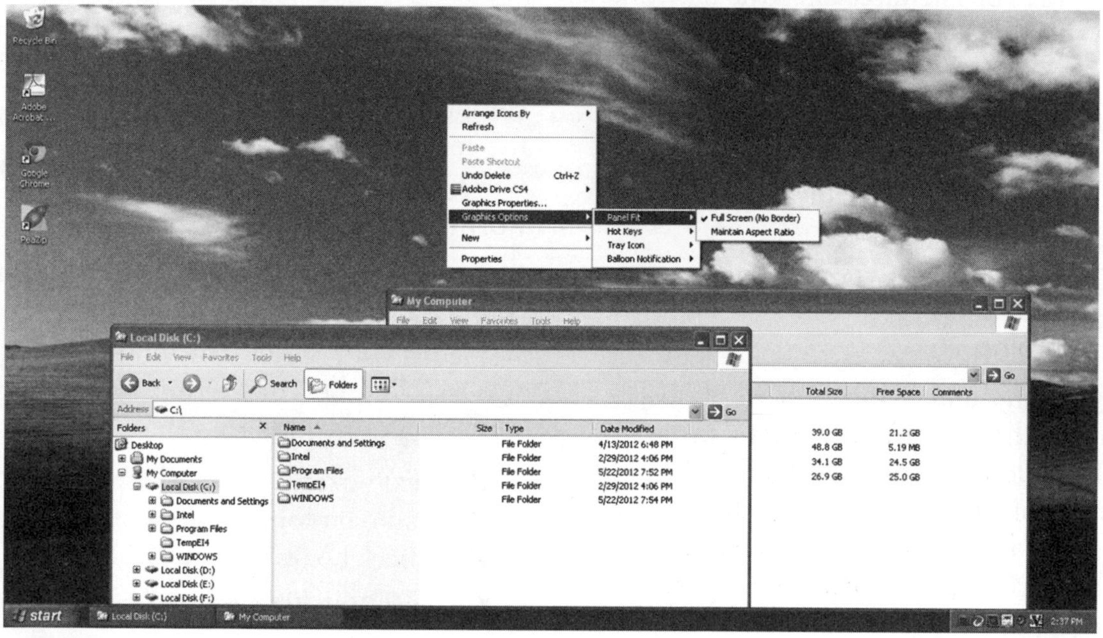

Figure 2.2

Graphical User Interface (GUI)

A GUI uses:

✓ windows (This means a 'program window' and not the Windows operating system)
✓ icons
✓ menus
✓ pointing device (for example, a mouse).

Hence a graphical user interface is called a 'WIMP' interface. This screen illustrates all these points. The Windows Explorer program uses multi-level menus (see screenshot). The desktop and taskbar has *icons* to represent various programs.

A more recent trend is to organise the menu selections using ribbons and tabs. This is illustrated with the Articulate Quizmaker software (Figure 2.3).

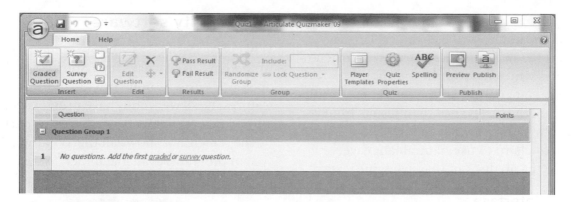

Figure 2.3

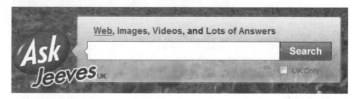

Figure 2.4

Command-line interface

The user is presented with a command line prompt. The user must learn and then use the commands. The traditional command-line interface on the PC was the early MS-DOS operating system from Microsoft.

One such command is 'dir' which displays a list of all the folders and files in the current folder/directory. Command line interfaces have the advantage that once the commands have been learnt an expert user can quickly use the computer system.

Natural language interface

Natural language processing is the ability to communicate with the computer system using **natural language**. This is one step on from simply carrying out a keyword search.

Figure 2.5

> ✎ **Note**
>
> There's an interesting paradox here in that natural language, the system that is easiest for humans to learn and use, is the hardest for a computer system to master and implement!

Consider a search for the text 'Which city in England has the largest population outside London'. A keyword search would only focus on the keywords 'population' and 'London'. A natural language search, attempts to use natural language to understand the nature of the question and then return matches which answer the question.

If the natural language search is successful, results should have a higher relevance than results from a keyword search using a search engine. The website Ask.com would claim to use natural language processing for the analysis of search engine text.

Menu-driven Interface

The majority of windows-based applications software is menu-driven. That is the user is presented – in various possible forms – with a number of menu choices. Making a selection may result in a second or more set of choices being presented.

The following screenshot is taken from the MediaFace software.

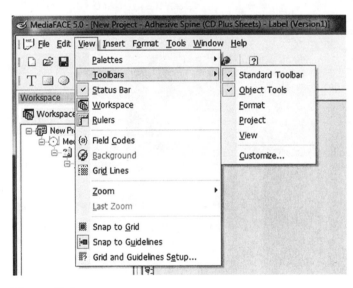

Figure 2.6

The user is presented with a horizontal menu with eight choices.

Selecting the 'View' menu choice opens up a further 13 choices (of which two are greyed-out to indicate unavailable) and finally the user has selected the Toolbars to be made visible.

> ← **Look Back**
>
> To Figure 1.2 in Chapter 1 to see where utility software fits in the general classification of software.

2.3 Utility software

What was classified as a utility some 15 years ago would have been clear. The issue now is that, as operating systems now provide more and more features, tasks we would have previously labelled a 'utility' may well now be packaged as part of the OS.

The screenshot shows all the Windows 7 operating system programs available under 'System Tools'.

The following are all examples of a utility program.

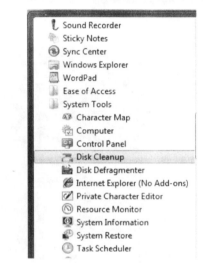

Figure 2.7

Disc formatter program

Formatting a disc requires the setting up of the block markers on each track. The screenshot shows the format of a pen-drive with Windows 7 and the screen shows the size of the blocks which the *FAT* filing system will use. The size of all blocks written to the disc is 16 kilobytes.

A disc must be formatted before it can be used.

Figure 2.8

📖 **Later**

In section 3.1 on discussion of the File Association Table (FAT).

Disc defragmenter

As the disc becomes more and more used for the saving of files, the blocks used for a file become scattered over various tracks and sectors. The result is that files may take longer to load, as all the required blocks need to be retrieved and this will require several movements of the read/write head of the disk drive.

Defragmenter software rearranges the blocks that are used for each file so that the blocks are contiguous. This will result in fewer movements of the read/write head and hence faster retrieval of the file.

Disc cleanup

Following heavy use, some of the blocks on the surface of the disc may become damaged. These blocks must be marked as unusable so that the file management module of the OS will not attempt to use them.

Virus checker

All computers should have one! The virus checker program will make reference to a database of known viruses and then report if a virus file is found on the computer. The virus checking software will then 'quarantine' the suspicious file, ready for its removal. The database of known viruses must be continually kept up-to-date. A virus is just one type of malware which can cause harm to the computer system.

Hardware driver

New hardware when developed will be designed so that it can be used with a variety of operating systems. What makes this possible is a program called a ***device driver***. A driver program is designed to allow successful communication between the operating system and the hardware device.

File management

The operating system will come with commands/programs to manage the files on the computer system.

File management includes:

- ✓ organising files into folders/directories
- ✓ deleting files
- ✓ moving/copying files.

File compression

Some files by their very their nature, for example, video and graphics files, are large.

Reducing the size of any file is clearly desirable as:

- ✓ it takes up less storage space on the secondary storage device
- ✓ the file size may be critical if the file is to be attached to an email and then sent over the Internet.

The WinZip program (Figure 2.8) has almost become a de-facto standard for file compression on the PC.

Figure 2.9

The overhead with file compression is that we need software to perform the task and then software to 'extract' a compressed file.

Archiving utility

This may be a utility in its own right or a feature which is part of an application such as an email client program. An email client program (such as Microsoft's Outlook) has a facility to archive old and unwanted emails. When the files are archived file compression will take place.

Top tip The list of possible utilities is huge – for an examination answer stick to these listed here which can be found on most computer systems.

1. (a) State what is meant by
      (i) operating system software

   ....

   .... [1]

   (ii) applications software

   ....

   .... [1]

> **Technique**
>
> ♦ The number of lines provided indicates the length of answer expected for each part.
> ♦ Note also the different keywords: State – Explain – Identify

   (b) Explain the difference between batch processing and real-time operating systems.

   ....

   .... [2]

   (c) Identify one application which would need to use batch processing and give a reason for your answer.

   Application ....

   Reason ....

   ....

   ....

   .... [2]

   Cambridge 9691 Specimen Paper 1 Q1

> **Technique**
>
> Needs careful reading, as the question requires:
> ♦ a description of the interface
> ♦ and then an application.

2. One purpose of most operating systems is to provide a human computer interface (HCI).

   (a) Describe the following HCIs and give an example of an application which would use each:

      (i) menu based

   ....

   .... [3]

(ii) natural language

....

.... [3]

(b) State **three** other purposes of an operating system.

1. ....

    ....

2. ....

    ....

3. ....

    .... [3]

Cambridge 9691 Paper 1 Q5 June 2009

Data Representation, Structure and Management

3

Revision Objectives

After you have studied this chapter, you should be able to:

☞ explain the use of codes to represent a character set (for example, ASCII and Unicode)

☞ explain the representation of different data types: integer, Boolean, date/time, currency, character and string

☞ express positive integers in binary form

☞ understand the structure of arrays (one and two dimensional), including initialising arrays, reading data into arrays and performing a simple serial search on an array

☞ describe the LIFO and FIFO features of stacks and queues

☞ explain how data is stored in files in the form of fixed-length records comprising items in fields

☞ define and explain the difference between serial, sequential, indexed sequential and random access to data, using examples and stating their comparative advantages and disadvantages

☞ describe how serial, sequential and random organisation and access to files may be implemented using indexes and hashing as appropriate

☞ select appropriate data types/data structures for a given problem and explain the advantages and disadvantages of alternative choices

☞ explain the procedures involved in backing up data and archiving, including the reasons for backing up and archiving.

3.1 The use of codes to represent a character set

Computers store and process numeric and character data. A digital computer stores all data as binary digits – hence characters must also be represented as numbers.

The character set used will have a different number to represent each character.

The character set must include upper case letters, lower case letters, the number digits and all the punctuation and other characters found on the standard QWERTY keyboard.

Progress Check 3.1

Will 4 and '4' be treated the same by the computer system?

ASCII (American Standard Code for Information Interchange)

This text suggests that we must have a standard set of character codes which is used by all computers (especially for transferring data between computers).

ASCII uses a 7-bit code to represent each of the characters and any programming text book should include this table of codes.

A selection of the codes is shown in Table 3.1.

✎ Note

Throughout the book we shall represent:

✓ single characters with single quotes

✓ a string of characters with double quotes

Table 3.1

Character	Decimal	Character	Decimal
\<Return>	13	…	…
\<Space>	32	z	122
A	65	0	48
B	66	1	49
C	67	2	50
…	…	…	…
z	90	9	57
a	97	$	36
b	98	%	37
c	99	&	38

The math tells us that 7-bits makes possible 128 different codes (with binary codes 0000000, 00000001, …, 1111111).

The computer stores all data as one or more bytes (8-bits) and so an extra digit is used in the most significant bit position (on the left) for a checking function called a parity check. This bit is called the parity bit.

Parity

A computer system uses either even parity or odd parity.

Even parity means that the total number of one bits (including the parity bit) must total to an even number.

Consider these characters:

1. 'A' has ASCII code 65 denary.

   7-bit binary for 65 is 1000001.

   This has two 1 bits (an even number), so the parity bit to be added will be a 0 bit.

   The 8-bit ASCII code for character 'A' is 01000001.

2. '8' has ASCII code 56 denary.

   7-bit binary for 56 is 0111000.

   This has three 1 bits (an odd number), so the parity bit to be added will be a 1 bit to make the total number of 1 bits even.

   The 8-bit ASCII code for character '8' is 10111000.

3.2 The representation of different data types

Data types

The computer system – or more precisely the programming language or applications software such as a spreadsheet – will distinguish between different types of data.

Integer

In math this is any positive or negative whole number.

Boolean

Some data only have values 'True' or 'False'.

- ✓ Is a customer allowed credit?
- ✓ Is a student aged over 18?

> 📖 **Later**
>
> The range of integers supported by the programming language is discussed again in Chapter 13.

> **Progress Check 3.2**
>
> Suggest a data value which would be stored as a Boolean data type.

Date and Time

There are considerable variations across different programming languages for how the language stores and processes a date value. Typical would be SQL which uses the format YYYY/MM/DD and encloses the characters inside the hash character.

The representation for the 13 April 2012 is #2010/04/13#.

Currency

The data type 'Currency' is available in Visual Basic. Net and applications such as MS Access and Excel. The data type is used for money values which have two digits after the decimal point.

📖 **Later**

The following data types are discussed later in Chapter 13:
- string of characters
- real number

Character

The ASCII code table was concerned with the number codes used for single characters.

Examples could include:

✓ gender – with possible value 'M' and 'F' only
✓ product type – 'E' used for electrical, 'C' for computer equipment etc.

Progress Check 3.3

What data type would be used for each of these items?

(a) A garment size to represent Small, Medium or Large (only these sizes).
(b) A game player's high score.
(c) The number of phone calls made this month.
(d) The date for the renewal of an insurance policy.
(e) Whether or not a person is married.

Strings

Most program applications will need to store string data. A string is a sequence of characters from the character set. So:
"President putin"
"14 The High Street"
"9876"
Are all examples of a valid string value.

✏️ **Note**

✓ The string may have no characters – called an 'empty string'
✓ The string may include digit or <space> characters – e.g. the address above
✓ The Programming language used may have an upper limit on the maximum length of a string
✓ The Programming language will have built-in functions for the manipulation of string data

3.3 Express positive integers in binary form

All data in the computer must be represented in binary form.

Consider a single byte used to represent a positive integer.

Think – just like we would in denary base ten – that each of the bits positions has a place value.

These are shown below:

✓ the most significant bit position has place value 128
✓ the least significant position has place value a 'unit' i.e. 0 or 1.

128	64	32	16	8	4	2	1

The following examples illustrate:

1. What positive integer is this?

0	1	1	0	0	1	1	1

$1 + 2 + 4 + 32 + 64 = 103$ denary.

📖 **Later**

Negative integers are not introduced until Chapter 20.

2. Represent 93 as an 8-bit positive integer.

$$93 = 64 + 16 + 8 + 4 + 1$$

128	64	32	16	8	4	2	1
0	1	0	1	0	1	0	1

Progress Check 3.4

1. A positive integer is represented using a single byte. What integers are these?
   (a) 0100 0001
   (b) 1010 1010
   (c) 1111 1111

2. What is the binary representation for these integers?
   (a) 3
   (b) 89
   (c) 257

3.4 Understand the structure of arrays

When we store three surnames with the identifier names – `Customer1`, `Customer2` and `Customer3` the variables will be declared in the program and this is the trigger for the interpreter or compiler to reserve three storage locations in memory ready to store the values assigned in the program. Appreciate that the data items have no relation to each other; the identifier names `Customer1`, `Customer2` etc., are as different as using names `NameA`, `NameB` etc.

Arrays

An array is a collection of data items which are referred to by the same identifier name.

♦ We should assume for this syllabus that the items will be of the same data type.

Example

A garage sells cars and stores data for the number of cars sold in each month of the year. The array will be called `MonthlySales` and we need to store twelve values. The array can be visualised as shown in Table 3.2.

The numbers alongside each value is called the *index* or *subscript* number of the array.

Typical values are:
`MonthlySales[1] = 13`
`MonthlySales[4] = 11`
This array is a *one-dimensional array*.

`MonthlySales` is storing integer values. We can have arrays that store values of any of the recognised data types, i.e. Char, Boolean etc.

Visual Basic.Net
♦ VB uses parentheses – (and) – to enclose the array subscript.
♦ Throughout the text we shall use square brackets.

Example

The garage has a site in three towns and records separately the monthly sales made on each site for the 12-month period.

This suggests we need to visualise the data as shown in Table 3.3. The columns represent each month and the rows represent the sites.

Note

It is usual to use the first subscript number for the row – the second subscript for the column – just like in a spreadsheet (row first).

Table 3.2

MonthlySales

1	13
2	15
3	5
4	11
...	
12	6

Table 3.3

SiteMonthlySales

	1	2	3	4	5	6	7	8	9	10	11	13
1	3	5	1	4	9	11	6	8	6	3	9	0
2	4	5	1	7	12	6	7	3	5	11	6	4
3	6	5	3	4	8	12	9	12	10	8	8	2

All values are represented with a single array. We shall use identifier name `SiteMonthlySales` which now needs two subscript numbers. This is called a *two-dimensional array*.

Typical values are:
`SiteMonthlySales[1, 5] = 9`
`SiteMonthlySales[3, 11] = 8`

If this was implemented with program code:
♦ For array `MonthlySales` subscript 0 is never used
♦ For array `SiteMonthlySales` column zero and row 0 are not used.

Initialising an array

The variable name use for the array must be declared in the program code.

Visual Basic.Net assumes the first subscript is zero, and the number shown is the highest subscript.

```
Dim MonthlySales(12) As Integer
Dim SiteMonthlySales(3, 12) As Integer
```

The smallest and largest subscripts are called the lower bound and the upper bound of the array.

If the array is to be given an initial value for all the cells in the array this can be done using a loop.

All the monthly sales values are to be assigned an initial value of zero.

```
Dim MonthlySales(12) As Integer
Dim Index As Integer

For Index = 1 To 12
    MonthlySales(Index) = 0
Next Index
```

Reading values into an array

This is what essentially has been done in the code above. Each element of the array was assigned the value zero.

We are to input the twelve monthly sales totals from the keyboard and store them in the array.

```
Note the Index variable is supplying both:
✓   the index number for the array
✓   the prompt for the data entry.
```

```
Dim MonthlySales(12) As Integer
Dim Index As Integer

For Index = 1 To 12
    Console.Write("Month: " & Index & " ...")
    MonthlySales(Index) = Console.ReadLine
Next Index
Console.WriteLine("Sales figures now stored in array ...")
```

Pseudocode

What follows is our first use of pseudocode to describe an algorithm.

You should be able to study this and then write the program code from it.

Serial search of an array

A serial (or linear) search means start with the first value and then consider each value in order.

Find the first month is which the total sales was below 10.

We shall write a pseudocode description for the search algorithm.

```
Index ← 1
Found ← False
REPEAT
    IF MonthlySales[Index] < 10
        THEN
            Found ← True
            OUTPUT "The month number was ..."
            Index
    ELSE
            Index ← Index + 1
    ENDIF
    UNTIL Found = True
```

📖 Later

The practical implementation for this is studied later in Chapter 13.

Progress Check 3.5

What would need to be added to the algorithm above to output a suitable message if there were no months below the critical value of 10?

3.5 The LIFO and FIFO features of stacks and queues

Stack

A stack is a collection of data items – which can continually have new items join and items leave – which behave in a certain way. A stack manages its data items as 'the last item to join the stack will be the first item to leave'. This can be abbreviated to 'Last in – First Out' (LIFO).

📖 Later

The stack and queue are studied in more detail in Chapter 20.

We shall see in Section 3 practical situations when we want a set of data value to behave in this way as a stack.

Queue

A queue behaves as follows. The first item to join the queue will be the first item to leave. That is 'First In – First Out' (FIFO). Again there are practical situations for a computer system where we would want data to be managed as a queue.

> 📖 **Later**
>
> The practical implementation of a queue is studied later in Chapter 13.

> ### Progress Check 3.6
>
> A queue data structure has the following activity.
>
> ✓ Items BAT, BADGER, HORSE join the queue
> ✓ Two items leave
> ✓ A new item GIRAFFE joins
>
> What is the final state of the queue?
> Which item will be the next to leave?

> ### Progress Check 3.7
>
> A stack data structure has the following activity.
>
> ✓ Items BAT, BADGER, HORSE join the stack
> ✓ Two items leave
> ✓ A new item GIRAFFE joins
>
> What is the final state of the stack?
> Which item will be the next to leave?

> 📖 **Later**
>
> The practical implementation of a stack is studied later in Chapter 13.

3.6 Storing data in files in the form of fixed length records comprising items in fields

Records

Data often consist of several data items which all relate to some entity. For example the collection of data for title, artist and release date all relate to the same 'recording' entity and we want to store the data for many recordings. The programmer would organise this data as a record. Using database terminology, each recording record would consist of three fields (title, artist and release date).

A collection of the data for (for example 150) recordings would be a file of recordings.

Fixed-length records

If the programming language was to store every record with the same number of characters then the records are said to be fixed length records.

In practice for the example given:

✓ Title of the recording
  ➤ would be a string of characters with a stated maximum length. If this was about 50 characters, then the title 'Abbey Road' could be stored either as:
    ♦ a string of 10 characters only, or
    ♦ a string with 'Abbey Road' followed by 40 characters so ensuring all title data was a fixed length. This second option ensures that the records will be *fixed-length records*.
✓ Artist field
  ➤ Same alternatives as for the Title data.
✓ Release date
  ➤ The programming language will have a standard format it uses for dates. If it was as suggested earlier YYYY/MM/DD, then all dates would be stored as 10 characters.

> 📖 **Later**
>
> The programming implementation of a record data type is explained in Chapter 13.

So the issue is that some data types will mean the number of characters is always fixed – but for the 'string of characters' data type the data value could be a variable or a fixed size.

3.7 Serial, sequential, indexed sequential and random access to data and implementing serial, sequential and random organisation of files using indexes and hashing as appropriate

Serial Access

Serial access to a set of data items is accessing them in the natural order in which they are stored. Access to the items held in an array would be serial if we started at the item with subscript 1, then subscript 2 etc.

Consider items held in a text file. Serial access would mean reading the line of text on line 1, followed by line 2 etc.

What serial access means in practice will depend upon how the items were originally stored or organised. If the file was a file of words stored in alphabetical order, then serial access would retrieve the data in alphabetical order. This is generally not so; serial access generally is retrieving the data items in the original order in which they were stored.

Advantage of serial access

✓ Easy to program and supported by all programming languages.

Disadvantage

✓ We do not have direct access to an individual record.

Sequential access

Sequential access assumes that the data items were stored with sequential organisation. One of the data items will be acting as a *key field*. For example a file of customer records could have the product code as the key field. The data items are then read starting with the first and this retrieves the items in (alphabetical) order, i.e. in sequential order.

For all applications where we are reading data from a file, the programming file processing methods have the major disadvantage that the data items can only be read in sequence. There is no way that we can immediately read the 12th item in the file.

> 📖 **Later**
>
> Implementing serial and sequentially organised files with program code are explained in Chapter 13.

Advantage

✓ Easy to program and supported by all programming languages.

Disadvantages

✓ We do not have direct access to an individual record

✓ The subsequent maintenance of the file (adding a new record, deleting a record) requires a lot of program code involving two files.

Random Access

This technique is designed to overcome the limitations of serial/sequential access.

A random access file uses a *record key number* allocated to each record. This number is used to calculate (or 'hash') the disc address where the data will be stored. The same record key can be used later to directly access this individual record from the file.

An array can be considered in the same way. The index number will be used when the data item is stored. The same array subscript can be used to directly access that individual array item.

There are issues to consider when deciding how each record key is generated. If we anticipate that there will be approximately 1000 records in the file, we need to use a hashing calculation which gives this range of key numbers. Also, we do not want two different numbers to generate the same record key. If this happens then potentially one of the records will be lost, or we need to anticipate this and have a strategy in place to deal with this situation of duplicate record key number.

Advantage

✓ Able to directly access individual records (without referencing any of the other records).

Disadvantages

- ✓ Storage space may be wasted as a result of a poor choice of hashing function (i.e. record key)
- ✓ Possible that two different records could generate the same record key number.

Indexed sequential

Index sequential organisation and access is designed to offer the benefits of both sequential and random organisation.

To understand index sequential organisation, we must appreciate that the data records will be written onto the disc in blocks. A block is the smallest unit of data which can be read/written. A block is typically 512 bytes and so could contain several logical (for example customer) records.

An indexed sequential file works as follows. Each record has a record key (just like a random file).

- ✓ An index which stores the highest record key in that block of records
- ✓ In practice this could be a multi-level index where:
  - ➢ the top-level is a track index for each track on the disc
  - ➢ each track then has its own block index.

The following *'track index'* is the first place to look when the program has to write a new record (Table 3.4).

Hence writing a new record with key 1926 would search the track index and establish this will be written somewhere on track 3.

We then consult the **block index** for track 3 (Table 3.5).

Table 3.4

Track index	
Track	**Highest key (on that track)**
1	946
2	1693
3	2030
4	5166

Table 3.5

Track 3: Block index	
Block	**Highest key**
1	1701
2	1754
⌇	⌇
14	1896
15	1944
16	2030

This tells the software to store this new record in block 14 (i.e. its home storage area). The problem arises when the track index tells us use block 14 but when the software reads block 14 it finds that it is full (It already has five records stored). This is the situation when an overflow area must be used.

The home storage area stores the blocks of records. A disc which used blocks of size 512 bytes and logical (fixed sized) records of 95 bytes would be able to store five records in each block.

An overflow area stores any records which could not be stored in their home block. Records stored here will have a link from the home area block in order that these can be retrieved.

Advantages

- ✓ Able to directly access individual records (without referencing any of the other records)
- ✓ Able also to access the records in sequence.

Many computing applications could benefit from both direct access and sequential access. Printing customer statements could use sequential access assuming the records are stored in customer name order.

Searching for a single transaction (to answer an on-line customer query) would use direct access to the customers record using the indexes.

Disadvantage

- ✓ Not supported by all programming languages.

Progress Check 3.8

1. What type of file organisation is best suited to the following applications?
   (a) A file of 10 000 customer bank accounts. Every month printed statements are produced and sent to all customers.
   (b) A file of 1 000 products. We frequently have to make an enquiry to see if a particular product is in stock.
   (c) As for (b) but we also need to regularly increase or decrease the prices for all products.
2. Select appropriate data types/data structures for a given problem and explain the advantages and disadvantages of alternative choices.

The data type to be used for any particular item should be self-evident and this issue is a fundamental one when we consider an initial program specification design.

As a general rule data items which are a 'one off' will be coded with a single variable whereas a collection of items – such as all the student surnames – would be represented with an array. A major advantage of using arrays is that separate arrays can be used for different data items. For example an array for the pupil's surname, an array for the form, and an array for the year the student joined the school. This way, we can assume that

```
Surname[56], Form[56] and
YearJoined[56] all refer to the same student.
```

A typical task such as searching for a student would search the surname array – find the array index where the surname is found – for example index value X – and then directly access Form[X] and YearJoined[X] to display this student's data.

The previous section on the use of files is a key consideration when designing the data structures to be used for a particular problem. We often have to think in reverse order. The data processing requirements will determine the file organisation and access methods to be used. For example if we

have to carry out frequent searches for individual records then direct access may be needed. An alternative approach could be to read all the data values into arrays at the start of any program session and save the data back to the file at the end of the session. This way the array indexes provide fast access to any data value.

3.8 Backing up data and archiving

Backing up data

The data that a company generates is one of its most important assets. All aspects of the business will generate data for order processing, research, manufacturing and general operational data. The loss of this data could prove disastrous for the company.

Safeguarding the companies' data is a *security* issue. Backing up the data means taking a complete copy of the data and is based on the worst-case scenario that this data could be completely destroyed. This could be the result of a hardware malfunction, some human error, a natural disaster or a member of staff not following the correct operational procedures.

The issues around backing up of the data are given here.

- ✓ Do we need to backup all the data?
- ✓ How often should this backup be taken?
- ✓ Where the backup data should be stored?
- ✓ What are the recovery procedures should the backups be required?

There is probably little to be gained in backing up program files. If a program fails then we will have the original program discs to re-install the software. However there may be configuration files which have been generated in the course of using the software which should be backed up.

The frequency of backup will be determined by the nature of the application. Consider a payroll application which uses batch processing and is run on the 28th day of each month. The processing is that the latest payroll *master file* is generated each month from the current payroll master and a monthly file of employee transactions. This produces the updated master file. The backup files should therefore be the original version of the master file and this month's *transaction file*. If the updated master became corrupted, then we could recover using the old master and the current transaction file. Hence a new backup set of files is effectively generated only every month.

Compare this with an order processing application which is receiving (for example) 50 new orders through its website every hour. What happens if this order processing file fails?

There will be changes made to the data every minute and it will not be possible to take a backup of the data every minute! It may be reasonable to backup the data every (for example) one hour. If we log all the transactions in a separate file then it should be possible the recreate master file(s) in the event of a failure.

An alternative strategy is the *mirroring* of the master files so that we always have a second 'live' copy of the important data. In the event of a disk failure, we can simply switch to the mirrored files.

Archiving files

We shall frequently get queries from customers about an order that was recently placed, but is it likely we shall get queries about orders which are two years old? This suggests that some data on the computer system could be removed from on-line availability.

Top Tip Don't confuse the terms backup and archive – they are not the same.

Archiving is the removal of files from online availability and moving (not copying) them to some form of off-line storage. In the unlikely event that the data will be needed, it can be accessed from the off-line storage.

Archiving is the process of freeing up files which are no longer in use but still having the files available if needed. Client email software typically asks the users if they want to 'archive' emails which are older than (for example) two months.

Exam-style Questions

1. (a) (i) Explain what is meant by the character set of a computer.

....

....

(ii) Explain how a character is represented in a computer.

....

.... [4]

(b) Explain the representation of integers in a computer.

....

.... [3]

Cambridge 9691 Paper 11 Q3 June 2011

2. (a) (i) Describe the structure of a one-dimensional array.

....

.... [2]

(ii) Explain how a simple serial search can be carried out to locate a specific item in a one-dimensional array.

....

.... [4]

(b) Describe how a queue is implemented using an array.

....

.... [4]

Cambridge 9691 Paper 11 Q5 November 2011

3. A bank has a customer file containing the transactions made by its customers.

The file is used to

- produce a bank statement for each customer once a month
- answer customer queries when the customer telephones the bank.

Data in the customer file is regularly backed up.

(a) Explain why taking back-ups is necessary.

....

....

(b) Describe a procedure for doing back-ups.

....

....

....

.... [4]

Cambridge 9691 Paper 11 Q7(b)(ii) November 2011

Hardware 4

Revision Objectives

After you have studied this chapter, you should be able to:

☞ describe the function and purpose of the control unit, memory unit and arithmetic logic unit (ALU) as individual parts of a processor
☞ explain the difference between types of primary memory and their uses (RAM, ROM)
☞ describe the basic features, advantages, disadvantages and use of secondary storage media, for example, magnetic, optical and solid state

☞ describe use of buffers and interrupts in the transfer of data between peripheral devices and primary memory
☞ describe a range of common peripheral devices in terms of their features, benefits, drawbacks and uses
☞ relate the choice of peripheral device to a given application, justifying the choices made
☞ understand the potential problem of speed mismatch between peripheral and processor.

We now need to consider more closely what makes up the computer's processor and how it interacts with the other components of the computer system.

The processor is purely electronic circuits. It will be mounted on a ***motherboard*** which has connectors to various buses used to communicate with input and output devices.

> ← **Look Back**
>
> To Chapter 1 for a basic picture of the components of a computer system.

4.1 A bus

> ✎ **Note**
>
> There would not be specific questions about buses in the examination.

A bus is a pathway along which data travels and consists of a set of parallel wires (lines). Each line can transmit a single bit. The bus is made up of a number of lines so be would described as (for example) a 16-line bus. 16 lines means 16 bits can be sent along

the bus at the same time, so a 16-line bus therefore can transmit a 16-bit number.

The address bus

All components of the system – including the primary memory – will be referenced by the processor using an ***address***. Since it is the only data that the processor understands an address will be a binary number.

The only component which can load an address onto the address bus is the processor. This address is then passed to the relevant component such as the main memory or an input or output device.

Device controllers

The processor has a fundamental problem. Manufacturers will want a particular processor to be able to communicate with thousands of different devices which are manufactured by various companies. It would be impossible for these connections to be hard-wired for all possible devices and so communication between the processor and the various devices is done through an intermediary ***device controller***.

The data bus

Data will be continually passed to and from the processor, the main memory and the devices.

Since data needs to be both read and written, the data bus will be bi-directional.

The control bus

Both the address bus and data bus use all the lines together to form a binary member. The control bus works very differently where each line is used for a different *control signal*. It is the task of the control bus to coordinate the various actions and send appropriate timing signals to indicate something has happened or been completed.

Consider when the processor has to read a value from main memory. The sequence of events would be as given here.

✓   Address bus is loaded with the address
✓   Data bus is loaded with the contents of this address and copies the value to a register in the processor
✓   Control bus sends a signal to confirm the 'data read' operation has been completed.

Other control bus signals include:

✓   memory write completed
✓   output completed – data on the data bus has been copied to the output device
✓   input completed – data has been copied from the input device to the data bus
✓   reset – the user has pressed the Reset button on the computer.

Putting all this together gives this picture of the internal make up of the computer system (Figure 4.1).

The vertical single arrow lines will themselves be made up of a number of lines.

> 📖 **Later**
>
> In Chapter 19 we shall study this in more detail – especially the *special purpose registers* which are involved in a data transfer.

Inside the processor

The processor will be continually receiving program instructions in sequence. Each time it must make sense of the instruction before it is able to execute the instruction.

A typical instruction could require the processor to:

✓   load the contents of a memory location
✓   add/subtract a number
✓   add/subtract the contents of a memory location
✓   manipulate the bits in some way, for example, shift them one place to the left.

Each instruction must be loaded from memory onto the data bus and it is one of the main roles of the *control unit* to manage the sequencing of instructions.

Arithmetic is done by circuits inside the processor called the *Arithmetic Logic Unit (ALU)*. The ALU is made up of logic circuits which are designed for various computations required.

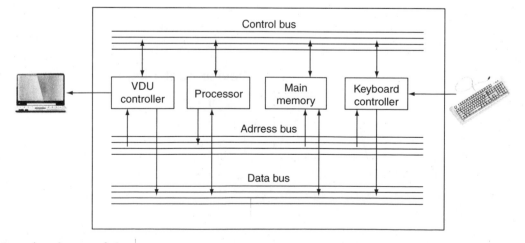

Figure 4.1   Internal make up of the computer system

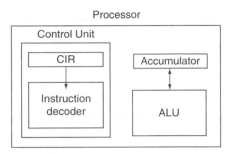

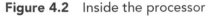

Figure 4.2   Inside the processor

Figure 4.2 assumes there is only one general storage location available inside the processor called the *Accumulator*.

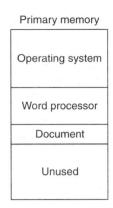

Figure 4.3   Primary memory

Progress Check 4.1

Which of the following statements are true?
(a) The processor is the only component which gives a value to the address bus.
(b) Data values are read from the address bus from the keyboard controller to the processor.
(c) If the processor has to read a value from main memory, the address bus must first be loaded with the memory address to be used.
(d) The control bus can communicate directly with all the components.

4.2 Primary memory (or Main memory)

Consider a session of word processing on a PC. The user will load the word processing software (from the secondary storage) – type the document and later save the document onto the secondary storage.

For this computer session the primary memory will contain both program instructions (the OS and the word processing software) and what the computer system will consider as 'data' (the document) (Figure 4.3).

The memory consists of a number of *memory cells* which are each referenced with a unique *memory address*.

Each cell of main memory on a PC will contain one byte (i.e. 8 bits); hence modern computers are described as '*byte-addressable*'.

It is a major job for the operating system to manage which memory cells are being used and

which cells are 'free'. When the word processing session finishes both the memory used for the program and the document will become free and available.

It is a fundamental concept that the computer system when reading/writing values to and from memory will treat the contents of all memory cells as a 'data' value. It is what it then does with that data value that will give the byte a context.

Random Access Memory (RAM)

'Random access' because the processor is able to go directly to a particular memory location (assuming it knows the address) to retrieve the data value from that cell.

For the most popular form of RAM – *Dynamic RAM (DRAM)* – each bit is formed from a capacitor and a transistor working together. The capacitor stores the charge representing the value 0 or 1. The transistor is the switch to this component which allows the value to be written or read.

Look Back

To Chapter 3 where we used the term random access.

RAM is *volatile* – that is its contents will be lost when the power to the computer system is switched off. Also the contents of the RAM can continually change (think back to our word processing session scenario).

Integrated circuit technology has progressed at such a rate that PCs with a memory size of

4GB are now common and this has implications for programming. In the early days of computing memory was at a premium and programming techniques were specifically designed to maximise the use of the available memory. One quote Bill Gates will want to forget is "640K ought to be enough for anybody!" (1981).

> 📖 **Later**
>
> You will need to know about the difference between *DRAM* and *SRAM*.
> This is covered in Chapter 10.

Read Only Memory (ROM)

'Read only' implies that the contents of this type of memory cannot be changed. The bit pattern in each cell of ROM is burned at the time of manufacture of the memory component. ROM also allows random access to cells. Because the contents of this memory cannot be changed this makes it suitable for storing the program instructions the computer needs for its start-up process (called booting the computer). The software on the ROM memory is called the *bootstrap loader*. The computer will be hard-wired to run the bootstrap loader software when the power is switched on and its main task will then be to load parts of the operating system from the secondary storage.

Progress Check 4.2

Which of the following statements are true?
(a) Random access means the hardware can go directly to any particular memory cell.
(b) Random access means memory cells are accessed in a purely random order.
(c) All Random Access Memory (RAM) is volatile.
(d) The bootstrap loader software is held on ROM.
(e) The bootstrap loader contains all of the operating system.

4.3 Secondary storage

Also called *auxiliary storage* or *backing storage*.
  If the RAM is volatile the computer system must use secondary storage for the permanent storage of programs and data.

Issues concerned with secondary storage will be:

✓ Is the device internal or external to the computer?
✓ Does the medium allow for direct access to particular files?
✓ Is the technology based on optical or magnetic methods of storage?
✓ Is the data effectively online or off-line to the computer system

Magnetic devices
Hard disk

A magnetic medium which has a number of surfaces (or disk platters) each divided into tracks and sectors. Data is read/written to and from the surface of a platter by a read/write head which floats above the surface of the disk. The disk rotates at high speed. To read a particular sector from the disc requires that:

✓ the head moves to a position over the correct track
✓ the head must wait until the disk rotates with the start of the sector under the head
✓ the head reads/writes the sector data.

> **Convention**
>
> ♦ 'Disk' for magnetic media
> ♦ 'Disc' for optical media

The hard disk is the device for secondary storage on all PCs and is an internal unit. External hard drives are available and are often used for archiving or the backing up of data.
  The hard disk is an *electro-mechanical* device. Read and writing the data is electrical but the positioning of the head to the correct track and waiting for the disc to rotate (the latency time) are all the result of a mechanical movement. The mechanical aspect has implications for the speed with which data can be retrieved and written to the device.

Optical devices – General operation

Like a hard disk, an optical disc is rotating at high speed. The disc consists of a protective plastic layer on top of a reflective layer (that looks like aluminium foil). The surface of the disc alternates between flat areas (called '*lands*') and tiny depressions (called '*pits*'). These two surfaces effectively encode the pattern of 0s and 1s.

A *laser* is shone onto the disc and light that strikes a land it reflected back to a detector – light that strikes a pit is scattered.

Unlike a hard disk, the data is written onto a single track divided into areas called sectors all of the same size. The speed of rotation of the disc is continually changing.

CD-ROM (Compact Disc-Read Only Memory)

Typically used for the commercial distribution of media files – software, audio and video/film. Typical capacity 600–800MB.

CD-R

A CD-R can be written to once and read many times. Capacity the same as for a CD-ROM. It is useful for the backup/archiving of data.

CD-RW

A CD-RW can be written to many times. Capacity the same as for a CD-ROM. It is useful for the backup/archiving of data.

DVD

Rapidly replacing the CD-ROM. Has a capacity approximately13 times that of a CD-ROM. Technology is similar to a CD-ROM but the DVD disc is multi-layered hence the increased storage capacity.

DVD-RW

A DVD-RW can be read and written to many times.

Blu-ray

Designed to eventually replace the DVD, Blu-ray discs store 25GB of data in each layer and are dual-layered. Hence they are used for High Definition (HD) media and games machines such as the Playstation 3. A Blu-ray player is becoming a standard household item to connect to the television monitor.

The media uses a blue laser (replacing the red laser used with DVDs) which allows data to be stored with a higher packing density.

Until 2008 there had been two competing optical formats Blu-ray and HD DVD and it was the announcement from Warner Bros that it was to adopt the Blu-ray format that made it become the de-facto standard.

Solid-state Storage

A Solid-state Storage Device (SSD) uses solid-state technology to store and retrieve the data. Unlike a hard disk (which is an electro-mechanical device) the SSD is only electrical. The benefits which result from this are that the device is silent and not susceptible to shock (such as a hard disk).

SSDs are increasingly being used as the main secondary storage in laptops, netbooks and other mobile devices.

Flash memory cards/Pens

In widespread use and capacities of 4GB now common. Fitted in portable devices such as a smartphone or a digital camera and used extensively for transferring files between two PCs.

Progress Check 4.3

Classify the following devices under the general headings 'Optical device', 'Magnetic device' or 'Solid-state Storage Device':
CD-ROM, Flash memory card, DVD-R, External hard disk, Blu-ray

Progress Check 4.4

Complete the entries in the table showing the capacity and which device is best suited to the list of applications given.

Application	Device	Capacity
Backup of all files on a PC		
Distribution of High Definition (HD) films		
Storage inside a digital camera		
Copying large images from a PC for distribution of other PC users		

Devices: DVD-RW, External hard drive, Flash memory card, Blu-ray
Capacities: 2GB, 13GB, 50GB, 250GB

4.4 Buffers

We have already described a hard disk as being an electro-mechanical device – compared with solid state memory which is purely electrical (there are no moving mechanical parts). This has implications for the operation of the computer system.

The processor executes its program instructions on a time scale of microseconds (i.e. millionth's of a second).

The mechanical parts of the disk drive operation (rotation of the disk and the movement of the head) are on a time scale of milliseconds (i.e. thousands of a second.

Consider these tasks:

✓ the output of data to a printer — this could take several seconds to print an A4 document.
✓ the user keying in data at the keyboard — even slower!

This suggests that all stages of operation of the computer, i.e. input, output and storing data are much slower than the speed at which the processor can operate.

A *buffer* is a temporary storage area between the device (for example, the hard disk) and the processor. Buffers are used when there is a speed mismatch between the speed at which data can be processed and input/output.

When data is read from the disk we can never read just a byte or a couple of bytes. The operating system will organise its available storage space into 'allocation units' which will typically be two of the sectors on the disc – this is called a *physical record*. An allocation unit which is read could contain (for example) 10 of the customer records we are storing so we say that one physical record from the disk is storing ten of the *logical records*.

A read operation of the disk head will copy this allocation unit to the disk buffer. And the operating system will then sort out the logical records and make them available to the application program (for example, the database).

Data transfer between the buffer and the processor is only electrical and so the use of a buffer is effectively speeding up the transfer of data between the secondary storage device and the processor.

> **Remember**
> ♦ When we discussed records stored on the disk for indexed sequential files.

Double buffering

More sophisticated is the use of *double buffering*. When one of the buffers is having its contents read by the application program a second buffer can be filling up by reading data from the disk (Figure 4.4).

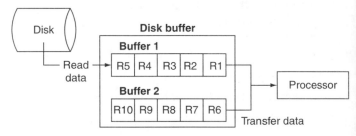

Figure 4.4   Double buffering

Print buffer

The buffering technique can similarly be applied to the output of data to a printer. Output is sent to a print buffer storage area and then the printer receives the data from the buffer. Double buffering would again speed up the operation.

4.5 Peripheral devices

A peripheral is any device which is not part of the Central Processing Unit. This includes any external input, output and storage device and also the internal hard disk.

Input devices
Keyboard

We expect to find a standard QWERTY keyboard on any PC. The keyboard may have a numeric keypad on the right hand side. Each key press generates the ASCII code for that character and the codes are stored in a *keyboard buffer* before transmission to the processor.

> **⟵ Look Back**
>
> To Chapter 3 for ASCII.

Concept keyboard

A keyboard device with a similar appearance to a touch screen. Different areas on the keyboard can be represented as a picture and each picture programmed to match a choice or action.

Mouse

Used by all computers with a graphical user interface. Original mice had the movement detected by the physical movement of a trackball, but newer mice use lasers and transit the movement signal wirelessly (rather that through a connecting cable).

Scanner

Most scanners are a photo-diode system which works on the following principle.

- ✓ A laser light is shone at the source document
- ✓ A moving mirror or prism moves the light across the source
- ✓ The light is reflected back; black areas reflect less light than white areas/bands
- ✓ A light sensor – typically a photo-diode – measures the intensity of the reflected light
- ✓ This level of reflected light is converted to an electrical signal which is encoded as a digital measurement.

Barcode reader

The following groups of devices – barcodes, OMR and OCR – are given the description *automatic data entry* as the data capture is done with some form other than the keying of data from the user.

A *barcode* is a series of vertical black bars with variable spacing of the width of the bars and the white space gaps between. The pattern of bars and gaps encodes the data value. The two coding systems in widespread use are the *Universal Product Code (UPC)*, a variant UPC-E and the *European Article Number (EAN)*.

A bar code is read by a peripheral device called a bar code scanner and there are variations:

- ✓ a horizontal flatbed panel – as used at the EPOS in a supermarket
- ✓ a hand held wand type scanner.

Optical Mark Reader (OMR)

Optical mark recognition uses 'marks' placed by the user at certain positions on a document. For example, the shading in one of a number of boxes coded (1 to 5) on a customer satisfaction survey form.

The positioning of the marks on the data capture form is the method for encoding the data. The form once completed is scanned. Some applications will have the ability to scan a whole batch of completed forms at high speed.

Typical applications include

- ✓ the input of an entry into the UK National Lottery
- ✓ students complete a multiple choice examination where the answer paper is designed for the OMR entry of the responses.

Optical Character Reader (OCR)

Uses *optical character recognition*. A document contains a numbers of characters which are printed in a stylised font which can be read by a scanner.

Typical applications include

- ✓ utility billing – the invoice sent to the customer is a document in two parts. The customer will return the bottom part of the form with their payment. This returned form has data such as the account number, printed in characters which can be scanned and captured.
- ✓ The basis of any OCR software on a PC. A document is first scanned and captured as an image. Software then processes the image and converts its contents into separate text characters (which could typically then be edited by word processing software).

Graphics tablet

The user draw on a glass plate with a digital pen and the movement of the pen is captured by software and mirrored on the screen.

Typically applications include

- ✓ capturing a handwritten signature
- ✓ tracing the outline of a shape from a paper copy (the paper document would be first secured on the tablet).

Touch screen

The visual display can detect the touching of the screen and translates the input as (for example) a menu choice and follows it with some action.

The obvious benefit of this device is that it does away with the need for an intermediary device such as a mouse.

Modern touch screens use one of two possible technologies:

Resistive – The screen consists of a number of layers, two of which come into contact as the result of a 'touch'.

Capacitive – the glass screen is coated with a layer of transparent conductor. Touching the screen causes the screen's electro-static charge to change and so its capacitance.

Typical applications include the primary communication for tablet PCs such as an iPad and smartphones such as an iPhone.

Radio Frequency Identification Reader (RFID)

An RFID chip or *tag* is embedded into an input device such as a plastic card.

- ✓ The RFID reader transmits a radio signal
- ✓ When the RFID tag comes into close proximity to the reader the signal from the reader activates (or 'energises') the tag
- ✓ The tag then transmits data to the reader by radio waves.

Typical applications include

- ✓ the identification of crates boxes of products in retail distribution (or even individual items)
- ✓ a microchip tag under the skin of a pet – when the tag is activated it sends

data to a central database so allowing the identification of the (lost?) pet
- ✓ tagging of new born babies in a hospital (to avoid them being wrongly identified).

Progress Check 4.5

Which media/device would you suggest for each of the following applications?
- (a) A school has a stock of surveying equipment which it loans out to students. The school needs a computer system for recording all loans.
- (b) Microchipping a pet.
- (c) A student has a number of images on paper which needs to be included in a word processed document.
- (d) A restaurant provides each waiter with a hand-held device to take the customer order.

Output devices

Monitor or the Visual Display Unit (VDU)

Monitors using cathode ray tube technology are rapidly being replaced by flat-screen LCD and TFT technology monitors. LCD monitors have the benefit that they use little power, but have the drawback that they are susceptible to temperature changes.

Laser printer

A laser is a page printer, i.e. it prints a whole page at a time. To print a page the following sequence is followed:

- ✓ the rotating print drum is negatively charged
- ✓ the printer generates a bitmap image of the page
- ✓ a laser beam is directed at the drum and removes the charge corresponding to the black areas of the image
- ✓ the toner is given a negative charge and is attracted to the positively charged areas of the drum
- ✓ toner is then bonded to the paper using heated rollers.

Typical application

The laser printer is the 'office workhorse'.

Dot matrix printer

A dot matrix printer has a print-head which moves laterally across the page and so prints a line of characters before advancing the paper to print the next line.

The print-head is made up of a matrix of pins and various combinations of pins form the different characters. The clarity of the printing will increase as the number of pins forming the matrix is increased. The pins strike a carbon ribbon which then impacts the character onto the paper.

Typical application

Although noisy and lacking in quality they are still in office use as their impact way of working makes them suitable for printouts which require one or more carbonised copies printed concurrently.

Inkjet printer

A print-head squirts coloured ink – black, cyan, magenta and yellow – onto the page from a piezo-electric crystal. Combinations of these four colours produce the coloured output.

- ✓ A heater behind the ink reservoir warms the ink
- ✓ This causes droplets of ink to vaporise and a small blob of ink is forced out onto the paper
- ✓ The print-head moves laterally across the width of the page and then prints the image line-by-line
- ✓ The ink dries on the paper before it is removed from the printer.

Typical application

Inkjet printers are in widespread commercial and home use for producing photo-quality printouts.

Plotter

The most common type is a ***flatbed plotter***. A sheet of paper is placed on the flat surface and a carriage mounted with pens of different colours moves above the paper. The carriage can move both horizontally and vertically so enabling the pens to be positioned anywhere on the page.

Typical application

Production of CAD drawings.

Speakers/Headphones

A loudspeaker is an analogue device and so the digital signals representing the sound wave must first pass through a ***digital-to-analogue converter*** before they are received by the loudspeaker.

Typical applications include

- ✓ the playback of media files
- ✓ signalling a warning message from a software application.

Storage devices

These can simply be summarised here as:

- ✓ an internal or external hard disk
- ✓ a variety of optical media storage devices.

These were discussed earlier in this chapter.

Exam-style Questions

1. (a) (i) Explain **two** differences between ROM and RAM as types of primary memory.

    1. ....

    2. ....

    (ii) State an example of what would be stored in ROM and justify your answer.

    Example: ....

    ....

    Justification: ....

    .... [2]

    (iii) State an example of what would be stored in RAM and justify your answer.

    Example: ....

    ....

Justification: ....

.... [2]

(b) (i) Explain the problem of speed mismatch between peripheral and processor.

....

....

(ii) Describe how this speed mismatch can be overcome.

....

.... [5]

Cambridge 9691 Paper 13 Q5 June 2011

2. A point-of-sale (POS) terminal in a supermarket has a number of input devices.
    State **two** different input devices used at the POS terminal and state the purpose of each.

1. ....

....

2. ....

.... [4]

Cambridge 9691 Paper 12 Q1(b) November 2011

3. State an example of each of the following types of storage medium and give a use for each.

(a) Magnetic
    Example: ....

Use: ....

.... [2]

(b) Solid state
    Example: ....

Use: ....

.... [2]

Cambridge 9691 Paper 12 Q6 November 2011

4. A mail order company allows customers to make orders by telephoning operators. The operators type the details of the order at a terminal.

On a regular basis, data is archived.

(a) Explain what is meant by archiving.

....

....

....

(b) Describe the reasons why it is necessary.

....

....

.... [4]

Cambridge 9691 Paper 12 Q7(b) November 2011

Data Transmission and Networking

5

After you have studied this chapter, you should be able to:

☞ describe the characteristics of a local area network (LAN) and a wide area network (WAN)

☞ show an understanding of the hardware and software needed for a local area network (LAN) and for accessing a wide area network (WAN)

☞ describe basic network topologies (bus, star and ring) explaining the benefits and drawbacks of each topology and typical applications where each topology would be used

☞ describe the different types of data transmission: serial and parallel; simplex, half duplex and full duplex modes

☞ explain the relationship between baseband and broadband

☞ recognise that errors can occur in data transmission; explain the use of parity checks, echoing and checksums in detecting and correcting these errors, and the use of parity blocks to aid self-checking

☞ explain the difference between packet switching and circuit switching

☞ define the term protocol

☞ describe the need for communication between devices, and between computers, and explain the need for protocols to establish communication links

☞ explain the need for both physical and logical protocols.

5.1 Local Area Network (LAN)

A collection of computers connected together over a geographical area such as the same building or site.

General benefits of networking

Most of these are the direct benefit of the computers being able to communicate with each other.

✓ Easier to transfer data from one user to another – no need to copy files to (for example) a memory stick and physically hand them over

✓ The network provides for the centralised storage and management of data files
  ➤ The ability to centrally store important company documents should avoid confusion over what is the latest version of an important document, for example, the Code of Conduct given to all employees
  ➤ Centralised files means we have easier control over backing up data

✓ The network allows specialist applications to be used
  ➤ such as internal email, diary scheduling applications

✓ Should encourage more flexible work practices

✓ Centralised management of software installation, patches/upgrades

✓ Allows the company to create an Intranet site

✓ Sharing of peripherals, for example, a printer

✓ A user can log on and work from any computer.

Peer-to-peer network

The first attempt at networking computers was in the late 1970s when computers were connected through the serial port.

All computers were 'peers' i.e. they had equal status and the benefits were that a user working at one computer could get access to the files on another computer. Security was not an issue. This encouraged collaborative working between users and was supported for example by features of the Windows operating system called *workgroups*.

Server based network

The next major development was to have all the user files centralised and available from a shared *file server*. This required the use of a network operating system which could:

✓   manage the organisation of users' files
✓   set up security controls
✓   manage user accounts for authentication and then authorisation of the use of resources network. For a large network this task would be done by a separate *domain controller server*, but for small business enterprise networks all networking functions are still carried out by a single 'multi-purpose' server.

As networking has developed the different facilities are provided for by a separate dedicated server such as an email server, web server, ftp server and many others.

Servers gave rise to a new model for computer applications called the *client-server model*. The server is providing a service to all the client computers on the network.

5.2   Wide Area Network (WAN)

A Wide Area Network is a collection of computers and possibly other networks which communicate over a wide geographical area such as nationally or globally.

A LAN is fine for connecting computers in the same building but large companies will have a computing facility in different countries and they need to be able to communicate.

Many communications over a WAN will use the existing land-line telephone network. But there is a fundamental problem with this. The telephone network was designed to carry voice traffic – which is analogue data, whereas all computers are digital machines. Hence data transmission using the telephone network requires the use of a *modem*. This is a hardware device which converts analogue signals to digital and vice versa.

5.3   Network topology

The topology is the physical layout of the devices and the connections between them.

Bus network

Early LANs used a bus topology which was a single cable segment with several computers connected onto the cable. In the early days this was done using a T-connector into the computer. Modern buildings are now wired with a cabling infrastructure and the connections are made from each device into a patch panel on the wall.

Figure 5.1 shows a typical bus network of four computers with a shared file server and printer.

✓   Each computer must be fitted with a *Network Interface Card (NIC)*
✓   The cable segment will be fitted with two *terminators*

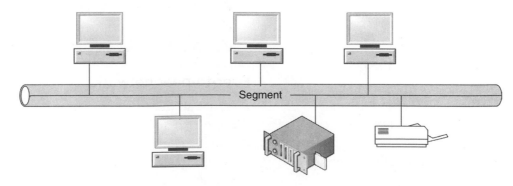

Figure 5.1   A bus network

✓ The file server will have the network operating system installed and each client computer must have the client network operating system software.

A bus network is a 'broadcast' system where data packets are sent along the network cable with the address of the receiving device. Packets are then received by the device which recognises the address of the packet.

The most widely used bus networking standard for the physical layer (see the discussion of protocols which follows) is called **Ethernet**. This has developed standards based on the transmission speeds called 10BASE-T (transmits at 10Mb/sec), 100BASE-TX (100 Mb/sec) or 1000BASE-T (1000 Mb/sec, i.e. 1 Gb/sec).

A bus network uses either:

✓ **coaxial cable**
✓ **twisted pair cable** (using a cabling standard called Cat5)
✓ **fibre optic cabling**.

Star topology

A star network has a separate communications link from each computer to a centralised computer (Figure 5.2). The connection from each computer will be into a separate port of the central hub and the types communications link may be different.

A star topology is used for WANs where the communications link may be already in place, for example, the telephone network.

The benefits of a star topology are obvious – if one of the communication links fails then the other computers are not affected.

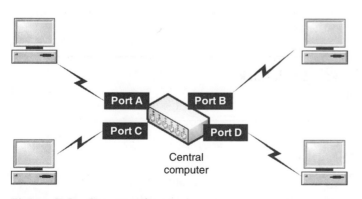

Figure 5.2   Star topology

Ring topology

A ring is a single cable forming a ring. The ring carries a single token which is the only carrier of data between the various devices attached to the ring. when a device wishes to send data it must wait until the token becomes availble and then 'grab' the token. The token circles the ring at very high speed. As it always travels in the same direction there is a possibility of collisions resulting in lost data.

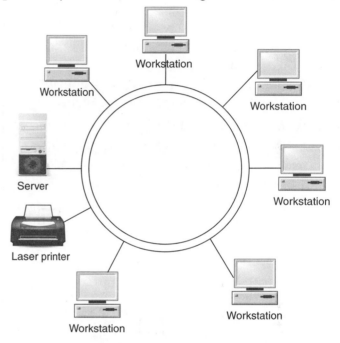

Token-ring networks from IBM were a popular LAN in the early days of networking.

Ring networks are potentially less secure as the token many pass between several devices before it reaches the intended destination device.

> 📖 **Later**
>
> Networks are studied again later in Chapter 24.

5.4 Different types of data transmission

The digital revolution has meant that every form of data – text, numbers, pictures, sound and all forms of media – can be represented, stored and processed by a computer system.

Data often has to be transmitted between two computers, between devices on a network or from a remote server to a computer.

All of these scenarios require the transmission of digital data along some form of communication channel.

Progress Check 5.1

A company has its computer system for the office, warehouse and call centre on different sites.

The office has a Local Area Network (LAN) consisting of:

✓ four computers
✓ file server (Server X) contains all the administration and order processing data for all shops
✓ file server (Server Y) acts as a domain controller and authenticates all logons.

The call centre and Warehouse each have a single computer which connects to the Office network. The computer systems are connected over a Wide Area Network using a star topology.

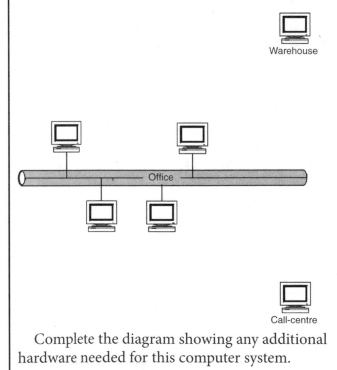

Complete the diagram showing any additional hardware needed for this computer system.

Serial transmission

A sequence of bits is sent along a single wire one after the other by varying the voltage on the wire.

Computers have always had a serial port for communication and the current de-facto standard for PCs is the **Universal Serial Bus (USB)**. The USB cable has separate wires for the sending and receiving of data and other wires for various control signals.

Serial transmission would be used for:

✓ transferring data from a USB memory stick to a computer
✓ for connecting two computers together using their USB ports for a data transfer.

A bus network cable segment we discussed earlier is another example of serial data transfer.

Parallel transmission

A cable would consist of several wires and bits are sent along each wire simultaneously.

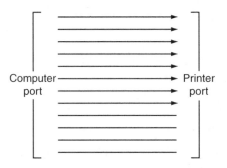

Until recently all PCs and laptops would have come with a Centronics parallel port. The cable consisted of 36 wires – 8 used for sending/receiving of the data bits and each of the others dedicated to a particular control signal. For example, a signal from the printer to inform the computer it is 'ready to receive data'.

Parallel transmission is only suitable for transmission over short distances due to the issue of **skew** – that is keeping the voltages changes on each wire in sync.

Parallel transmission is used for a computer to printer device connection and all the internal busses on the motherboard.

> ← **Look Back**
>
> To Chapter 1 for the discussion of busses.

Simplex

The simplest form of transmission. Data can be transmitted in one direction only. An example of simplex transmission is the sending of Teletext or picture data from the mast to the user's television receiver. Data is only ever transmitted in one direction only – from the mast to the television.

Half duplex

Data can be transmitted in both directions but only in one direction at any instance in time.

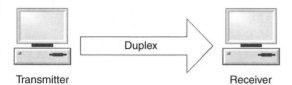

Transmitter   Receiver

Figure 5.3   Simplex

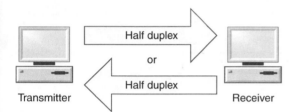

Transmitter   Receiver

Figure 5.4   Half duplex

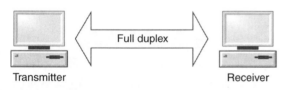

Transmitter   Receiver

Figure 5.5   Full duplex

An example of half duplex is CB radio where the communicating devices are set at any one time to send or receive.

Full duplex

Data can be simultaneously transmitted in both directions. A telephone conversation is an example of full duplex. Both persons are able to talk and receive voice traffic at any time.

5.5 Baseband and broadband

Baseband

Baseband communication is where all the available bandwidth is dedicated to a single data channel only which connects a single sending and receiving device.

The ring and bus LAN topologies – including Ethernet-are examples of baseband communication.

Progress Check 5.2

Which of these are true statements?
(a) Serial communication between two computers will always use a cable with a single copper wire.
(b) The data transmission rate is expressed as the bit rate.
(c) The data transmission rate is expressed as the baud rate.
(d) Parallel data transmission is only suitable for long distances.
(e) For parallel transmission, transmission of a single data byte would require 8 separate lines.
(f) For parallel transmission, some additional lines are used for control signals.
(g) Half Duplex means communication is only ever possible in one direction only.
(h) Full Duplex means communication is possible in both directions – but not at the same time.

Broadband

Broadband is a multi-channel system where the available bandwidth is used across several data channels.

Broadband communicationis usually provided with either a fibre-cable or **Asymetric Subscriber Digital Line (ADSL)** communication. In the UK ADSL uses the existing copper wire telephone subscriber network but using a frequency range different to that used for voice communication. ADSL is and example of full duplex communication.

Since ADSL is a shared service its performance in terms of upload and download speeds is determined by the number of users at any time.

5.6 Detecting and correcting errors in data transmission

Data transmission may be made up of millions of bits – just one bit being received incorrectly will cause problems.

Echo back

This and parity which follows, is a technique designed to achieve a successful data transmission.

'Echo back' is a form of verification check. The data received is sent back to the sending device and software can then check if the two binary values match.

Parity

We described a parity check when discussing ASCII codes in Chapter 3.

A parity bit is a bit in addition to the seven bits which encode the character and is used to check the byte.

The computer system will work on either even parity or odd parity.

Is a parity check foolproof?

No – because if two or more of the bits were received incorrectly then the byte could still pass the parity check even though the data is wrong.

> ← **Look Back**
>
> To study the examples given in Chapter 3 for the calculation of a parity bit.

Progress Check 5.3

A computer system using odd parity transmits the following sequence of four bytes.

Byte 4	Byte 3	Byte 2	Byte 1
0101 1110	1100 0000	0010 0001	0111 1111

→

Which byte(s) will fail the parity check?

(See Case II in Example which follows).

Parity block check

A further check can be performed on a block of bytes called a *parity block check*.

Data is saved onto the hard disk in blocks (typically each of 512 bytes) – it is a block which will be read/written in a single read/write operation. For the illustrations which follow, we shall consider for simplicity a block of size 5 bytes made up of four data bytes + a parity byte. The calculation can be illustrated by considering the five bytes as rows and columns. The final row is

the parity byte. The final column for all five bytes is the parity bit.

The parity byte is a sequence of parity bits each calculated from the four bits in the rows above.

Example

Consider the structure described – four data bytes and a parity byte – for a computer system using odd parity. The correctly transmitted data block should look like this:

Bytes transmitted are:

1	1	0	0	1	1	0	1
0	0	1	0	0	0	0	0
1	0	1	1	1	1	0	0
1	1	0	0	0	0	1	0
0	1	1	0	1	1	0	0

Data bytes

Parity byte

Assume that there was an error in the transmission and the bytes were received by the device as follows:

Case I – Actual bytes received

One of the bits in data byte 3 has been incorrectly received as a 0.

Data byte 3 has its parity bit calculated as a 1, but as a 0 bit was received in the parity position, the receiving software will conclude that there must be a error with byte 3.

1	1	0	0	1	1	0	1
0	0	1	0	0	0	0	0
1	0	0	1	1	1	0	0
1	1	0	0	0	0	1	0
0	0	1	0	0	1	0	1

The parity byte will calculate a parity bit of 0 and so conclude there is a error with the column 3 calculation for the parity byte.

The conclusion is that the bit in byte 3 which must be in error is in column 3.

Case II – Actual bytes received

Here for byte 3, two bits are in error from the same data byte and the result is that it passes the parity bit check.

```
1  1  0  0  1  1  0  1
0  0  1  0  0  0  0  0
1  0  1  0  1  1  0  1
1  1  0  0  0  0  1  0
0  1  1  0  1  1  0  0
```

The parity byte however will conclude that there is an error – as the bits in positions 4 and 8 do not match the calculation of the parity byte for columns 4 and 8.

It is claimed that a combination of using parity bits and a parity block check will identify 99 per cent of all transmission errors.

Progress Check 5.4

A computer system using odd parity transmits data as 'parity blocks' each made up of four data bytes followed by a parity byte.

Parity byte	Byte 4	Byte 3	Byte 2	Byte 1
?	1101 1110	1100 1000	1111 0111	1111 1110

What is the parity byte?

Progress Check 5.5

The following sequence of five bytes are received – the final byte is the parity byte and the system uses odd parity.

Parity byte	Byte 4	Byte 3	Byte 2	Byte 1
0000 0110	0010 0000	1101 0000	1110 0111	1111 1110

Explain how the system can detect that there is an error in the transmission of byte 2.

What was the binary for byte 2 originally transmitted?

Checksums

A checksum is a number or pattern of bits which is hashed from some existing data values. To carry out a checksum on some data which has been transmitted, the bytes transmitted would be hashed in some way prior to transmission and then the same *hashing function* applied to the bytes after they are received. The calculated checksums will be the same following an error-free transmission.

Checksums are commonly used during the startup (boot) process of the computer system. A checksum is hashed from the BIOS data held on CMOS memory and compared to the checksum calculated on the previous boot-up session.

Checksums are also commonly used during a file download and are designed to check that users are downloading the proper program and that no data was corrupted during the download process. An example is the Python programming language download site where the site has quoted a checksum string, for every available download, for the user to verify after a download from the site.

5.7 Difference between packet switching and circuit switching

Circuit switching

When two computers wish to exchange data, they establish a path – called a circuit – through the network. After they have established a circuit, all data exchanged between the two computers flows through this circuit. Once the data transfer is complete the circuit is released.

Packet switching

Messages are broken into small blocks called *packets* or *datagrams*, which are routed individually through the network.

Packets for a particular message may travel along different routes through the network. At the receiver, the packets are reassembled to construct the complete message. Packet switched nodes have the capability to store packets until the node is ready to transmit the packets. Packets have a destination address and a sequence number to enable the message to be constructed by the receiving device. See the discussion of TCP/IP which follows.

On the Internet and a LAN it is the role of a *router* to handle packet transmission.

📖 **Later**

More detail about a router in Chapter 24.

5.8 Protocols

A *protocol* is a set of rules about the transmission of data between two computers, in order that computers can communicate.

Standard protocols

A standard protocol conforms to a standard laid down by a standards authority (for example, the ISO) to allow data/information exchange between any computer systems conforming to the standard.

A standard protocol usually consists of several separate *layers* which are used for the various stages of the communication process.

Analogy

An analogy could be the receipt of a parcel from a mail order company. There will be various protocols about the way in which the goods are packaged for the various stages of the process – putting the goods in its original packaging by the manufacturer, then the sending of the goods from the warehouse to the courier may involve a second packaging protocol, as the goods are to be sent with other parcels.

> The term 'Protocol' is not only used for computing.

5.9 The need for both physical and logical protocols and the need for layering in an interface

In a computing context:

- ✓ lower level protocols are concerned with establishing and maintaining connections
- ✓ higher level protocols are concerned with the transfer of messages once a connection has been made
- ✓ still higher levels are concerned with the transfer of programs, files etc., as a sequence of messages to the applications software.

The various layers which make up the communications protocol is called the *protocol stack*.

TCP/IP

The standard protocol which is used to send data Across the Internet is *TCP/IP*. TCP stands for *Transmission Control Protocol* and IP stands for *Internet Protocol*.

TCP/IP protocol stack

Communications and network protocols are developed in layers, with each layer responsible for a different part of the communication process. The TCP/IP protocol suite is normally considered to be a four-layer system as shown in Table 5.1.

Table 5.1

TCP/IP protocol suite	
TCP/IP Protocol Stack	
Application	Web browser, FTP
Transport	TCP
Network	IP
Link	Network card

Link layer

Handles all the physical details of interfacing with the cable including the network interface card and a device driver. This will depend on the hardware and protocols include Ethernet and Token Ring.

IP layer

IP forwards each packet using a four byte destination address (the IP number). Each computer on the network will have its own unique IP address.

TCP layer

This layer is responsible for:

- ✓ assigning a sequence number to every packet in the message.

Data will be sent/received from several applications so:

- ✓ allocation of a *port number* to different applications and then
- ✓ routing packets to the correct application program.

Data could be lost in the intermediate network, so the TCP layer must:

- ✓ verify the correct delivery of data from client to server and vice-versa

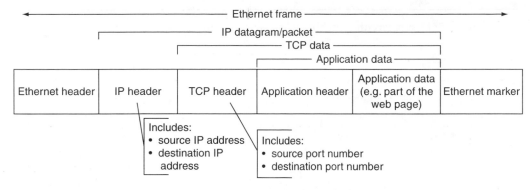

Figure 5.6 Ethernet frame

✓ detect errors or lost packets of data
✓ TCP will trigger re-transmission until the data is correctly and completely received.

Application layer (or Sockets)

This layer is a package of subroutines that provide access to TCP/IP on most systems.

The application layer handles the details of the particular application. It uses different protocols depending on the application. One example is File Transfer Protocol (FTP).

The Ethernet frame shown in Figure 5.6 would be the basic unit of data transmission on an Ethernet bus network and illustrates the concepts of layering of the communications protocol.

Port numbers

A connection made to a server may be for a variety of different reasons as servers offer a dedicated service.

These include:

✓ *http:* access to web pages
✓ *ftp:* access to a server providing file transfer, for example, downloads
✓ *IRC:* access to a server offering Internet Relay Chat.

Each service is identified by a port number. Most PCs have access to their:

✓ web pages set to port 80
✓ ftp file transfer using port 21.

Sockets

To access a service from a server we need to specify two things:

✓ the IP address of the server
✓ the port number of the service required.

The *(IP address + the port number)* is called a *socket*.

Exam-style Questions

1. (a) State what is meant by a protocol.

....

.... [2]

(b) Communication across a network can be done by using circuit switching or packet switching.

(i) Explain the difference between circuit switching and packet switching.

....

.... [2]

    (ii) Give one advantage of using circuit switching when sending data across a network.

....

....

    (iii) Give one advantage of using packet switching when sending data across a network.

....

.... [2]

Cambridge 9691 Specimen Paper 1 Q8

2. (a) State two differences between a Local Area Network (LAN) and a Wide Area Network (WAN).

    1. ....

    ....

    2. ....

    .... [2]

(b) State what is meant by each of the following types of data transmission. Give an advantage of each.

    (i) Serial   ....

    ....

    Advantage   ....

    ....

    (ii) Parallel   ....

    ....

    Advantage   ....

    .... [4]

    ....

(c) The following bytes were received during a data transmission.

    01101101 10101010 10111101 10110001

    Parity is being used as an error check.

    State which one of the bytes has been corrupted. Explain why you chose the one that you did.

    Corrupted byte   ....

    Reason   .... [3]

Cambridge 9691 Paper 11 Q8 June 2011

3. The computers in a school classroom are networked. It is decided that this network should be linked to the Internet.

(a) State **two** items of hardware and one type of software which would be necessary to connect this network to the Internet.

    Hardware 1   ....

    ....

    Hardware 2   ....

    ....

Software ....

.... [3]

(b) When a video file is accessed on a network it can be watched as it is downloading or it can be stored for watching at a later date. Explain the relationship between the required bit rates and the data being transmitted.

....

....

....

.... [4]

Cambridge 9691 Paper 11 Q8 November 2011

4. A Supermarket has a number of point-of-sale terminals.

Data is read from goods at the terminals and information is produced.

(a) State **two** output devices which would be used at the point-of-sale, justifying their use.

Device 1 ....

Justification ....

....

Device 2 ....

Justification ....

.... [4]

(b) State **three** types of output needed at the point-of-sale terminals. For each type of output explain why the output is needed.

Output 1 ....

....

....

Output 2 ....

....

....

Output 3 ....

....

.... [6]

Cambridge 9691 Paper 11 Q1(b)&(c) June 2011

System Life Cycle

6

Revision Objectives

After you have studied this chapter, you should be able to:

- explain the importance of defining a problem accurately
- describe the function and purpose of a feasibility study
- explain the importance of determining the information requirements of a system and describe different methods of fact finding, highlighting the advantages and disadvantages of each method
- describe what is involved when analysing the requirements of a system, explaining the nature of the requirements specification and its content, identifying inefficiencies/problems, user requirements and hardware and software requirements
- design the data structures, inputs, outputs and processing using diagrammatic representations where appropriate (including the use of Data Flow Diagrams (DFDs) and system flowcharts)
- explain the importance of evaluating the system against initial specifications
- explain the content and importance of documentation in the system life cycle, including the requirements specification, design specification, program specification and documentation
- explain the importance of testing and installation planning, including the method of installation
- explain the reasons for maintaining the system.

6.1 The importance of defining a problem accurately

The saying 'Chinese Whispers' makes the point that as more people are involved in any communication the risk increases that the message will change as it is passed from one person to the next. There will be many people involved in the development of a new information system!

Terminology

Computer system
Used already to describe the 'hardware'

Information system
The 'business application'

"Code this program for the computer system."
"Design the program for the computer system."
"Test the program for the computer system."

This illustrates that a difference of just one word defines very differently the task to be done.

The problem to be solved and tasks required must be clearly defined.

Overview – The system life cycle

All the stages involved in producing a new information system is called the ***systems (development) life cycle*** and the stages are shown below:

- ✓ Feasibility study
- ✓ Analysis
- ✓ Design
- ✓ System development
    - ➢ System testing
- ✓ Implementation
- ✓ System maintenance

For the development of most systems the stages will be sequential, for example, the design stage follows on from the analysis.

📖 **Later**

There are many different variations of these stages in different textbooks.

Look at the Section 4 requirements and match these stages to what you will be asked to do for your project work.

6.2 The function and purpose of a feasibility study

We shall assume we are to develop a new information system for a company or organisation.

Examples might include:

- ✓ call centre monitoring software for insurance company ABC
- ✓ new payroll software for large company XYZ
- ✓ a government's new information system for the processing of visa applications
- ✓ new payroll software which is to be developed and then commercially sold to as many clients as possible.

They all require the writing of software and all except the last example are for a particular client. The final example is not for the development of a information system but a particular software package only and will not feature in the coverage which follows.

It is highly unlikely that no current system exists. The proposed information system is likely to be:

- ✓ a replacement system for a procedure which is currently operated as a 'manual system'
- ✓ a replacement system for a currently information system which has become outdated for a number of reasons
  - ➤ The hardware is out-of-date
  - ➤ The software features no longer matches with the business needs.
- ✓ the current computer based information system is to have new features added
  - ➤ for example, a web site is to have added content. Online retailer Amazon recently added the feature of setting up your personal Christmas present list!
  - ➤ for example, a retail shop wants to be able to order an item it does not have from another store, which it cannot currently do.

Feasibility study

This is an initial study – before any development work starts in earnest – to confirm or otherwise the proposed information system is 'feasible' i.e. possible.

The feasibility study will describe the context of the problem.

"This system is for Company *X* and is designed to replace the current system for the picking and dispatch of orders from the warehouse".

The issues the feasibility study will consider are discussed here.

Technically feasible

Does currently technology exist which would be the vehicle for the development of the proposed system?

Socially feasible (i.e. acceptable)

The proposed system will have many objectives one of which will be to make cost savings for the client. Its impact could be the loss of jobs, the need to re-skill staff or even locate staff to work at a different geographical location.

There is likely to be a social impact on staff and the client will need to justify that these changes can be managed.

Economically feasible

The client will carry out a 'costs verses benefits' study before the project gets the go-ahead. The client will be thinking long-term and have to justify that the new computer system will result in cost benefits after (about) three years. This has to be balanced against the initial cost of paying for the new system.

What follows assumes that the proposed new system gets the go-ahead.

6.3 Different methods of fact finding

Analysis

The task of finding out precisely what the client wants is a specialised job and is done by a ***systems analyst***. The analyst should have:

- ✓ excellent communication skills
- ✓ sound all-round computing skills.

> Remember, the system does not exist at this stage so call it the '**proposed system**' (not the new system).

The key roles of the analyst include:

✓ carry out the analysis, i.e. the *fact finding* for the information requirements
✓ design the new information system
✓ supervise the implementation of the system.

The fact finding is done using a number of common-sense techniques.

Discussion with staff

✓ The managers of the system
✓ The staff who operate the current system.

It is important that both are involved as the reason why the current system is not operating efficiently could be that the manager's perception of the current system is very different from that of the staff who work in (for example) the Call Centre or operate the picking of orders from the warehouse.

This will be a 'face to face' interview. The analyst should go into the interview with a list of prepared questions.

Advantages of interviewing

✓ Able to clarify any points of misunderstanding
✓ Change the questioning, for example, follow up specific points of detail by asking additional questions.

Disadvantage of interviewing

✓ Face-to-face interviews are very time-consuming.

The alternative is to collect the responses from staff using questionnaires.

Questionnaires

A large national company may use the same (for example) point-of-sale system in all its retail shops and it will not be possible within the time available to interview all staff.

Advantage

✓ A large number of responses can be obtained with little involvement of the systems analyst

Disadvantages

✓ Staff may be unable to seek clarity about questions
✓ Questionnaires often have a low-return rate.

Current system documentation

The current system will have **documentation** containing the procedures for its operation. The analyst may find that there is a difference between what is written down and what s/he has learnt from earlier discussions with staff. This should give clues as to why the current system is not working and provide pointers to what is required by the proposed system.

Observation

Perhaps the best possible information about how (say) the warehouse operator processes and 'picks' an order from the shelves is to observe this at first hand. Again there may be differences between what is actually happening in the warehouse and what the documentation contains or what the manager has already told the analyst.

Past experience

The analyst or colleagues may have past experience of similar systems from other projects on which they have worked.

6.4 Requirements of a system

The analyst must collect as much information as possible from as many different sources as possible within the limits of the time made available.

The key skill of the analyst is then to process and analyse the information and identity:

✓ points where information collected from different sources appears to conflict
✓ points of agreement from different sources.

From this will come:

✓ the weaknesses of the current system
✓ the core parts of the proposed system
  ➤ for example, some managers may have suggested features which will be rarely used.

The analyst must now summarise their findings.

The requirements specification

This formal document summarises the work of the analysis stage and contains:

- ✓ a list of **criteria** or **objectives** against which the success of the project can be measured
- ✓ a **data dictionary** of what data is needed to operate the system
- ✓ various **chart**s which describe the processes involved in the system.

This *requirements specification* document is the starting point for the next stage in the system life cycle – the design.

6.5 Design the data structures, inputs, outputs and processing

Design

There is often more than one way to solve a problem and the design stage must consider a system which is less costly, efficient and less complex whilst still meeting all the objectives in the requirements specification.

The information system involves people, hardware, software and operating procedures which must all be considered.

Software requirements

The way forward will be one of the following approaches.

- ✓ Buy a commercially available software solution which requires only a minimal amount of tailoring
  - ➤ This is a very tempting option as commercial software is available for a vast range of business functions – order processing, payroll and thousands more – even for e-commerce.
- ✓ Write new software. There are still possible short-cuts including:
  - ➤ the use of *software components*
  - ➤ the use of *program libraries*
  - ➤ write applications programs which access data stored in a *Database Management System (DBMS)* – since DBMS software is widely available.

> 📖 **Later**
>
> **DBMS** covered in more detail in Chapter 24.

The discussion which follows assumes the second approach to the design of the proposed system – we are writing new software.

Hardware requirements

Following the fact finding the analyst should have an idea about what hardware will support the proposed system.

- ✓ Will additional computers be needed?
- ✓ Will the system operate on the existing network?
- ✓ If so, will a new file server be needed?
- ✓ Is the project a web-based system?

If new hardware is needed, this must be carefully costed, alternative suppliers asked to provide a quotation and the final decision approved by the client.

The detailed design work must consider:

- ✓ the *input*s to various processes which make up the system
- ✓ the *processing* which takes place to this data
- ✓ the *outputs* required
  - ➤ output to the screen or is hard copy output required?
- ✓ *Data storage*
  - ➤ The information system will need to save data generated by its business operations. The analyst must decide what files will be used including methods of organisation and access.

> ⬅ **Look Back**
>
> To Chapter 3 for a discussion of files.

Data Flow Diagram (DFD)

A DFD illustrates the input-processing-output and storage sequence and considers also the data items from the data dictionary which form the flows of information (Figure 6.1).

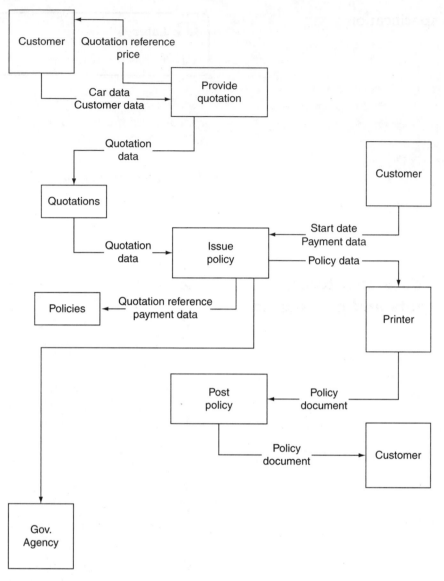

Figure 6.1 A Data Flow Diagram (DFD)

Example

Consider an insurance company which provides motor insurance quotes from its web site.

Customers key in their profile and the vehicle profile; the company then provides a quotation with a reference number.

The customer can then (or later) accept the quote and the company will issue a new policy number and take the customer's payment. A paper copy of the policy is posted to the customer.

The insurance company must notify all new policies issued to a Government Agency.

Key points about a DFD are listed here.

✓ The **process box** will describe a 'doing' action
➤ Issue quotation, Issue policy and Post policy.
✓ The **flow lines** show the actual data items involved
➤ These data items would have been documented in the data dictionary and include the Customer data, Vehicle data, Start date etc.
✓ The **entities** show the staff, department or even a physical device such as a printer

➢ Customer, Government Agency and Printer.
✓ The DFD may have a 'boundary box'. This shows the boundary for the information system operated by the company
✓ A *data store* will be labelled with the file name or data being stored.

Systems flowchart

A systems flowchart is an alternative to using a DFD and shows:

✓ the source of any inputs
✓ the program(s) which should match to the DFD's processes

✓ the file(s)
✓ document(s).

The equivalent systems flowchart for our insurance information system is shown in Figure 6.2.

The symbols used are for a document, keyboard, pre-defined process (usually a program), a data store, general data input and a communications link. The systems flowchart illustrates that:

✓ the customer is providing the data from printed documents. Entering this data to the website form is shown as a new process
✓ there is no indication of the flow of actual data values and who is involved, for example, the customer, the government agency etc.

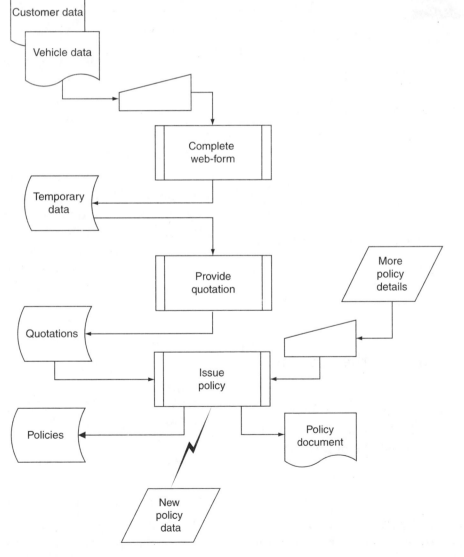

Figure 6.2 A system flowchart

Progress Check 6.1

In the UK a person learning to drive must take a theory test. These are done at test centres with about one sitting each week. The driver telephones for a booking and a date is confirmed. The driver attends on this date and sits one of a number of tests selected from a tests database. They are told on the day if they have passed or failed and given a results certificate.

Draw the DFD to describe this computing application.

Hint: there are two processes – 'Book Test' and 'Take Test'.

Progress Check 6.2

Draw the systems flowchart for the same scenario.

6.6 The importance of evaluating the system against initial specifications

The requirements specification document may form the basis of the formal contract between the client and the developer. The client therefore will assess carefully if all the *objectives* have been successfully implemented before payment is made. Conversely the developer may ask to client to formally 'sign off' the project as written confirmation that the work has been completed and the system fully implemented.

6.7 Documentation in the system life cycle

The purpose of documentation is to communicate effectively between the different stakeholders in the project – the client, the analyst, the programming team and users.

Project brief

The project brief is given by the client to the development team in order to access the feasibility of the project.

Requirements specification

This is the summary of the analysis stage. It contains a number of objectives and criteria. On completion of the project, what has been produced and the performance of the new system will be matched to these objectives.

Design specification

The analyst and the programming team work closely together to produce the *design specification*.

The design specification is a reference point for all members of the programming team as different parts of the system will be developed and programs produced by different programmers. The system will have been divided up into sub-tasks and the design of each sub-task will use a *top-down approach* to the program specifications.

> 📖 **Later**
>
> A discussion of using a top-down approach is covered in Chapter 11.

Program specifications

The design of the programs is part of the overall design process. Note that 'program design' does not mean the writing of the code – we are not yet ready for this. Using approaches such as the use of program libraries and object-oriented programming it is even more important.

The specifications will have pseudocode descriptions for various algorithms which provide the solution; from these, writing the program code can be started.

> 📖 **Later**
>
> 'Maintenance documentation' is discussed later in this chapter.

User support

There are different forms in which documentation for the user can be provided.

- ✓ Paper based *manual*
- ✓ *On-screen help* which is context sensitive.

A user manual would contain:

- ✓ installation instructions and guidance
- ✓ sample input screens

✓ sample output screens/printouts
✓ explanation of error messages which appear and the action to take when they do
✓ explanation of backup and archiving procedures
✓ a 'Frequently Asked Questions' (FAQ) section
✓ a 'knowledge base' of previously reported issues and suggested fixes
✓ telephone numbers for any Help Desk facility
✓ tutorials.

These help files would until recently have been available as part of the software installation and the files saved on the file server or PC. With the widespread availability of the Internet at a workstation, the developer will instead make the help files available through a web browser from the developer's web server.

6.8 Testing and installation

Testing

Testing will occur at two key stages in the system life cycle.

✓ Testing following the coding of the programs
✓ Testing the system following its installation in the client's workplace.

> 📖 **Later**
>
> The different types of program testing are discussed later in more detail in Chapter 16.

Program testing

The first level will be to test that individual program works. A top-down approach will have been used so the next stage will be to test that programs work successfully with each other – this is *system testing*.

Acceptance testing

All the testing so far has been carried out in-house by the developer. The programs must then be installed onto the client's computer system and further testing carried out to prove to the client that all the objectives have been met.

If the system does not meet any of the objectives in the requirements specification then the developer will be obliged to carry out further work.

Installation of the system

Direct changeover

The old system is deactivated and at this precise time the new system becomes active. For a system such as online retailing over the Internet this could be done at off-peak times.

Direct changeover is risky. If there are problems then we could re-activate the old system. The problem then is that all transactions saved by the new system must be transferred.

Parallel conversion

This is designed to avoid the problems which could occur with a direct changeover. The old and new systems are run together alongside each other for a limited period of time. Results from the new system can be compared to establish if the new system is functioning correctly. The drawback is that the period of parallel running may involve more work by staff, for example, the double entry of data.

Phased conversion

The introduction of parts of the system is staggered over a period of time. Consider a school which was introducing a Management Information System for all aspects of the school's operation. It could introduce the enrolment system, then three months later the examinations system and in a further three months the timetabling system etc.

As each new module is activated and confirmed to be working the next module can be installed. It is likely that some modules will work with each other. For example, the timetabling module assumes we have all the student data – and so the order in which they are introduced must be considered.

Pilot conversion

The complete system is first introduced and made operational at a single shop only (not at all shops in the chain). Once the system is confirmed to be fully working at this shop then the system can be introduced at all the other shops. There could be issues which result from a mixture of the old and new system at different shops.

Progress Check 6.3

An examination board currently marks all scripts (for around 150 different subjects) by hand (i.e. examiners using a red pen!). The board are developing a computerised system for the scanning of the scripts and marking scripts on-line by examiners at home on their PC.

Which method of implementation would you suggest for this system?

6.9 Maintaining the system

The client will want to review the working of the system after (for example) three months and may conclude that changes need to be made to the system.

Perfective maintenance

The system is working but not as well as it was hoped.

> **Note**
>
> Do not confuse the term 'Maintenance' with the basic updating of a file's contents – such as changing the price of the product.

Examples

- ✓ Customers who place an order on the website are complaining that the response time for a search for a particular item takes a long time. We need to carry out work to improve this
- ✓ The volume of orders we are now taking on the website has increased from around ten an hour (the figure predicted in the requirements specification) to double this and this is causing poor performance.

Corrective maintenance

Despite all the program and system testing some errors have appeared after the system was formally handed over. This will be due to some unforeseen set of events or data.

We need to go back to the developer and ask that the bugs are fixed.

Adaptive maintenance

The system needs to be changed in some way.

Examples

- ✓ The changes have been forced on the client due to a change in Government legislation – rates of tax have changed. This will require changes to be made to either program code and/or data files.
- ✓ The network file servers have been updated and this requires the transfer of data files to a new server.
- ✓ The client wants to add new features to the system which requires new work to be done by the developer.

Technical/Maintenance documentation

This is written for the developers (not the client or end-users). The programmers who carry out the maintenance may not be the ones who coded the original software. It is important therefore that all aspects of the system design and program code listings are documented.

Progress Check 6.4

You buy a game for your PC and it comes with a user manual. List the contents you would expect to find in the manual.

Progress Check 6.5

Make a list of all the documents which are produced throughout the systems life cycle. Show the timing at which each document is produced.

Document	Timing
–	–
–	–

Progress Check 6.6

A company uses a website for order processing. For each of the following issues name the type of maintenance which will need to be carried out.

(a) A user keys in their address and then has to later key in the address a second time for the 'delivery address'. The data capture form is to be changed to provide a button with 'Delivery address the same?' to avoid in most cases keying a second time.

(b) Customers are complaining that the website is frequently unavailable at certain times of the day.

(c) The Government has brought in new legislation that requires a message on all order forms stating that the customer has the right to return the goods within 14 days.

(d) The company needs to be able to change a product description or availability at any time.

(e) The website is to add feature allowing customers who make a purchase to later leave feedback.

(f) A user reports that after selecting the items to be purchased the web page 'froze' and did not let then continue to the payment stage.

Exam-style Questions

1. A systems analyst is employed to produce a new stock control system for a company. The manager of the company is not satisfied with the present system.

(a) Explain the importance to both analyst and manager of defining the problem accurately. You should make clear the part played by each person.

....

....

....

....

....

.... [4]

(b) (i) Explain how the evaluation of the new system will be carried out.

....

....

....

....

(ii) Explain why the evaluation is important to both the analyst and the manager.

....

....

....

.... [4]

Cambridge 9691 Paper 11 Q2 June 2011

2. (a) In the systems development life cycle, describe what is involved when designing a system.

....

....

....

.... [4]

(b) When a new system has been developed it must be installed into the organisation for which it has been produced. Describe the tasks involved in installation planning and of implementing the system into the organisation.

....

....

....

.... [4]

Cambridge 9691 Paper 11 Q2 November 2011

3. A systems analyst is employed to produce a new computer system. The systems development life cycle includes a feasibility study. Explain the purposes of the feasibility study.

....

....

....

....

....

....

....

....

....

.... [5]

Cambridge 9691 Paper 11 Q5 June 2012

4. The analyst needs to collect information about the present system.

State **one** advantage and **one** disadvantage of each of the following methods of information collection.

(i) Observation..[2]

(ii) Interviews...[2]

(iii) Document collection..[2]

Cambridge 9691 Paper 11 Q8 November 2010

Choosing Appropriate Applications Software

7

Revision Objectives

After you have studied this chapter, you should be able to:

☞ distinguish between custom-written software and off-the-shelf software packages, and discuss the benefits and drawbacks of each in given situations

☞ identify the features of common applications found in business, commercial and industrial applications, for example, stock control, payroll, process control, point-of-sale systems

☞ identify suitable common generic applications software for particular application areas, for example, word processor, spreadsheet, desktop publishers (DTP), presentation software, graphics packages (bitmapped and vector graphics)

☞ identify application areas for which generic applications software is not appropriate

☞ describe the purpose and impact of different types of generic applications software, for example, word processors, spreadsheets, desktop publisher (DTP), presentation software, drawing packages, graphics packages.

7.1 Application software

We have already discussed the production of software in the chapter on the systems life cycle.

Custom-written software

Also called *bespoke software* it is software written for a particular client.

Custom-written will enable the software to match exactly with a list of requirements drawn up by the client.

Advantage

✓ The software will be exactly what the client wants.

Disadvantages

✓ There will be a long time lag between the start of the production and its completion

✓ Software is a human activity and its design, coding and testing usually involves a large amount of 'man hours'; hence the cost of the production of the software will be high and will be charged to the client

✓ When the software is released there could still be errors in the software.

Custom-written software will also be required in many manufacturing processes. For example, a company who makes a new washing machine or a new printer will require software designed to operate the machine, for example, a printer driver.

Off-the-shelf software

Off-the shelf can mean either:

✓ Software which is designed for a mass market and is purchased in a retail shop. This includes all the software we use on a PC – operating system, generic software such as an office suite, word processor or any of the vast range of special-purpose applications software available.

✓ Software for a specialised business application but which is already available from a software house. The program will only require some tailoring to meet each business' needs. For example, a software house has produced a point-of-sale system (see later) for use by a small business which uses a single terminal. The software house hopes it will sell the software to hundreds of small shops.

Advantages

- ✓ A choice of products, for example many different garden design programs are readily available for the PC, should drive down the cost, or several software houses have available software for stock control
- ✓ The cost will be competitive as all the initial development costs are now being effectively shared by the large number of customers
- ✓ All errors should have been identified due to its widespread use
- ✓ User forums and user groups will spring up for popular software
- ✓ The software licence may include an option to upgrade the software at a competitive price when a new release becomes available.

Disadvantage

- ✓ There may not exist a single program which has all the features the user requires and so the purchase of a product will mean accepting a compromise solution.

Progress Check 7.1

A company is to employ more staff and needs to purchase payroll software for the first time.
(a) What will be the benefit of a software house producing a custom-made solution?
(b) Off-the shelf payroll software is available – what will be the benefits of this approach?

7.2 Features of common applications

Stock control

A large or small business must keep control of its stock. The processes involved will be:

- ✓ the creation of a file/database of all items held with their current stock levels
  - ➢ data will include a product code, description of the product, retail price, wholesale price, name of the usual supplier, the 'minimum stock level' i.e. the level at which we order new stock for the item.

- ✓ keeping the database up-to-date including:
  - ➢ the sale of stock items
  - ➢ the re-ordering of stock
  - ➢ the updating of the stock file
    - ◆ add new items
    - ◆ reduce the price of an item
    - ◆ delete an item from the database.
- ✓ ordering of new stock
- ✓ recording the arrival of new stock.

Managers will frequently ask for management reports to highlight issues such as products which are not selling well or to make a comparison of the sales made by different shops.

Payroll

All employees want to be paid!

Payroll software manages the payment made to all staff including a regular monthly salary and various expenses they have incurred that month, for example, for the use of their car at work or the train fare for travelling to a course.

The payroll file or database will include data for each employee: payroll reference number, full name, grade, location where they work, number of contracted hours, tax code etc.

Each month the payroll software will be run and produce:

- ✓ a payslip for each employee
- ✓ an automatic money payment into their bank account or a printed cheque
- ✓ a management report showing all payments made.

Payroll software is a good example of an application which can be purchased off-the-shelf. It is also a good example of a batch processing system since all the input data is entered in a batch, the processing is done on all employee records at the same time and all the outputs are produced as a batch.

↩ Look Back

To Chapter 2 for discussion on batch processing systems.

Order processing

A company which sells goods or services needs a computerised system for the recording of all transactions. Ecommerce has meant that many companies do this business over the Internet with a website which allows the placing of orders.

The order processing system must have a file/database of all products and a stock control system to manage stock (see earlier).

Placing an order will follow the following sequence:

✓ record an order (through the website or receiving a paper based 'purchase order' document sent by the customer) and either:
  ➤ take the customer's payment
  ➤ if the customer is allowed credit, prepare an 'invoice' document.
✓ process the order – the goods have attached a paper document called the 'delivery note'
✓ send the goods (and the invoice).

The computerised system will be able to:

✓ make order enquiries from customers – "has my order been sent yet?"
✓ produce management reports, for example, list which products are selling well.

Process control

An industrial process is controlled by a computer system. The input to the computer system will come from **sensors** and the computer will then act upon this data it receives.

This has already been discussed in Chapter 1.2.b when we considered a real-time operating system and used the example of a computer controlled greenhouse.

The sequence for any process control system is:

✓ Data captured from a sensor, for example, a temperature sensor records a temperature reading
✓ Data is sent to the processor as a digital signal
✓ Processor processes the reading, for example, decides that the greenhouse temperature is too cold

✓ Processor decides what action is required, for example, signal is sent to an **actuator** to drive a motor to close the greenhouse window. The sequence is continually repeated with data sent from the temperature sensor (for example) every 30 seconds.

Point-Of-Sale (POS) systems

Also called **Electronic Point-Of-Sale (EPOS)**.

A shopper in a retail shop makes payment for the goods at the 'Point-Of-Sale' (the checkout).

The till is connected online to the shop's product file/database and has a communications link to enable online cashless payments.

This is a computerised till where each sale will follow this sequence:

✓ a barcode reader scans the barcode on each item
✓ the POS software will search for the barcode in the products database
✓ the data for that product is sent to the POS – which includes the price
✓ repeat this sequence for all items
✓ software calculates a total for the goods and any discounts due
✓ a till receipt is printed and given to the customer
✓ the customer makes payment either with cash or a debit/credit card.

As each product transaction is recorded in the product database stock control software deducts the number sold from the stock level.

The major advantage for the shop is that all transactions are electronically recorded and the shop will be able to:

✓ produce useful management information. For example, how much more barbeque food did it sell on a hot day?
✓ record the transactions against a customer's store card so that a purchasing profile for that customer can be generated.

7.3 Categories of software

Applications software

There are two main categories of software – **systems software** and **applications software**.

Applications software is any program which is designed for a task which would still need to be done without the availability of a computer. For example producing a presentation – we would have to use instead acetate sheets and an overhead projector.

Applications software can be divided into special-purpose applications software and generic (or general purpose) applications software.

Generic software (or general purpose) applications software can be used as the starting point for a variety of different tasks.

See the following examples for spreadsheet software.

Special purpose applications software is designed for one particular task only. For example route planner software used in a SatNav system.

Generic software

Word processor

Software used for text creation, text editing and the storage of text documents.

Word processing software has become increasingly 'full-featured' and more advanced features now include:

- ✓ use of style sheets and document templates
- ✓ spelling and grammar checker
- ✓ the inclusion of graphic images embedded in the text
- ✓ page numbering, headers and footers and tables
- ✓ the generation of a table of contents
- ✓ and hundreds of others.

Word processing applications include:

- ✓ letters, reports and all business documents
- ✓ the creation of the text and then making it available to other software such as a DTP program
- ✓ integration of the word processor with a database program to carry out a ***mail merge***. A mail merge is the sending of a standard letter to a large number of clients whose data is stored in a database. The mail merge facility makes the letter appear personalised for each client.

Mail merge sequence will be:

- ✓ create the standard letter
- ✓ include in the letter 'field markers' to indicate where items of data from the database will be positioned
- ✓ create a database query which specifies which records are to be included
- ✓ 'Run' the mail merge based on the query to produce the printed letters.

Spreadsheet

A spreadsheet consists of a grid of rows and columns which form cells. A cell can contain text, a number or a formula. A formula computes a value from on other numbers or formulae the sheet.

For example a spreadsheet could be used:

- ✓ to manage a list of data such as football fixtures
- ✓ to produce a set of financial accounts
- ✓ to produce charts such as showing examination performance in different subjects
- ✓ the export of data to other applications
- ✓ to do a '***what if***' exercise such as the costing for a pop concert where we ask 'what if' we increase the cost of a ticket to $30 – what effect will this have on the overall profit?

This final point is the most powerful use of spreadsheet software where it is used for ***forecasting*** and to make ***predictions***.

A spreadsheet is like a single sheet of paper and modern spreadsheet software such as Microsoft Excel allows several sheets (called a 'workbook') to be saved in the same file.

Desktop publisher (DTP)

This has become a grey area with many features which were previously only found in DTP software now available with a word processor.

DTP allows the design and creation of ***complex page layouts*** and the use of 'containers' which each store particular content.

The content will have been produced using software which is best suited to the task:

- ✓ text is best initially created in the word processor

✓ tables will be created in either the word processor or spreadsheet
✓ graphics will be created using the drawing software.

DTP applications include the creation of posters and the composition of the pages of a catalogue or book.

Presentation software

Microsoft's PowerPoint has become a de-facto standard for this type of software. A presentation is made up of a number of *slides* each containing:

✓ mixture of text and graphics
✓ animation type features and sound
✓ movie clips and other media content.

The presentation is stored electronically and so can be easily distributed – for example, for a member of staff who was unable to attend a training course.

The slides can be set to produce a rolling display. The slides are shown in sequence for a set time of (each of about 20 seconds). This could then be used at a marketing event.

Presentation software is used extensively in schools and Colleges in lessons for the display of subject material.

Progress Check 7.2

Explain the information processing which takes place when a customer takes their basket of goods to the supermarket's EPOS checkout.

Drawing (or Graphics) software

There are two distinct types of drawing software which are used to create either:

✓ *bitmapped graphics*
✓ *vector graphics*.

Bitmapped graphics

A bitmap graphic is built up from a number of *pixels*, where a pixel is the smallest addressable picture element. The term bitmap comes from the concept that the bytes which make up the file are 'mapped' to an area in the main memory.

There are several types of *encoding* and file formats for bitmap images:

✓ *Monochrome* i.e. black and white pixels only
✓ *16 colour* i.e. 16 available colours for the pixels
✓ *256 colour* i.e. 256 possible colours
✓ *24-bit colour* (or true-colour) where millions of different colours are possible.

The encoding for each type can be worked out.

✓ *Monochrome* – Only two colours needed so store each pixel as a single bit. A byte stores 8 pixels.
✓ *16 colour* – Requires 16 different numbers (to represent each of the 16 possible colours) so 4 bits needed. A byte would store 2 pixels.
✓ *256 colour* – Requires 256 different numbers which needs 8 bits, so a byte would store one pixel.
✓ *24-bit colour* – Each pixel is stored using 24 bits or 3 bytes, So the number of different colours possible is 2^{24} i.e. 16,777,216!

Bitmaps are stored as a rectangular image with the 'data bytes' storing the pixel data and also a *header*. The header data will give the size of the bitmap (width and height measured in pixels) and the type of bitmap (monochrome, 256 colour etc.)

Bitmaps have the drawback that:

✓ they have a large file size
✓ if an attempt is made to over-enlarge the bitmap with image editing software the individual pixels may become visible. This is called the staircase-effect. Figure 7.1 shows the mouse on the left after it has been enlarged – the pixels can clearly be seen.

Figure 7.1 Stair-case effect in the enlarged image of mouse

The clarity with which a bitmap image is viewed on a monitor screen will depend on two factors:

1. **Screen resolution** – the number of pixels which can be viewed horizontally and vertically on the screen. A typical PC screen resolution is 1680 pixels x 1080 pixels. This is a key factor to consider when purchasing a monitor – what is the highest possible screen resolution?
2. **Resolution of the image** – the number of pixels per centimetre. A small image size made up from a large number of pixels will produce a sharper display.

Vector graphics

A vector graphic is made up from a number of **drawing objects**. A vector graphic program such as Microsoft Visio comes with a vast number of different objects organised into groups.

The screenshot (Figure 7.2) shows a typical vector graphics session. The user has started to draw a network diagram. Objects are organised into groups of shapes – the creator has selected a straight line from the 'Connectors' group and an LCD screen from the 'Computer' group.

Objects have **properties**. These properties determine the size and appearance of each object. If an object is re-sized its properties are simply recalculated.

The screenshot shows the current size and position properties for the line object.

The line will have other properties stored including its line thickness and colour.

The advantage of vector graphics is that changing the size of any object will not affect the quantity of the drawing's appearance.

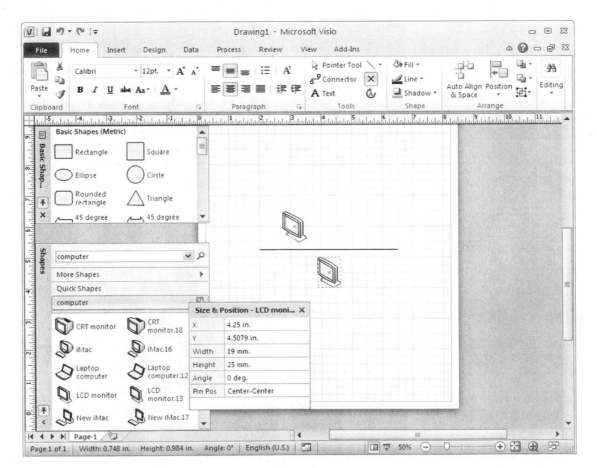

Figure 7.2   A typical vector graphics session

Progress Check 7.3

Explain the difference between bitmap graphics software and vector graphics software.

Progress Check 7.4

A vector graphic has available a rectangle, circle and a straight line object. Tick the cells showing the properties which are relevant for each shape.

	Rectangle	Circle	Straight line
Line colour			
Line thickness			
Centre coordinates			
Radius			
Fill (yes/no)			
Fill colour			
Start coordinate			
End coordinate			
Shading style			

7.4 Application areas for which generic applications software is not appropriate

There is a limit to what can be done with generic software. If a user wants to maintain the data for (about) 100 business contacts they will decide that a spreadsheet can do this.

However none of the generic programs will be suitable to solve a problem if:

✓ the nature of the task is very specialised
✓ no available generic software can provide the features and functionality which the task requires.

The next step is to look for a special purpose applications program which can meet the user's needs. We already have a definition for this – special purpose software is designed for one particular task. These programs are many and varied and are usually 'off-the-shelf' software and include:

✓ Games
✓ Tax calculator
✓ Management of a football league
✓ Audio recording and editing
✓ Internet browser
✓ And thousands of others.

Progress Check 7.5

What generic software would you use for each of the following tasks? If none is suitable state 'special purpose software needed'.

(a) Produce a list of employee travelling expenses for the firm's five sales staff.
(b) Produce some text about the firm's new office block, which you have to prepare and then pass on to a colleague
(c) You have to edit a number of photographs for your colleague, who is producing a glossy two page leaflet about recent company developments.
(d) Software for recording the student exam entries at a school and sending these entries to the Exam Board three months before the exams.
(e) An IT Help desk in a College has digital cameras available for student loan. A record must be kept of all loans.
(f) A rolling display about healthy eating is to be designed and then displayed on a 'big screen' in the firm's canteen.

1. The management of a supermarket use a number of different types of software. State what each of the following types of software would be used for.

   Give a feature of each which makes it suitable for your use.

   (a) Desktop publishing (DTP)

   Use ....

   ....

   Feature ....

   .... [2]

   (b) Presentation software

   Use ....

   ....

   Feature ....

   .... [2]

   Cambridge 9691 Paper 11 Q1(d) June 2011

2. (a) Define the following types of software:

   (i) operating system

   ....

   .... [1]

   (ii) applications software

   ....

   .... [1]

   (b) (i) Explain the difference between custom-written software and off-the-shelf software.

   ....

   ....

   ....

   .... [2]

   (ii) Explain **four** advantages of using off-the-self software.

   ....

   ....

   ....

   ....

   ....

   ....

   ....

   ....

   ....

   .... [2

   Cambridge 9691 Paper 11 Q2(a)&(b) June 2012

Handling of Data in Information Systems

8

Revision Objectives

After you have studied this chapter, you should be able to:

☞ describe manual and automatic methods of capturing and inputting data into a system, including form design, keyboard entry, barcodes, Optical Mark Recognition (OMR), magnetic stripe cards, Optical Character Recognition (OCR), sensors and data logging, touch screens, chip and pin

☞ describe image capture by use of a scanner, video capture card and digital camera/camcorder

☞ explain the techniques of validation and verification, and describe validation tests which can be carried out on data

☞ describe possible output formats such as graphs, reports, interactive presentations, sound, video, images and animations stating the benefits and drawbacks of each format

☞ discuss the need for a variety of output formats according to the target audience

☞ describe knowledge based (expert) systems, how they are created and how they function

☞ explain the use of knowledge based (expert) systems as a diagnostic tool.

8.1 Manual and automatic methods of data capture

> ← **Look Back**
>
> To Chapter 4 for discussion on peripherals used for data input.

We shall briefly re-visit each one – this time the emphasis is not on the hardware but the method of data capture.

Manual data entry is done by the user typing in characters at the *keyboard*. We would not use the term 'data entry' for a word processed document. Data entry assumes this is a data set which will then be used for some form of processing; ordering a new coat from a website, registering your details on a forum, etc.

Web forms are usually made up of standard controls such as a text box for text entry, making a single selection from a group of radio buttons, making one or more selections from a group of

check boxes, making a single selection from a drop-down list. The choice of which controls to use for which data value will consider the accurate capture of the data from the form.

Automatic data capture methods

The methods which follow all have the objective that they avoid the manual keying of data. Some of the methods are designed for the fast entry of a volume of data.

> ← **Look Back**
>
> To Chapter 4 for a description of how a scanner works.

Barcode

A barcode, with its pattern of black and white bars of varying thickness, provides a way of encoding a sequence of digits.

The barcode is scanned with a laser beam and the computer system captures the digits which make up the code. There is nothing automatic about this but the reader makes it possible to quickly capture the code – quicker than keying the digits.

Optical Mark Recognition (OMR)

A pre-printed form has set positions at which the user can 'shade in' and leave a mark. A multiple choice examination paper with questions which each have five alternative answers would have boxes labelled 1 to 5 and invite the student to shade in the box corresponding to the correct answer to each question.

The student answer documents will be scanned as a batch – definitely automatic data capture. The position of the marks on the paper is then interpreted by software to determine correct and incorrect answers for all questions for all students.

Optical Character Recognition (OCR)

A document contains pre-printed characters in a stylised font. The characters are read by a scanner and captured as text characters. This again would be suitable for the reading and processing of a batch of similar documents.

Magnetic stripe card

Although gradually being replaced by chip-and-pin technology they are still in widespread use. The front of the card has information presented visually with embossed characters for the name, account number and expiry date. The back of the card has a *magnetic stripe* with other data such as a password encoded and a signature strip. Like a barcode, the data capture is designed for fast and accurate data capture which avoids keying data.

Chip-and-pin

The replacement technology for magnetic strip cards. The plastic card has visual embedded characters on the front and an embedded *microchip* in the card. The chip contains personal data and has a larger capacity than a magnetic strip.

Sensors and data-logging

A sensor is a device which records some physical characteristic of the real-world environment such as air pressure or humidity. A *data-logger* is a device which captures data readings from one or more sensors over a period of time. A digital data-logger will have all the basic components of a computer system with a processor and main memory. The device will either act as a stand-alone device able to process the data readings, or the alternative is a device which interfaces to a PC so that the processing and analysis of the data is done with software on the PC.

The data-logger will be programmed to switch on and off the taking of data readings. The simplest data-logger is a single channel device which records data from a single sensor. More complex multi-channel devices would require some form of *multiplexor* to relay the data from a number of sensors to the PC through a single port.

Touch screen

A combined input and output device. The screen has a number of touch sensitive areas which are mapped by software to menu selections or other choices. Smartphones such as the iPhone and devices such as the iPad and other tablet devices use a touch screen, which includes an on-screen keyboard.

8.2 Image capture

Scanner technology

> **← Look Back**
>
> To Chapter 4 for a description of how a scanner works.

Video capture and digital camera/camcorder

Video capture means recording a video sequence on a device such as a camcorder and then transferring this media content to the computer. Early camcorders used tapes but modern recorders all now use some form of digital storage such as a hard drive, solid state storage or a flash drive. Transfer from a hard drive to the computer is done with a cabled or wireless connection and the appropriate software.

Software on the computer can be used for video editing such as the removal of sections of the recording, splicing content together and adding caption text.

For examples of what is a possible with a PC and the appropriate software just log on to YouTube!

Digital cameras are now common and can be one of the features of a mobile or smartphone. Pictures are stored either on internal memory or onto a flash memory card. Images can be immediately browsed after a shot is taken and the user can make an instant decision to retain or delete a shot. Images can be saved in a variety of standard file formats (for example JPEG) and different resolutions. A digital camera is often able to record video.

Progress Check 8.1

What method of data capture would you suggest for the following applications?
(a) A college student ID card is to contain a photograph of the student.
(b) A web site contains a page to be completed for a person who wants to be included on the companies' mailing list.
(c) A college IT Support desk has a number of digital cameras which it loans to students and staff. What method could be used to identify each camera?
(d) A student has taken a number of photographs (using a film camera) which have been printed. They need to be included in a word processed report.

8.3 The techniques of validation and verification

Validation

Data validation is any technique to ensure the correctness or 'validity' of the data.

Validation checks will take place at the data entry or capture stage.

The following all refer to Figure 8.1

'From a list'

The Title and Country fields have a drop-down list in order that the customer makes one of the permitted entries only.

Figure 8.1

Required entry

The asterisk alongside a field indicates that data must be entered – it cannot be left blank. Also the 'terms and conditions' check box must be checked.

Format check

The characters allowed must be in a particular format. For example, UK post codes have the format CCNN NCC or CCN NCC only.

The Day Phone and Eve Phone boxes will accept numbers only.

Length check

The number of characters entered must not exceed a maximum length.

Uniqueness check

A field cannot take the same value as another record in the file/database.

Range check

A number entered must be within a permitted range.

Data Verification

Verification means that a comparison will be made between two copies of the data.

Examples

✓ Change of a network account password, where the user is required to enter the new password twice (to check that they match)

✓ Data copied to a CD-R. The software will check that the data copied to the CD matches exactly with the files on the PC, i.e. checking that an exact copy has been made.

Progress Check 8.2

A gym is to design a web form for application for membership. These are some of the fields the applicant will complete.

✓ Name
✓ Date of birth (members must be over aged 18 and under 80)
✓ Forenames
✓ Address
✓ Email address
✓ Membership: A – Adult, J – Junior, S – Senior citizen
✓ Type of membership required (F – Full, L – Limited to certain times of the day)
✓ Number of times likely to visit the gym in any one week
✓ Have you been a member of a gym before?

Suggest validation checks which could be used on the web form.

8.4 Output formats

Reports

Consider a company selling second-hand cars. They employee five sales staff and produce detailed data (Figure 8.2) about the breakdown of all sales made.

All sales are recorded in a database. The database has the facility to produce various reports. The report above shows the sales for the month grouped by salesperson. The report could have included sub-totals

Figure 8.2 Car sales data

for each salesperson and a total for the month of all sales made.

> ✎ **Note**
>
> The report has a clear heading and is dated showing the date on which it was produced.

Graphs

The car sales company also sell new vehicles and the graph (Figure 8.3) shows the sales of new and used vehicles for the 12-month period.

Advantages

✓ More than one data set can be shown on the same graph to give a comparison

✓ The graphs can be produced by software – such as a spreadsheet and then included in a written report.

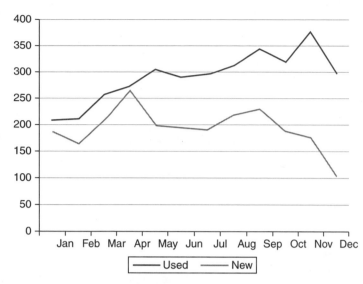

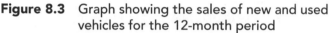

Figure 8.3   Graph showing the sales of new and used vehicles for the 12-month period

Disadvantage

✓ Difficult to read the exact value for any given month.

Interactive presentation

Presentation here is taken with a general meaning. A presentation created with software such as a PowerPoint is usually not interactive; the only interaction by the user is to advance the display on to the next slide.

Multimedia software can provide interaction such as a lesson on a particular topic. There could be (for example) four instructional slides followed by a slide which asks the user questions which they must get correct in order to progress to the next set of slides. A wrong response could navigate to display the instructional slides a second time, or to a slide giving feedback.

Sound

All PC computer systems support sound and this is used for:

✓ warning messages to the user
✓ the playback of media content such as video clips or a film
✓ specialist applications where a text document is spoken to the user.

Video, Images and Animation

Video is now widely used on the computer for a variety of objectives.

✓ Recreational such as the millions of 'home' video clips posted onto the YouTube site
✓ Instructive such as a video demonstrating the use of a piece of equipment or software.

Advantages

✓ The video can include not only 'live' footage of some event, but also sound and screens of explanatory text.

Disadvantages

✓ Video player software is required and may not support the file format in which the file was saved.
✓ Reasonable computing power needed, i.e. processor and memory, to playback video clips. There have been lots of recent developments and an example is Sky Television who are now able to offer the screening of live television pictures on a mobile smartphone.

🔙 **Look Back**

To Chapter 7 for discussion of bitmap and vector graphics.

Images

Images are widely used on the computer system as part of webpage content, instructional booklets and reports.

Most software supports a wide variety of file formats – the most popular are .PRG, .BMP and .JPEG.

Animation

Animation is a sequence of images which when viewed creates movement. Web pages often contain small graphics used as icons which are 'animated JPEGs or GIFs' – an image file which includes simple movement.

A variety of output formats are needed according to the target audience. This is self evident and the above discussion has mentioned several software applications where each output format would be appropriate.

Progress Check 8.3

What output formats would be used for the following applications?

(a) A teacher is preparing on-line some self-study materials for students to use for revision for an exam.

(b) An instruction manual for a new vacuum cleaner.

(c) A sales summary is produced for the Managing Director of a company which operates supermarkets in five towns.

(d) You want to make available on a social networking site your version – singing and playing the guitar – of a recent pop song.

8.5 Knowledge based (expert) systems

An expert system is software designed to 'capture' the expertise of a human expert, in order that this expertise can be made more widely available.

📖 Later

Prolog is discussed in more detail in Chapter 21.

The software which makes the data capture possible is called an *expert system shell* and would be the starting point for developing an expert system application.

The expert's knowledge is captured by the software as a large number of *facts*. Two facts could be that:

✓ copper is a metal
✓ one of the uses of copper is for cabling.

Expert systems are developed from a *declarative programming language* such as Prolog where the facts are presented as follows:

```
metal(copper)
application(copper, cabling)
```

The facts are then related with **rules** and this combination of the facts and rules form the **knowledge base** for the expert system application.

An **inference engine** allows **queries** to be set for the knowledge base. For example the query:

```
application (X, cabling)
```

would list all values of variable X, i.e. all materials which are used for cabling.

The use of the expert system by the non-expert would be through a **user interface** which shows query results.

More sophisticated features would include:

✓ assigning probabilities to certain facts and rules
✓ the ability of the inference engine to, not only reports the results of a query, but also to show the reasoning as to how the results were deduced.

8.6 The use of knowledge based (expert) systems as a diagnostic tool

The most common applications of expert systems are for diagnostics.

Examples

✓ A knowledge base of all the known facts about some medical condition has been created by a senior consultant. The junior doctor could key in the known facts about a patient's symptoms and the expert system would report the likely diagnosis.

✓ An expert system on plumbing and heating. The plumber could key in the known symptoms, for example, the heater is failing to heat the water, and the expert system would suggest possible reasons.

Progress Check 8.4

Name and describe the component parts which make up an expert system?

Exam-style Questions

1. The computer system in a factory is used to store personnel records and to manage the payroll. Workers in the factory register when they arrive for work by placing a card in a machine (clocking on) and repeating the process when leaving (clocking off). This machine is not connected to the main computer system, although the information collected will eventually be used as the input to a device which will provide data for the payroll program. The data on the cards consists of a barcode and OCR data.

   (a) Describe how these two types of data are read by the input device.

   ....

   ....

   ....

   ....

   (b) State what the data are used for in this application.

   ....

   .... [6]

   Cambridge 9691 Specimen Paper 1 Q5

2. Explain how a knowledge based (expert) system can be set up and used to help oil companies search for oil-bearing rocks.

   ....

   ....

   ....

   ....

   ....

   .... [6]

   Cambridge 9691 Paper 11 Q4 November 2011

3. A supermarket has a number of point-of-sale terminals. Data is read from goods at the terminals and information is produced.

   (a) State two output devices which would be used at the point-of-sale, justifying their use.

   Device 1 ....

   Justification ....

   ....

   Device 2 ....

   Justification ....

   .... [4]

   (b) State three types of output needed at the point-of-sale terminals. For each type of output explain why the output is needed.

   Output 1 ....

   ....

   ....

   Output 2 ....

   ....

   ....

   Output 3 ....

   ....

   .... [6]

   Cambridge 9691 Paper 11 Q1(b)&(c) June 2011

Designing the User Interface

9

Revision Objectives

After you have studied this chapter, you should be able to:

☞ discuss the importance of good interface design

☞ discuss human computer interaction (HCI) design issues such as the use of colour, layout, and content

☞ identify the required characteristics of a user interface with respect to information, type of interface, type of user, type of application, physical location and current technology.

9.1 The importance of good interface design

In Chapter 2 we gave as one of the definitions of the operating system 'the interface between the user and the hardware'. This definition implies that the interface is designed to make the hardware usable. The interface will consist of several screens shown to the user which may then require a response from the user.

How the user reacts to information presented to them is a complex issue and will draw upon research in the field of psychology.

The HCI is the space between the computer system and the user and its aim is to facilitate the successful use of the computer system.

The interface will be crucial for all aspects of the application – input (for user data entry), processing (where the user may be required to confirm certain results) and the output (where the user interprets the results and responds accordingly).

Operating a piece of machinery – such as driving a car – requires the user to be familiar with certain basic controls, i.e. the steering wheel, accelerator, brake and clutch pedals etc. This way a competent driver would be expected to be able to drive a car with which they have no previous experience. This idea of 'transferability' also applies to be use of

computer systems and applications software. A user looking for the 'Save' option would expect to find this either as separate button or on the left hand side of a *menu bar*.

The effectiveness of a human computer interface is determined by:

✓ the graphical, textual and auditory information presented to the user
✓ control sequences – such as keystrokes and mouse clicks required
✓ selections the user makes to *navigate* through the software.

9.2 Human Computer Interaction (HCI) design issues

Before considering each of these design features, think about what information is being presented to the user at any time.

At the start of a word processing session the user will make a menu selection to (for example) load an existing document. The implication is that the user will be expected to know where to find this menu selection.

Keying in of text

The implication is that the user will be aware of software features which are relevant, for example, highlighting text, deletion and movement of text.

Help features

The user will do a keyword search, for example, the user needs to edit a footnote and has forgotten how to do it. This is a transferable skill which has already been used with other software.

These are very different components of the task and the user interface will reflect this.

Consistency

For the two issues of *colour* and *layout* a key consideration is consistency. That means both consistency within the same piece of software and existing software with which the user is familiar.

Intuitive

When students produce documentation for their coursework report they often set as an objective in the requirements specification that the software is 'user friendly'. When queried they will agree that this is a meaningless phrase to use. What is meaningful is a statement that the software should be intuitive to use. The user should – at any point in the use of the software – be clear what options are possible and what response is required from them. There is no worse feeling when using a program than sat there asking yourself "What do I do next?".

Colour

This is best illustrated with simple examples.

✓ On a web form the labels for the various controls could be a different colour to explanatory text

✓ Text which gives a warning message could be red to attract the immediate attention of the user.

The use of 'loud' colours is generally to be avoided.

Modern generic software – such as Microsoft Office PowerPoint – has pre-defined colour combinations – called themes – which can be selected by the user (Figure 9.1).

There may be an outside influence on the choice of colours. For example, web site pages may need to use corporate colours which have been adopted by the company in all its materials and so colours must be carefully chosen.

Colour blind users may be unable to distinguish between green and red or other colour combinations.

Progress Check 9.1

Name some of the content of a screen for which you would consider carefully the colours used.

Layout and Content

The design needs to be consistent, for example, different fonts and font sizes will be consistently used for headings, warning text, explanatory text, labels for controls and for any data entered.

There is a limit to the amount of information a user can process from a single screen – and this is where research from psychology is relevant.

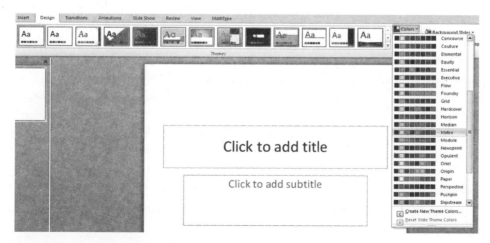

Figure 9.1 Microsoft Office PowerPoint themes

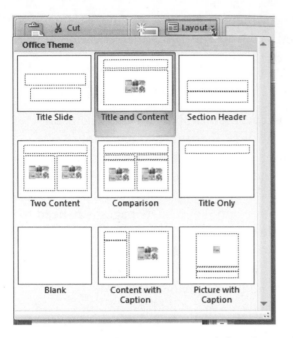

Figure 9.2 MS PowerPoint pre-defined templates

A data entry screen may require the information to be either:

✓ split across several inputs screens – a good example of this would be a web form for ordering goods where the data entry is organised as a sequence of screens for the input of the goods data, then the customer data, followed by the delivery data and finally the payment data
✓ or presented using a vertical scroll bar.

Software such as PowerPoint has a number of pre-defined templates for the layout of page content (Figure 9.2).

Data entry may be done by copying the information from a paper form. The order of the fields on the computer form should match the order on the paper document.

As a general rule English users would expect to scan the content of a screen from the top left to the bottom right corner of the screen. Content should therefore reflect this. Initial instructions would be at the top of the screen and a 'Save' or 'Next screen' button positioned bottom right of the screen.

Progress Check 9.2

What do you understand by a screen design which is described as 'intuitive' to use?

9.3 The required characteristics of a user interface

We have already introduced the different types of interface in widespread use:

✓ **Command driven**
✓ **Graphical User Interface (GUI).**

⬅ Look Back

To Chapter 2 for different types of interface.

Characteristics of a user interface

The categories of interface are only two:

✓ Graphical User Interface
✓ Command driven

However, a GUI may take a number of styles as these include: forms-based, menu-driven and natural language.

These style are not mutually exclusive and It is common, for example, for a forms-based interface to be menu-driven. Also, a forms-based interface would be a GUI.

The suitability of the style will depend upon the software application and the anticipated end-user.

History illustrates well the type of interface needed will be reflected by the application. Early computing was done only by systems programmers and then later by applications programmers. Application then became more widespread and avilable to the end-user who would be using software as a tool for their particular application area. Computing has now developed to the point where 'everyone' is using the computer as a tool – with the possible exception of the computing profession developers who are creating the tools for others.

Matching interfaces types to application areas is almost impossible to do. Whereas previously a programmer would require access only to a simple text editor and a compiler which could both be simple menu-driven interfaces, modern Integrated Development Environment (IDE) now has a wealth of features and such an interface is complex.

The move towards even increasing web applications supporting applications such on-line transaction processing has with it developed styles of interface to support this need.

Progress Check 9.3

The tailoring of the appearance of the screen used with a command driven interface will be limited. What features could be changed?

📖 **Later**

We shall consider the actual design of an interface in Section 2. This discussion will be highly relevant for your coursework for Section 4. The design of your application will include the design of the various interface screens used by the application.

Exam-style Questions

1. A building firm has expanded rapidly. A systems analyst is employed to plan the introduction of a computer system which will store customer records and details of stock and also keep the firm's accounts.

   Communication between the computer system and the administration staff employed by the firm is to be through a Human Computer Interface (HCI).

   Discuss the importance of:
   (a) colour,

   ....
   ....
   ....
   ....

   (b) layout,

   ....
   ....
   ....
   ....

   (c) content,
        in the design of the HCI.

   ....
   ....
   ....
   .... [9]

   Cambridge 9691 Specimen Paper 1 Q4(c)

2. An interactive computer system in a shopping mall is intended to give information to customers.

   Discuss how the use of colour, layout and content will influence the design of the Human Computer Interface (HCI).

   (a) colour ....

   ....
   ....
   ....

(b) layout ....
....
....
....

(c) content ....
....
....
.... [6]

Cambridge 9691 Paper 11 Q7 June 2011

3. A navigation system is designed to be mounted in a car in order to show the driver how to reach the destination. Describe the characteristics of the user interface and why they are appropriate to the application.

....
....
....
....
.... [5]

Cambridge 9691 Paper 11 Q3 November 2011

4. A bank has a customer file containing the transactions made by its customers.

   The file is used to

   • produce a bank statement for each customer once a month
   • answer customer queries when the customer telephones the bank.

   Explain why the telephone operator uses a forms-based interface when taking details of the query from the customer.

....
....
....
.... [3]

Cambridge 9691 Paper 11 Q7(a)(i) November 2011

Logic Gates 10

Revision Objectives

After you have studied this chapter, you should be able to:

☞ understand and define the function AND, OR, NOT, NAND and NOR logic gates including the binary output produced from all possible binary inputs

☞ calculate the outcome from a circuit of logic gates given the input by producing truth tables for given logic circuits

☞ produce a simple logic circuit from a given written statement (e.g. if A AND B are on and if C is on, then the lights will be on).

10.1 Effects of logic gates on binary signals in a processor

The second generation of computers followed the invention of the transistor in 1947. A logic gate is a unit made up from one or more transistors. There are no moving parts and one or more input signals produce an output signal. Because of the way in which a transistor works the least complicated to produce are the NOT, NAND and NOR gates. These assume the more fundamental gates of AND and OR.

We must understand the behaviour of these five gates.

Note

We shall deal with gates with no more than two inputs.

AND gate

An AND gate has two or more inputs and a single output. The table show all the possible combinations of input and the output each produces. This is called a *truth table*.

Inputs		Output
A	B	X = A AND B
0	0	0
0	1	0
1	0	0
1	1	1

The AND gate produces a 1 output only when input A is 1 *and* input B is 1.

OR gate

An OR gate has two or more inputs and a single output.

Inputs		Output
A	B	X = A OR B
0	0	0
0	1	1
1	0	1
1	1	1

The OR gates produces a 1 output when either A is 1 <u>or</u> B is 1 <u>or</u> both are 1.

> ✎ **Note**
>
> The 'exclusive OR' gate is not in the syllabus.

NOT gate

A NOT gate has a single input and a single output.

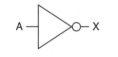

Input	Output
A	X = NOT A
0	1
1	0

The NOT gate – called an *inverter* – simply changes the value of the input.

NAND gate

A NAND gate has two or more inputs and a single output. It is equivalent to an AND gate followed by a NOT gate.

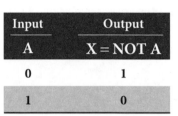

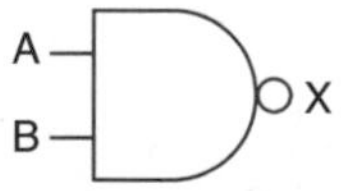

Inputs		Output
A	B	X = A NAND B
0	0	1
0	1	1
1	0	1
1	1	0

The NAND gate produces a 0 output when both A and B are 1 – all other outputs are 1.

NOR gate

A NOR gate has two or more inputs and a single output. It is equivalent to an OR gate followed by a NOT gate.

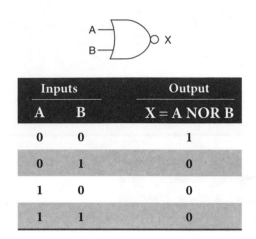

Inputs		Output
A	B	X = A NOR B
0	0	1
0	1	0
1	0	0
1	1	0

The NAND gates produces a 1 output when both A and B are 0 – all other outputs are zero.

10.2 Calculating the output from a set of logic gates given the input

Logic gates can be connected to produce a particular set of outputs from the different input combinations.

Appreciate that a logic circuit with:

- ✓ two inputs (A and B) would have four possible combinations
- ✓ three inputs (A, B and C) would have eight combinations.

> **Progress Check 10.1**
>
> A logic circuit has five inputs. How many different input combinations does this produce?

Consider the logic circuit below.

> ✎ **Note**
>
> Since it will be difficult to calculate the final X outputs 'in one go' we have labelled some intermediate points (P and Q) in the logic circuit and shall show these in our truth table.

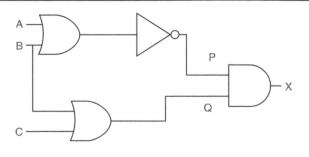

The circuit has three inputs so there will be eight possible combinations of inputs – that means eight rows in our truth table.

Inputs					Output
A	**B**	**C**	**P**	**Q**	
0	0	0	1	0	0
0	0	1	1	1	1
0	1	0	0	1	0
0	1	1	0	1	0
1	0	0	0	0	0
1	0	1	0	1	0
1	1	0	0	1	0
1	1	1	0	1	0

The final column shows the output.

Progress Check 10.2

Draw the truth table for the circuit shown below.

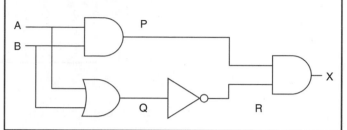

Progress Check 10.3

Draw the truth table for the circuit shown below.

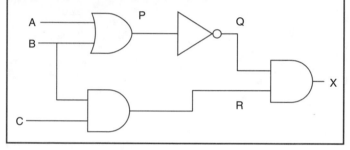

Exam-style Questions

1. (a) Complete this table for an OR gate.

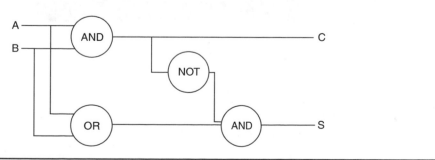

A	B	Output
0	0	
0	1	
1	0	
1	1	

> ✎ **Note**
>
> When the specimen paper was written it did not use the particular logic gate symbols.

[2]

(b) (i) Complete this table for the circuit.

A	B	C	S
0	0		
0	1		
1	0		
1	1		

[4]

(ii) Give a possible use for this circuit in a processor, explaining your answer.

....

.... [2]

Cambridge 9691 Specimen Paper 1 Q7

2. Complete the truth table to show the outputs from the logic circuit shown.

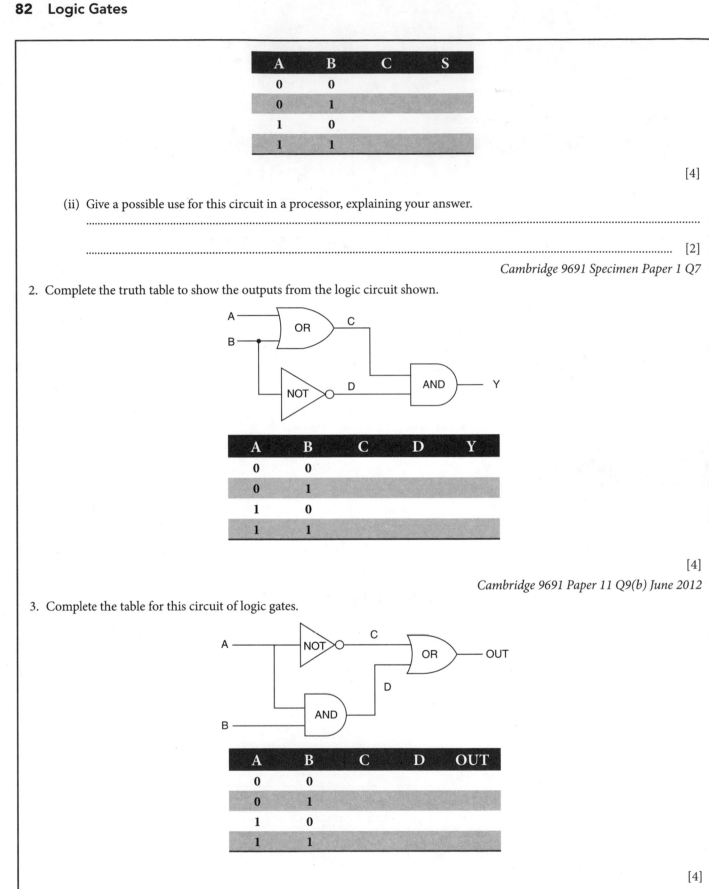

A	B	C	D	Y
0	0			
0	1			
1	0			
1	1			

[4]

Cambridge 9691 Paper 11 Q9(b) June 2012

3. Complete the table for this circuit of logic gates.

A	B	C	D	OUT
0	0			
0	1			
1	0			
1	1			

[4]

Cambridge 9691 Paper 13 Q6 June 2011

4. (a) Complete the table to show the outputs for the possible inputs to this circuit.

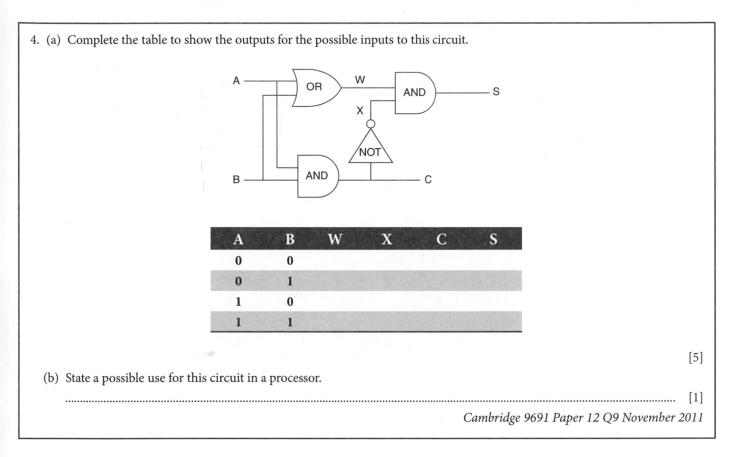

A	B	W	X	C	S
0	0				
0	1				
1	0				
1	1				

[5]

(b) State a possible use for this circuit in a processor.

.... [1]

Cambridge 9691 Paper 12 Q9 November 2011

Section 2

Data Types and Data Structures

Designing Solutions to Problems

11

Revision Objectives

After you have studied this chapter, you should be able to:

☞ discuss the importance of good interface design

☞ design and document data capture forms, screen layouts, report layouts or other forms of input and output (for example, sound) for a given problem

☞ explain the benefits of designing a solution to a problem by splitting it up into smaller problems (top-down/modular design)

☞ produce and describe top-down/modular designs using appropriate techniques, including structure diagrams, showing stepwise refinement

☞ produce algorithms to solve problems using both a program flowchart and pseudocode

☞ understand algorithms presented in the form of program flowcharts and pseudocode.

11.1 The importance of good interface design

The term 'interface' is widely used in computing. Here it is used to describe the means of communication between the computer system and the user. Hence this is also called the Human Computer Interface (HCI).

Good interface design is fundamental to the likely success the user will have working with a particular software application.

11.2 Design and document data capture forms, screen layouts, report layouts or other forms of input and output

Console mode

The user may not have a lot of choice about the design of the interface. If they are presented with any kind of Console Mode application then the only choices will be:

✓ the console window can be re-sized
✓ the background colour used for the console window
✓ the font and text size used for the text.

A simple interface like this will be appropriate for an application where the user is doing little more than keying in commands and reading some response.

Graphical User Interface (GUI)

Here the user/developer will have a lot more options about the appearance of the software interface.

> ⬅ **Look Back**
>
> To Chapter 2 for discussion on different types of user interface.

✓ The different types of user interface
✓ How is navigation made clear to the user?
✓ What key colours will be used?
✓ Does the overall style have to match that for any existing software?
  ➢ For example, most Windows based software has as the first two menu bar options File – Edit with the final option Help.

Screen content

What the screen is use for will determine many of its design features.

- ✓ Data capture screens
  - ➤ may be *forms* based
- ✓ A screen where we wish to indicate to the user that some processing is currently taking place and no further interaction is required for the moment
- ✓ An output screen where the user is presented with the results of some processing such as a database report or query.

Input screens

These are varied and some are shown here.

In Figure 11.1, the user is required to select logic gates from the palette of shapes shown and then construct a logic circuit.

The horizontal menu allows four selections File–Edit–View–Help which each offer a number of choices.

In Figure 11.2, the user is invited to key in a 'search string'.

> ✍ **Note**
>
> The user is helped and offered suggestions as more characters are keyed in.

Figure 11.2 Web page used for a key word search

Figure 11.3 A data form where the user is copying the data from a paper document

---

> ✍ **Note**
>
> The use of textbox and drop-down list controls and the validation of fields where the requirement is that data must be entered by the user.

Key features

1. Consistency: The software may need to be familiar to users of some existing software package.
2. Layout: On a forms based layout, the form will be built-up from the standard widget controls – see the 'glasses direct' form above: Similar forms will be constructed using a selection of these standard form controls:

- ✓ Text box
- ✓ Drop-down list
- ✓ Check box
- ✓ Radio button
- ✓ Button

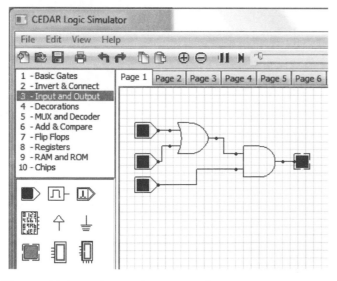

Figure 11.1 A menu-driven interface

3. Fonts etc.
  - ✓ The layout of the form will have all the controls left-aligned and each control will be labelled
  - ✓ The font used throughout will be consistent, for example, all labels use 10 pt Ariel
  - ✓ The general order of controls for browsing the form
    - ➤ start at the top-left and finish in the bottom-right
    - ➤ the button control to save the data will be positioned bottom right.
  - ✓ Clear headings and instructions should be at the top of the form
  - ✓ Any supplementary information such as advice about how to complete a particular control could be in a smaller front size or available as a 'pop-up'.
4. Colour: On a forms based interface the text boxes which require data entry will have a different background colour to text boxes which only display information.
5. Icons: On a graphical user interface icons provide a key way of communicating with the user.

Progress Check 11.1

What controls would you expect to find on a forms-based interface?

Progress Check 11.2

State five key features which would be considered in the design of any user interface.

11.3 Structure diagram

A structure diagram is a block diagram which shows the initial design of some problem for which a computer program is to provide a solution. The diagram is hierarchical and will show at each lower level a more detailed breakdown of the task. This is not specific to computing – it is the basic strategy we might use to think through the various *sub-tasks* of any real-world problem.

Example

A computer program is to be developed which simulates a game of 'noughts and crosses' between two players. Players need to be shown the board each players move. The following structure diagram (Figure 11.4) shows the initial design.

The diagram makes clear that the essential steps are:

- ✓ The use of a 2-dimensional array to store the move data as a grid.
- ✓ The cells will:
  - ➤ contain the empty string value at the start of the game
  - ➤ the 'x' character when a player moves to a cell
  - ➤ the 'o' character when a player moves to a cell.

Stepwise refinement

The designer will keep breaking each task down into smaller sub-tasks (Figure 11.5) until s/he is satisfied that the design can be implemented with program code.

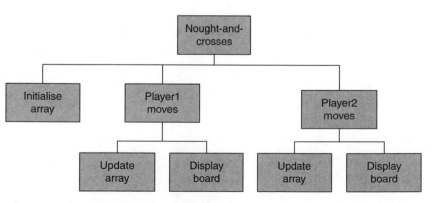

Figure 11.4 Structure diagram showing the initial design

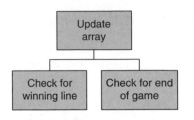

Figure 11.5

A structure diagram is used when we take a task and break it down into a number of sub-tasks.

This is taking a *modular approach* to the problem.

Continually breaking the problem down into smaller tasks is called *stepwise refinement*.

Modular design

We can adopt the same approach when we are designing, not just one program, but a large computing application.

Example

Consider the design of a new application for order processing (Figure 11.6).

Here the tasks are not just a stage in a program, but each task in the application will be written as a separate program. Each task will be coded as a program module, so the final application is built as a collection of program modules.

A modular approach has benefits. Each program module:

✓ can be worked on by a different programmer
✓ written and tested independently from the other modules.

11.4 Program flowchart

One of the key features of a procedural high-level language is that statements are executed in sequence. A *program flowchart* will show the sequential nature of a problem and any repetition.

Program flowchart symbols

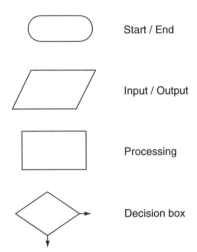

Example

A program is to input a student's exam mark. The program will output a PASS/FAIL message.

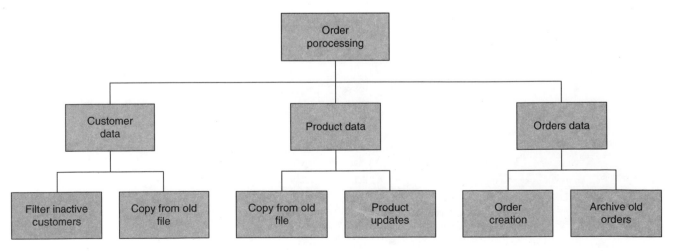

Figure 11.6

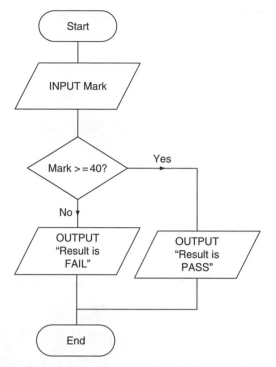

The program will terminate when the user enters a mark of −1, i.e. a 'rogue value'.

We can modify the design so that the user may input a sequence of marks for a number of students.

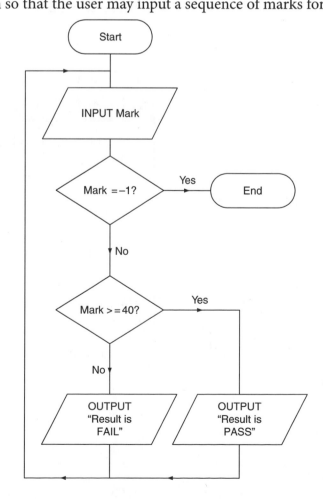

11.5 Pseudocode

Pseudocode is what it says – it's not quite program code, but close enough that a programmer should be able to look at the pseudocode and then write the actual program code from it.

If you have not already done so, go back and do Progress Check 11.1.

Pseudocode is made up of:

✓ keywords (just like the keywords in a programming language)
✓ the variables and constants that are required by the problem.

The following is a pseudocode description for the processing of the student mark we introduced earlier with a flowchart.

```
INPUT Mark

// now compute the result ...
 INPUT Mark
 IF Mark >= 40
   THEN
     OUTPUT "Result is PASS"
   ELSE
     OUTPUT "Result is FAIL"
 ENDIF
```

We have used a number of pseudocode keywords. These are explained in Table 11.1.

The variables used by the problem can be summarised with an identifier table as shown in Table 11.2.

Table 11.1

Pseudocode keywords	
Keyword	**Explanation**
INPUT	To input a value
OUTPUT	Displays a string of text to the user
IF-THEN-ELSE-ENDIF	A selection statement
//	Comment line

Table 11.2

Identifier table		
Identifier	**Data type**	**Description**
Mark	INTEGER	The mark out of 100 for the exam

That's enough for the time being. We shall soon need to extend our list of pseudocode keywords, but will wait until we need them in section 2.2.

Convention

Throughout the book all pseudocode is shown using the courier new font as above.

Note

The exam-style questions for section 2 of the syllabus can be found following chapter 16.

The Structure of Procedural Programs

12

After you have studied this chapter, you should be able to:

☞ define and correctly use the following terms as they apply to procedural programming: statement, subroutine, procedure, function, parameter, loop

☞ identify the three basic programming constructs used to control the flow of execution: sequence, selection and iteration

☞ understand and use selection in pseudocode and a procedural programming language, including the use of IF statements and CASE/SELECT statements

☞ understand and use iteration in pseudocode and a procedural programming language, including the use of count-controlled loops (FOR–ENDFOR loops) and condition-controlled loops (WHILE–ENDWHILE and REPEAT–UNTIL loops)

☞ understand and use nested selection and nested iteration statements

☞ understand, create and use subroutines (procedures and functions), including the passing of parameters and the appropriate use of the return value of functions

☞ use subroutines to modularise the solution to a problem

☞ identify and use recursion to solve problems; show an understanding of the structure of a recursive subroutine, including the necessity of a stopping condition

☞ trace the execution of a recursive subroutine

☞ discuss the relative merits of iterative and recursive solutions to the same problem.

12.1 Procedural programming languages

Examples of these languages include Visual Basic, Pascal, Java, Python, C and C++ and literally hundreds of others.

All procedural programming languages are based on three fundamental concepts.

Sequence

The statements in the program will be executed in sequence. There will be exceptions to this where the flow of control causes the program to return to an earlier statement in the program, or branch to the code for a procedure or function.

Iteration

A number of statements in the program – or a 'block' of program code – is repeated a number of times. Hence procedural languages are also called '*block* *structured*' languages. The repetition of a number of statements is implemented in a program with a *loop*.

⬅ Look Back

To Chapter 11 to see an example of a flowchart containing a loop.

Selection

A statement in the code asks a question and a different route is taken through the code depending on whether the condition is true or false. The question is called a *condition*.

⬅ Look Back

To Chapter 11 to see an example of 'Selection'. Here the algorithm computed a PASS or FAIL result. This was shown with an IF statement in the pseudocode.

There are many variations of the IF structure.

IF – THEN – ENDIF

```
IF <condition>
  THEN
    <statement(s)>
ENDIF
```
The grade is a PASS for a mark of 40 and above.

The Visual Basic Code:
```
    If Mark >= 40 Then
      Console.WriteLine("grade is PASS")
    End If
```

IF – THEN – ELSE – ENDIF

The grade is a PASS for a mark over 50 otherwise the program reports a FAIL.

```
IF <condition>
  THEN
    <statement(s)>
  ELSE
    <statement(s)>
ENDIF
```
Code example:
```
If Mark >= 40 Then
    Console.WriteLine("Grade is a PASS")
    Else
    Console.WriteLine("Grade is a FAIL")
    End If
```

12.2 Selection

Assume that a grade is now awarded as follows:

Mark	Grade Awarded
Under 40	FAIL
40 and under 75	MERIT
75 and over	DISTINCTION

The algorithm could be structured with three separate IF statements.

The alternative is to use '*nested IF statements*'; this means we have one IF statement sitting inside another.

```
INPUT Mark
IF Mark <40
   THEN
      OUTPUT "FAIL"
   ELSE
      IF Mark >= 40 AND Mark < 75
         THEN
            OUTPUT "MERIT"
         ELSE
            OUTPUT "DISTINCTION"
      ENDIF
ENDIF
```

The IF statement inside the box is nested inside the original IF statement.

The Visual Basic code:

```
If Mark < 40 Then
  Console.WriteLine("FAIL")
Else
  If Mark >= 40 And Mark < 75 Then
    Console.WriteLine("MERIT")
  Else
    Console.WriteLine("DISTINCTION")
  End If
End If
```

This is fine but will get messy when we have several alternatives.

The solution is to use the alternative CASE – ENDCASE structure.

Case

A grade is awarded as shown by the table below.

Mark	Grade Awarded
Under 40	FAIL
40 and under 50	E
50 and under 60	D
60 and under 70	C
70 and under 80	B
80 and over	A

```
INPUT Mark
CASE Mark
<40            : OUTPUT "FAIL"
>=40 AND <50   : OUTPUT "E"
>=50 AND <60   : OUTPUT "D"
>=60 AND <70   : OUTPUT "C"
>=70 AND <80   : OUTPUT "B"
>=80           : OUTPUT "B"
ENDCASE
```

The Visual Basic code:

```
Select Case Mark
    Case 0 To 39
        Console.WriteLine("FAIL")
    Case 41 To 50
        Console.WriteLine("E")
    Case 51 To 60
        Console.WriteLine("D")
    Case 61 To 70
        Console.WriteLine("C")
    Case 71 To 80
        Console.WriteLine("B")
    Case 80 To 100
        Console.WriteLine("A")
    Case Else
        Console.WriteLine("INVALID mark")
End Select
```

12.3 Iteration

If something is 'iterated' it is repeated. If a program has a loop, the code inside the loop will be iterated (or repeated). In all high-level programming languages there are three alternative structures available for implementing a loop.

FOR – ENDFOR

This is the choice to use if we know, by the nature of the problem, the number of iterations to be made.

Example

We need to process the exam marks for seven students.
   The code will require an integer variable to act as the loop counter.

```
FOR Student ← 1 TO 7
   ...
   ...
ENDFOR
```

The Visual Basic code:

```
For Student = 1 To 7
    Console.Write("Mark ...")
    Mark = Console.ReadLine
    If Mark < 40 Then
        Console.WriteLine("FAIL")
    Else
        Console.WriteLine("PASS")
    End If
Next Student
```

Readability

It is good practice to indent the statements inside the loop – it makes the start and end of the loop stand out.
   This issue is covered extensively in Chapter 15.

The `Student` variable is the loop counter.
   The FOR structure is called a 'count controlled' loop.

Progress Check 12.1

Six product descriptions are to be keyed in and stored in array `Description`.
   Write the pseudocode.

REPEAT – UNTIL <condition>

Here the number of iterations cannot be predicted and the <condition> to test for more iterations is done at the end of the loop.

```
REPEAT
   ...
   ...
UNTIL <condition>
```

Example

Process the student marks until a mark of −1 is entered.

```
Do
    Console.Write("Mark ...")
    Mark = Console.ReadLine
    If Mark <> −1 Then
        If Mark < 40 Then
            Console.WriteLine("FAIL")
        Else
            Console.WriteLine("PASS")
        End If
    End If
Loop Until Mark = −1
```

> ✍ **Note**
>
> The Visual Basic keywords are different to the pseudocode used:
>
> Do – Loop Until
>
> The code is 'clumsy' as we do not want to process the mark of –1. Hence the need for a third alternative loop structure.

Using REPEAT – UNTIL will always perform at least one iteration of the loop.

WHILE – END WHILE <condition>

The problem of 'at least one iteration' is overcome with this third alternative structure which tests for the condition at the start of the loop. If the condition is false the first time, then the statements inside the loop are never executed.

```
WHILE <condition>
  ...
  ...
ENDWHILE
```

The Visual Basic code:

```
Console.Write("Mark ...")
Mark = Console.ReadLine

While Mark <> -1
  If Mark < 40 Then
    Console.WriteLine("FAIL")
  Else
    Console.WriteLine("PASS")
  End If

  Console.Write("Mark ...")
  Mark = Console.ReadLine
End While
```

> When a problem design requires a loop, the first question is always to consider:
>
> "Do we know how many iterations"?

The second and third loop structures are called a '**condition controlled**' loop.

> **Progress Check 12.2**
>
> A number of car registrations are keyed in and terminated with the registration "XXX". Registrations are to be stored in array Reg. The rogue value used to terminate the loop should not be stored.
>
> Write the pseudocode.

12.4 Procedures and functions

We have already stated that it is a good practice to design the algorithm for our problem using the idea of sub-tasks which are coded separately.

Procedures and functions are called **subprograms** or **subroutines** and fit with this idea of using a modular approach to both the problem design and coding.

Procedures

Consider any application where the user is continually presented with a main menu and (about) three menu choices are available.

```
Sub Main()
    Dim MyChoice As Integer
    Do
        Call DisplayMenu()

        MyChoice = Console.ReadLine()

        If MyChoice = 1 Then Call MyProcedure1()
        If MyChoice = 2 Then Call MyProcedure2()
    Loop Until MyChoice = 3
End Sub

Sub DisplayMenu()
    Console.WriteLine("=====================")
    Console.WriteLine("1. Make available the student marks")
    Console.WriteLine()
    Console.WriteLine("2. Process the student marks")
    Console.WriteLine()
    Console.WriteLine("3. End")
    Console.WriteLine()
    Console.Write("Your Choice ? ")
End Sub

Sub MyProcedure1()
    ' code
    ' code
End Sub

Sub MyProcedure2()
    ' code
    ' code
End Sub
```

This would be a typical program structure for any 'menu driven' program.

> ### ✎ Note
>
> ✓ Consider the .main program' as `Sub_Main`
> ✓ Three sections of code have been written as a procedure:
> ➢ `DisplayMenu`
> ➢ `MyProcedure1`
> ➢ `MyProcedure2`
> ✓ Each procedure is called from the main program when required.

Procedures have the possible benefit that the procedure code can be written and defined once only and then called as many times as needed from the main program.

> ### 🗐 Key Points
>
> A procedure must have an ***identifier name***.
> The procedure is called (i.e. run) using its identifier name.

Functions

Built-in Functions

There are two kinds of functions. The programming language will have hundreds of **'*built-in*'** functions, i.e. functions which come as part of (for example) the Visual Basic programming language.

Section 2.4. of the syllabus requires you to be familiar with the built-in functions which are available to manipulate string data. For example, compute the number of characters in a string.

User-defined Functions

The programmer can define their own functions which will be designed for a particular purpose.

This is best illustrated by an example before we try to introduce the technical terms.

> A little confusing as it's not the user who will define and code the function but the programmer.

Example

A student takes three papers for each subject and their final subject grade is computed from the total for all three papers. A total of 120 or above means they can progress to the second year of the course; less than 120 requires them to repeat the year of study.

The pseudocode for the problem is:

```
TotalScore ← 0
FOR Paper ← 1 To 3
  INPUT NextMark
  TotalScore ← TotalScore + NextMark
ENDFOR
// then decide if they can progress...
```

> ### ✎ Note
>
> We are using the // syntax to indicate a comment line in the pseudocode.

`CanProgress` and we shall define a function with identifies.

It will need to be given the value for `TotalScore` and this value is called a ***parameter***.

The function will do its working out and return a value to variable `Decision` in the main program.

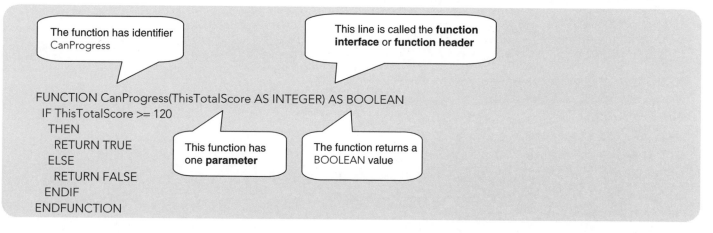

The function has identifier CanProgress

This line is called the **function interface** or **function header**

```
FUNCTION CanProgress(ThisTotalScore AS INTEGER) AS BOOLEAN
IF ThisTotalScore >= 120
  THEN
    RETURN TRUE
  ELSE
    RETURN FALSE
  ENDIF
ENDFUNCTION
```

This function has one **parameter**

The function returns a BOOLEAN value

The early use of functions did not use the keyword RETURN.
    The value to be returned was assigned using the function name:

CanProgress=TRUE
CanProgress=FALSE

The remainder of the main program then becomes:

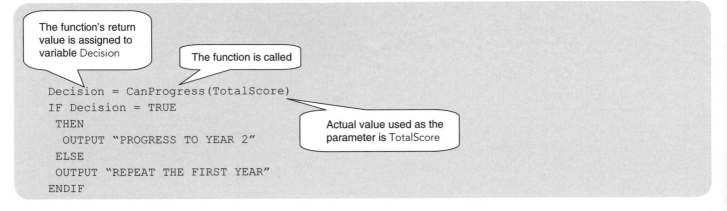

The function's return value is assigned to variable Decision

The function is called

```
Decision = CanProgress(TotalScore)
IF Decision = TRUE
  THEN
    OUTPUT "PROGRESS TO YEAR 2"
  ELSE
  OUTPUT "REPEAT THE FIRST YEAR"
ENDIF
```

Actual value used as the parameter is TotalScore

The Visual Basic code:

```
Sub Main()
    Dim NextPaper As Integer
    Dim Paper As Integer
    Dim TotalScore As Integer
    Dim Decision As Boolean

    TotalScore = 0
    For Paper = 1 To 3

        Console.Write("Paper score ...? ")
        NextPaper = Console.ReadLine
        TotalScore = TotalScore + NextPaper
    Next
    Decision = CanProgress(TotalScore)
    If Decision = True Then
        Console.WriteLine("PROGRESS TO YEAR 2")
    Else
        Console.WriteLine("REPEAT TO YEAR 1")
    End If

    Console.ReadLine()
End Sub

Function CanProgress(ByVal ThisTotalScore As Integer) As Boolean
    If ThisTotalScore >= 120 Then
        Return True
    Else
        Return False
    End If
End Function
```

– Function call
– TotalScore is the **argument**

Function definition

Progress Check 12.3

What is missing from this function header?

```
FUNCTION CountVehicleByType(Vehicle[]:
STRING,
  VehicleType:CHAR)
```

Progress Check 12.4

What is missing from this function header?

```
FUNCTION IsCharacterPresent(ThisString,
ThisChar) RETURNS BOOLEAN
```

What missing from this function definition?

Summary of functions

- ✓ Functions always have an identifier name
- ✓ The definition line of the function is called the *function header* or *function interface*
- ✓ The function can have any number of *parameters* (including none)
- ✓ The parameters must be used in the correct order and have the correct data type
- ✓ A function always returns a value to a variable in the main program
- ✓ In the function call the parameter(s) are called *arguments*

Passing value by reference - passing values by value

Consider the following:

The main program will not compute the total mark first. The three paper marks are passed as parameters to the function `CanProgress`. A fourth parameter shows if there is to be a percentage increase in the marks (for example, +10% could be the adjustment if the Exam Board decided these were exceptionally hard papers).

```
FUNCTION CanProgress (P1 : INTEGER, P2 : INTEGER, P3 : INTEGER,
         Change : Integer) : RETURNS BOOLEAN
 DECLARE TotalScore AS INTEGER
 P1 ← P1 * (100 + Change) / 100
 P2 ← P2 * (100 + Change) / 100
 P3 ← P3 * (100 + Change) / 100
 TotalScore = P1 + P2 + P3
 IF TotalScore >= 120
  THEN
   RETURN TRUE
  ELSE
   RETURN FALSE
  ENDIF
 ENDFUNCTION
```

A typical function call would be:

```
CanProgress(13, 56, 44, 5)
```

Meaning that the scores on the three papers were 13, 56 and 44 respectively and the marks are all to be adjusted up by 5%.

Implement the Visual Basic code:

```
Sub Main()
    Dim Paper1 As Integer
    Dim Paper2 As Integer
    Dim Paper3 As Integer
    Dim Decision As Boolean
    Dim PerCentChange As Integer

    Console.Write("Next paper ...? ")
    Paper1 = Console.ReadLine
    Console.Write("Next paper ...? ")
    Paper2 = Console.ReadLine
    Console.Write("Next paper ...? ")
    Paper3 = Console.ReadLine
    Console.Write("Percentage change to marks...? ")
    PerCentChange = Console.ReadLine
    Decision = CanProgress(Paper1, Paper2, Paper3, 5)
    If Decision = True Then
        Console.WriteLine("PROGRESS to YEAR 2")
    Else
        Console.WriteLine("REPEAT YEAR 1")
    End If
    Console.WriteLine()
    Console.WriteLine("Paper 1 is ... " & Paper1)
    Console.WriteLine("Paper 2 is ... " & Paper2)
    Console.WriteLine("Paper 3 is ... " & Paper3)
    Console.ReadLine()
End Sub

Function CanProgress(ByVal P1 As Integer, ByVal P2 As Integer,
            ByVal P3 As Integer, ByVal Change As Integer) As Boolean
    Dim RevisedTotalMark As Integer

    P1 = P1 * (100 + Change) / 100
    P2 = P2 * (100 + Change) / 100
    P3 = P3 * (100 + Change) / 100

    Return RevisedTotalMark = P1 + P2 + P3
End Function
```

A run of the program gives:

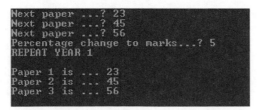

This demonstrates that the paper scores were changed inside the function. When control returns back to the main program the original paper values are unchanged.

Consider the function header changed to:

This time when the values are changed inside the function their new values are mirrored back in the main program.

```
Next paper ...? 23
Next paper ...? 45
Next paper ...? 56
Percentage change to marks...? 5
REPEAT YEAR 1

Paper 1 is ... 24
Paper 2 is ... 47
Paper 3 is ... 59
```

```
Function CanProgress(ByRef P1 As Integer, ByRef P2 As Integer,
        ByRef P3 As Integer, ByRef Change As Integer) As Boolean
```

Passing parameters by reference

A memory reference is now passed to the function. If the values of the variable changes inside the function, the value is retained back in the main program.

Passing values by value

A copy of the value is used as the function argument. If the value changes inside the function this change is not carried back to the variable(s) in the main program.

Conclusion

Passing values into a function can be either:

♦ *By value*
♦ *By reference.*

12.5 Recursion

Not an easy concept to grasp. A recursive procedure is:

✓ one which is defined in terms of itself
✓ a procedure which calls itself.

Coded as a function, there must be a stopping condition to make the recursion terminate.

Example

The first example is from maths where the 'factorial of number N is defined as:

Factorial N (written as N!) = N x (N–1) x (N–2) x .... x 3 x 2 x 1

This means that the Factorial 5 = 5 x Factorial 4.

Written as a function `Factorial` it would have a single parameter, i.e. the number and will be defined as follows:

```
FUNCTION Factorial(ThisNumber)
   IF ThisNumber = 1
    THEN
      RETURN 1
    ELSE
      RETURN ThisNumber x Factorial(ThisNumber - 1)
   ENDIF
ENDFUNCTION
```

The Visual Basic code:

```
Sub Main()
    Dim Number As Integer
    Dim FactorialOfNumber As Integer

    Console.Write("Number ...? ")
    Number = Console.ReadLine
    FactorialOfNumber = Factorial(Number)
    Console.WriteLine("The factorial is ... " & FactorialOfNumber)

    Console.ReadLine()
End Sub

Function Factorial(ByVal ThisNumber As Integer) As Integer
    If ThisNumber <= 1 Then
       Return 1
    Else
       Return ThisNumber * Factorial(ThisNumber - 1)
    End If
End Function
```

Call to function `Factorial`

Here's where we know the function is recursive – it refers to itself

12.6 Recursive or iteration algorithm

The Factorial algorithm could have been designed with a loop instead of using a recursive solution. Here is the code:

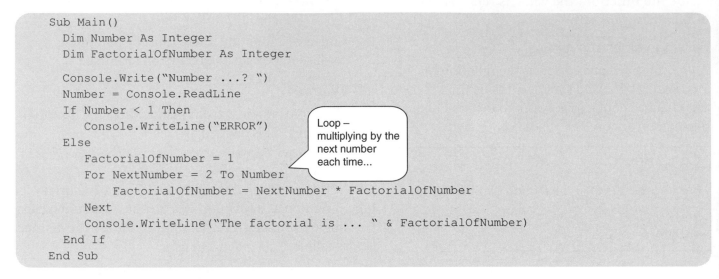

```
Sub Main()
  Dim Number As Integer
  Dim FactorialOfNumber As Integer

  Console.Write("Number ...? ")
  Number = Console.ReadLine
  If Number < 1 Then
      Console.WriteLine("ERROR")
  Else
      FactorialOfNumber = 1
      For NextNumber = 2 To Number
          FactorialOfNumber = NextNumber * FactorialOfNumber
      Next
      Console.WriteLine("The factorial is ... " & FactorialOfNumber)
  End If
End Sub
```

Loop – multiplying by the next number each time...

So which should we design – a recursive or an iterative algorithm?

Requirements of a recursive solution

✓ Every new call with recursion requires the computer system to remember this return point in the current call. These return points must be stored and retrieved using "last return point stored will be the first to be retrieved" – i.e. last in – first out – so we need a stack

✓ There is the danger that after many calls that the stack space could be full and generate a 'stack overflow' error

✓ Recursive solutions tend to require less steps for the algorithm and therefore less code.

📖 **Later**

We shall return to recursion in Chapter 20 when we discuss:

✓ a binary search
✓ a binary tree traversal.

Data Types and Data Structures

Revision Objectives

After you have studied this chapter, you should be able to:

☞ define and use different data types, for example, integer, real, Boolean, character and string

☞ declare and use arrays (one- and two-dimensional) for solving simple problems (this should include initialising arrays, reading data into arrays and performing a simple serial search on a one-dimensional array)

☞ design and implement a record format

☞ estimate the size of a file from its structure and the number of records

☞ store, retrieve and search for data in files

☞ use the facilities of a procedural language to perform file operations (open, read, write, update, insert, append and close) on files and use appropriate file handling functions.

13.1 Data types

We are already familiar with using identifiers for any data values which are used by the problem under investigation.

The issue for the programmer is to decide for all data values which is most appropriate – a *variable* or a *constant* – and then to choose an *identifier name*.

The programmer must then decide what data type is appropriate for each variable and constant.

For Visual Basic the data types most widely used are given in Table 13.1.

> The actual data type names used will differ for different programming languages. For example, Pascal uses Real for real numbers.

Declaration statements

The programmer lists the variables and constants that the program will use.

```
Dim Surname As String
Dim SexCode As Char
Dim NoOfChildren As Byte
Dim NoOfPoints As Integer
Dim AveragePoints As Decimal
Dim IsMarried As Boolean
```

> Some languages will allow a variable to be used without declaring its data type – this is considered 'bad practice' in traditional programming.

Table 13.1

Data types used in Visual Basic	
Data Type	**Explanation**
Byte	A positive integer between 0 and 255
Integer	An integer between −32657 and +32658
Decimal	A real number, i.e. a number which may have a fraction part
Char	A single character
String	A sequence of characters
Boolean	A True/False value

Progress Check 13.1

A program is to store the surname and initials (separately) for a number of employees who each have an employee code (typically D768). The program also stores the number of years of service and whether or not they are a full-time employee.

13.2 Arrays

If the program had to store data for twenty employees, a possible design would be to use variables:
`Surname1, Surname2, Surname3, …,`
`Surname20`.

However, these names have no relation to each other and are as different as using A, B, C etc., for the surnames.

> Arrays are sometimes called lists.

An array is a data structure (i.e. 'a way of structuring our data') so that:

✓ all the data items are referred to by a common *identifier* name
✓ each value is identified by a *subscript* number or an *index* number
✓ all items in the array must be of the same data type.

> Some languages – including Visual Basic – will start the index at zero.
>   One strategy is to go along with this but never use subscript 0.

The array data can be visualised as a one-dimensional table as shown in Table 13.2.

Table 13.2

Index	Surname
1	"Patel"
2	"Adams"
3	"Nani"
…	…
20	"Viovanni"

Individual array items are then referred to using the subscript number. For example, `Surname[3]` is assigned "Nani".

The `Surname` array is a one-dimensional array.

> Some languages – Pascal and C++ – use square brackets.
>   Visual Basic uses parentheses.
>   In our pseudocode we shall use [ ].

The highest and lowest index number used by an array is called its ***upper bound*** and ***lower bound***.

Declaring the array

In pseudocode we shall use the keyword `DECLARE`.
`DECLARE Surname[20]: STRING`
In Visual Basic code:
Dim Surname As String

> Dim Surname(20) As String

Initialising the array

Assume all array elements are given an initial value of empty string.

```
For Index = 1 To 20
    Surname(Index) = ""
Next
```

> Initialising all the values can be done using a For – Next loop.
>   Note the use of the Index variable (data type Integer or Byte) to act as the loop counter and the index for the array.

Assigning values to the array

```
Surname(3) = "Nani"
Surname(20) = "Viovanni"
Etc.
```

2-Dimensional arrays

Visualise this as a two-dimensional table.
Six employees are sales staff. We are to store the number of sales made by each employee over 12 months.

Table 13.3

Sales	1	2	3	4	5	6	7	8	9	10	11	12
1	0	0	0	3	4	0	0					
2	1	12	12	6	7	8	9	18	8	12	11	6
3	2	4	5	1	2	3	11	6	7	2	3	1
4	11	12	3	4	6	7	1	2	6	7	11	4
5	1	0	0	8	0	0	1	1	2	3	4	
6	0	0	1	2	3	4						

The rows represent each salesperson. The columns represent each month.

Declaring the array

```
Dim Sales(6, 12) As Integer
```

Initialising the array

Assume all array elements are given an initial value of zero.

```
For SalesPerson = 1 To 6
   For MonthNo = 1 To 12
      Sales(SalesPerson, MonthNo) = 0
   Next
Next
```

> **Note**
>
> This uses a **nested loop** – the inner loop is for the 12 months – the outer loop for each salesperson. We have already used the concept of 'nesting' with IF statements.

Assigning values to the array

```
Sales(3, 7) = 11
Sales(6, 4) = 2
Etc.
```

> **Progress Check 13.3**
>
> Use the data from Table 13.3
> (a) How many sales were made by salesperson 4 in April?
> (b) What array value describes the 18 sales made by person 2 in August?

Searching the data in a 1-dimensional array

The user inputs the surname to be found. Output the array position at which the item is found, or the message "Name NOT FOUND". Assume the upper bound of the array is 20.

The algorithm is a simple **serial search**. We consider the first item in the array, then the second etc. We stop searching when the item is found or we reach the end of the array.

The variables needed are shown in Table 13.4.

Table 13.4

Variables needed for searching data in a 1-dimensional array		
Identifier	**Data Type**	**Description**
Surname	ARRAY[20]: STRING	The surname data
Index	INTEGER	Index position in the surname array
IsFound	BOOLEAN	Flags whether or not the requested surname has been found

> A pseudocode description of the algorithm is the best starting point.
>   First decide what variables are needed.

> **Note**
>
> The choice of a REPEAT – UNTIL loop in the pseudocode which follows, as we may not need to consider all items in the array.

```
INPUT SearchName
IsFound ← FALSE
Index ← 1
REPEAT
  IF Surname[Index] = SearchName
    THEN
       IsFound ← TRUE
       OUTPUT "Surname was FOUND – at position" Index "in the array"
  ELSE
       Index ← Index + 1
  ENDIF
UNTIL (IsFound = TRUE) OR (Index = 21)

IF IsFound = FALSE
  THEN
     OUTPUT "Name NOT FOUND"
ENDIF
```

 Note

The algorithm will only find and report the **first** occurrence of the requested surname.

- Pascal uses the keyword TYPE
- Visual Basic calls the type a STRUCTURE
- C++ uses STRU.
  We shall use TYPE in our pseudocode.

13.3 Record structure

Most programming languages support the use of a 'record' data structure.

As well as the surname, there may be other data values we wish to store for each employee.

Consider each employee has recorded:

✓ surname
✓ employee code(typically D758)
✓ a code to indicate Full-time (F) or Part-time (P).
✓ the number of years they have been employed by the company.

We first define a data structure called EmployeeData (this is the identifier for the record).

Each data item which makes up the record is defined together with its data type.

```
TYPE EmployeeData
   Surname       : STRING
   EmployeeCode  : STRING
   Status        : CHAR
   YearsService  : INTEGER
ENDTYPE
```

Now we must declare a variable of type EmployeeData. As we have several employees we shall use an array.

```
DECLARE MyEmployee[20] : EmployeeData
```

Assigning values

```
MyEmployee[1].Surname ← "Pollard"
MyEmployee[1].EmployeeCode ← "Y568"
MyEmployee[1].Status ← 'F'
MyEmployee[1].YearsService ← 8
```

The 'dot notation' is generally used with a record data structure.
  Note, in our pseudocode we shall use double quotes for a string and single quotes for a single character.

And similarly for all other employee data.

Progress Check 13.4

A companies' product file consists of the following fields:

- ✓ product code
- ✓ quantity in stock
- ✓ retail price
- ✓ wholesale price.

(a) Design a record type structure to describe the product data.

(b) Declare an array of size 200 to store this product data.

(c) How would you refer to:
   (i) the product code,
   (ii) the wholesale price

   for the product record with index 57 in the array?

Files

Files are needed to permanently store data. The term 'file' is generally used to describe any type of data which needs to be permanently stored by the computer system and so a file could include:

- ✓ program files
- ✓ image files
- ✓ sound files
- ✓ data files
- ✓ data files which are organised in a format specific to a particular software product, for example, a Word document with a .docx file extension.

For this section of the syllabus we are using 'file' to describe a *data file* with a consistent structure.

When data is stored by a variable or constant in a program the data will be lost as soon as the program terminates.

The general use of files by a high-level programming language is called ***file handling***.

There will be variations in the language keywords used by different programming languages so we shall again use pseudocode.

13.4 File handling basics

The following are basics which could apply to all programming languages.

Open the file

The file must be opened and usually the file cannot be both written to and read from in the same session.

The file is opened as an 'output' file when we are to write data to it.

Once the file exists then we can open the file as an 'input' file for reading its contents.

Writing records to the file

```
OPEN "MyDatFile.dat" FOR INPUT AS 1
```

Says, open the file with name `MyDataFile.dat` for writing to.

The following statement then writes a new record to the file:

```
FILEWRITE #1, Surname, EmployeeCode,
         Status, YearsService
```

Since a program may be reading/writing data from more than one file, the file is allocated a **channel** or **disc buffer number**.

Reading a record

```
OPEN "MyDataFile.dat" FOR INPUT AS 1
```

Says, open the file ready to read its contents.

The following statement then reads a new record from the file and stores the data in the variables shown:

```
FILEREAD #1, ThisSurname, ThisEmployeeCode,
         ThisStatus, ThisYearsService
```

For reading or writing data the programmer must know the structure of the data in the file.

Appending to the file

A third mode of opening the file is to add new data items to the end of the file and this is called ***appending*** to the file.

```
OPEN "MyDataFile.dat" FOR APPEND AS 1
```

Followed by one or more new records written:

```
FILEWRITE #1, Surname, EmployeeCode,
         Status, YearsService
```

Close the file

```
CLOSE #1
```

File operators

The programming language will have a number of functions available to test for certain conditions. These would include:

```
EOF( )    will test whether we have reached the
          end of the file
EXISTS ( )   will test for the existence of the file.
```

File contents

Consider this file:

> Pollard, T009, F, 12
> George, T008, F, 11
> Harrison, R001, P, 1
> Veale, R007, P, 2
> Patel, G008, F, 23
> Osman, G009, P, 0

Here the data items are organised one record per line, with commas separating each field – called a **comma separated (CSV) file.**

This shows the typical contents of the file after six customer records have been entered.

Serial file organisation

Records are written into the file in no particular order. The file is said to have **serial organisation**. When the file is opened for reading, the records can only be read from the file in sequential order. For example, the record for Veale can only be read after the three earlier records have been read. This is a major drawback when using data files with serial or sequential organisation.

> When using the terms serial and sequential, be clear – are you referring to the way the records are stored or accessed?
> That is, file 'organisation' or file 'access'.

Sequential file organisation

A possible improvement is to have the records ordered in some way, for example, ordered in surname order.

The file is said to be a **sequentially** organised file, with Surname chosen as the **key field.**

> George, T008, F, 11
> Harrison, R001, P, 1
> Osman, G009, P, 0
> Patel, G008, F, 23
> Pollard,T009, F, 12
> Veale, R007, P, 2

We still have the limitation for a sequential file that records can only be read in sequence starting with the first record in the file.

13.5 Estimating the file size

We must be clear if each field is a fixed size or a variable size.

> **Look Back**
>
> To chapter 3 for the discussion of fixed length and variable records.

✓ A character is stored as a single byte
   ➤ so string and character data is straight-forward – 30 characters will use 30 bytes of storage
✓ For integers and real numbers the programming language will use a constant number of bytes
   ➤ in Section 2 we stated an Integer is stored with four bytes.
✓ Boolean data is stored as a single byte.

Calculate the file size (in Kbytes) for a file of 2000 employees.

The discussion for our employee file would go as shown in Table 13.5.

Table 13.5

Calculating the file size		
Field	Fixed/ Variable	
Surname	Variable	Estimate maximum 30 characters
EmployeeCode	Fixed	4 characters (4 bytes)
Status	Fixed	1 character (1 byte)
YearsService	Integer	Languages uses 4 bytes for all integers

Total number of bytes for a single record $= 30 + 4 + 1 + 4 = 39$ bytes

Estimate 200 employees in the file

Total file size: $2000 \times 39 = 78000$ bytes.

If this is a file which is likely to have records added then we should allow for a 10 per cent increase in the file size. So,

$78000 + 10\% = 85800$ bytes

1024 bytes $= 1$ kilobyte

So file size (including expansion) is

$85800/1024 = 83.8$ kilobytes.

13.6 File processing

Assuming a file can only be opened for either reading (input) or writing to (output) then *file maintenance*, i.e. add, delete or amend records will always involve the use of two files.

To add a record into a sequentially organised file

Records from the file will be read until the position at which the new record to be inserted is found. As each existing record is read it is written to the new file. The new file will finally contain all the original records plus the new record at the correct position.

Assume the file has Surname as its key field.

Delete and amend a record

The algorithms are very similar to the one below so these are set as a progress check exercise.

Progress Check 13.5

Study the algorithm given below for adding a record. Describe in words.

(a) the algorithm needed to delete a record.

(b) the algorithm to amend a record.

Hint: Both algorithms require the existing DATA file for input and a new empty NEWDATA_ file for output.

```
OPEN the existing file DATA for INPUT
OPEN (a new empty) file NEWDATA for OUTPUT
INPUT NewSurnamePosition
Found ← FALSE
REPEAT
    READ the next record from DATA (including Surname)
    IF NewSurname < Surname
      THEN
        PositionFound ← TRUE
        INPUT other new record data (EmployeeCode, etc.)
        WRITE new record to NEWDATA
        WRITE current record from DATA to NEWDATA
    ELSE
      WRITE current record to NEWDATA
    ENDIF
UNTIL PositionFound = TRUE

// now write all the remaining records from DATA to NEWDATA
WHILE NOT EOF(DATA)
    DO
      READ next DATA record
      WRITE this record to NEWDATA
ENDWHILE

//the latest version of the file must be NEWDATA so
DELETE DATA
RENAME NEWDATA AS DATA
```

Exam-style Questions

1. A database of properties in an estate agency displays on the screen a form to allow the user to enter queries.

(a) The system stores details of the last 100 queries made. These are held in a file which contains, for each query made, the following:
   • the name of the customer
   • the number of bedrooms requested
   • the date on which the query was made
   • whether the customer asked for details of a property or not.
   Complete the following table.

	Data Type	Field Size (bytes)
Name		
Number of Bedrooms		
Date		
Details Requested		

[8]

(b) Estimate the size, in kilobytes, of the file of 100 records. Show your working. [5]

(c) The records are held in a serial file. Describe the process for adding a new query into the file that already contains 100 queries. There should be no more than 1 entry per customer. If there is already a record for that customer it should be replaced by the new one. [5]

Cambridge 9691 Specimen Paper 2 Q1(b)(c) & (d)

> Don't be put off by the word 'Estimate'. It means we shall have to make a sensible guess for the number of characters needed to store a customer name.

2.

(a) Students take exams in all their subjects at the end of every year. A procedure is to be written which inputs the marks of a student from the STUDENT file and calculates the mean mark for that student.
   Produce an algorithm which will carry out the above task. The procedure is to be called MEAN. [4]

> Our preferred technique throughout the textbook has been to use pseudocode.

(b) The school awards a prize each year to the students who achieve the highest mean mark in their form.
   Produce an algorithm for a procedure called PRIZE which will determine which student will win the prize for a particular form. The name of the form and the name of the student should then be saved to a file called PRIZES.
   You should use MEAN in this final algorithm without reproducing the detail in part (a). [7]

Cambridge 9691 Paper 13 Q9 June 2010

> **Note**
>
> This question draws on the content from several sections of the Section 2 syllabus.

Common Facilities of Procedural Languages

14

Revision Objectives

After you have studied this chapter, you should be able to:

☞ understand and use assignment statements

☞ understand arithmetic operators including operators for integer division (+, −, *, /, MOD and DIV) and use these to construct expressions

☞ understand a range of relational operators, for example, =, <, <=, >, >= and <> and use these to construct expressions

☞ understand the Boolean operators AND, OR, and NOT and use these to construct expressions

☞ understand the effects of the precedence of standard operators and the use of parentheses to alter the order of evaluation

☞ evaluate expressions containing arithmetic, relational and Boolean operators and parentheses

☞ understand and use a range of operators and built-in functions for string manipulation, including location (LOCATE), extraction (LEFT, MID, RIGHT), comparison, concatenation, determining the length of a string (LENGTH) and converting between characters and their ASCII code (ASCII and CHAR)

☞ understand that relational operations on alphanumeric strings depend on binary codes of the characters

☞ input and validate data

☞ output data onto screen/file/printer, formatting the data for output as necessary.

14.1 Assignment

We have already used assignment in both pseudocode and actual program code.

Pseudocode: `NoOfChildren ← 3`
Visual Basic statement: `NoOfChildren = 3`

The number or expression on the right-hand side is assigned to the variable on the left-hand side of the statement.

14.2 Arithmetic operators

In computer programming we shall need exactly the same set of operators used in mathematics.

Operator		Expression	Result
+	Add	14 + 7	21
-	Subtract	14 − 4	9
*	Multiply	6 * 11	66
/	Divide	11/6	1.83333333
^	Raise to the power	2^4	16
Modulo arithmetic			
DIV	Integer division	11 DIV 4	2
MOD	The remainder following integer division	11 MOD 4	3

14.3 Relational operators

These will typically be used to form a <condition>. For example, as part of an IF statement or to test for the end of a loop.

Operator		Expression	Returns
=	Equals	1 = 4	False
>	Greater than	8 > 4	True
>=	Greaten than or equal to	"Bob" >="Brian"	False
<	Less than	9 < 10	True
<+	Less than or equal to	5 <= 5	True
<>	Not equal to	"Ant" <> "Rat"	True

> **Not equal to**
>
> C++ uses !=

14.4 Boolean operators

These will also be used to form a <condition>. For example, as part of an IF statement or to test for the end of a loop.

Operator	Expression	Returns
AND	(13 = 2) AND (4 = 4)	False
OR	(13 = 2) OR (4 = 4)	True
NOT	NOT (13 = 2)	True

These expressions can get long-winded and the intended logic may need to be made clear with the use of brackets.

Consider:

A = 16

B = 4

C = 3

IF C = 4 OR (A = 16 AND B = 5) THEN ......

The condition here returns False.

14.5 Parentheses and precedence

Parentheses

The term for the use of brackets within an expression.

Precedence

Precedence means that the order in which the various parts of the expressions must be evaluated

must be made clear. The use of brackets will do this as the agree order of precedence is:

1. evaluate the contents of brackets first
2. then compute any multiply or divide calculations
3. and finally any add or subtract calculations.

Example

$$(13 - 12/4) / 5$$

Computes the contents of the brackets first to give 10.

Note the 'order of precedence' inside the bracket required that 12/4 was computed first, then subtract the result 3 from 13.

The final division by 5 computes the expression as 2.

> **Progress Check 14.1**
>
> Evaluate these expressions:
>
> (a) (11/2 + 2.5) / 4
> (b) (2^3 + 5) / (3+1)

> **Progress Check 14.2**
>
> Evaluate these expressions when:
>
> a = 6
>
> b = 3
>
> c = 2
>
> (a) (a + 2b) +2/c
> (b) 3 (a + b + c) / (2a – 3b)

14.6 String manipulation built-in functions

The syllabus specifically includes these string handling/manipulation built-in functions.

LOCATE

`LOCATE (String1, String2)`

Searches for the occurrence of `String1` within `String2` and if found returns the position of the first character.

```
LOCATE ("Bull", "New York Bulls")
Returns 10.
```

LEFT

`LEFT(ThisString, Number)`
  Start at the left hand side of the string and retain the number of characters shown.

```
LEFT("Queens Park Rangers", 6)
Returns the string "Queens".
```

RIGHT

`RIGHT(ThisString, Number)`
  Similar to the LEFT function, but start at the right-hand side of the string.

```
RIGHT("Nottingham Forest", 6)
Returns the string "Forest".
```

LENGTH

`LENGTH(ThisString)`
  Returns the number of characters in the string.

```
LENGTH("Real Madrid")
Returns 11.
```

Progress Check 14.3

```
ThisString = "Liverpool FC"
  NewString = RIGHT(ThisString,
2) & " " & LEFT(ThisString, 9)
```
  What value is assigned to `NewString`?

Progress Check 14.4

```
Position = "Potter", "Harry Potter")
```
  What value is assigned to `Position`?

Concatenation

The technical term for 'joining together' two or more strings.

Concatenation

The language may have a CONCAT function.

```
CONCAT("Will", "Smith")
Returns the string "WillSmith"
```

Or, using the concatenation operator:

```
Surname = "Ahmed"
FirstName = "Reymond"
FullName = FirstName & " " & Surname
```

  Assigns the string "Raymond Ahmed" to variable `FullName`.

Concatenation operator

Visual Basic will allow either & or +.

ASCII Function

All characters in the ASCII character set have a unique code number.
  Ones to remember are:

✓ the upper case letters start with 'A' with code 65
✓ the digit characters start with '0' with code 48, '1' with code 49, etc.

```
ASCII('A') returns value 65.
ASCII('2') returns 50.
```

The Visual Basic function is ASC ( ).

⬅ Look Back

To Chapter 3. where we introduced the ASCII character set.

CHAR Function

Works in reverse to the ASCII function – converts the number code to the character.

```
CHAR(67) returns the character 'C'.
CHAR(57) returns the character '9'. CHAR(67)
```

The Visual Basic function is CHR ( ).

Progress Check 14.5

```
No1 ← ASC('B')
Final ← No1 + 10
```
What value is assigned to `Final`?

14.7 Relational operations on alphanumeric strings depend on binary codes of the characters

This simply means that we can use the relational operators to compare strings. What the high level language will be doing behind the scenes is to compute the ASCII code values for each character and then make comparisons between these numbers.

Some examples to illustrate are shown below.

Expression	Returns
"Monkey" = "Monkey"	True
"monkey' <> "MONKEY"	True
"MONKEY" > "monkey"	True
"ANT" < "ANTELOPE"	True

All these expressions can be tested using Visual Basic's IDE Immediate Debug window:

```
Immediate Window
? "monkey" > "MONKEY"
True
? "MONKEY" <> "Monkey"
True
```

14.8 Input and validate data

We shall show here practical examples which effectively validate some data value on input.

Range check

Suppose a main menu offered six choices: 1 2, 3, 4 and 5 and finally 6 to exit.

Any other input from the user will be refused.

Other practical examples could include the following.

Length check

Checking on the length of a product code since all product codes are exactly six characters.

Format check

> **← Look Back**
>
> To Chapter 8 where Data Validation is extensively covered.

Checking on the format of a product code as all codes start with a two character code followed by four digit characters.

'From a list' check

The first two digits of the product code are from the list:

✓ EL – electrical
✓ CO – consumables
✓ HA – hardware

```
Sub Main()
    Dim InputIsValid As Boolean
    Dim Choice As Integer

    Call MainMenu()

    InputIsValid = False
    Do
        Console.Write("Choice ...? ") : Choice = Console.ReadLine
        If Choice >= 1 And Choice <= 6 Then InputIsValid = True
    Loop Until InputIsValid

    If Choice = 1 Then Call ....
    If Choice = 2 Then call ....
    etc.

End Sub
```

Presence check

A field must contain a value (it cannot be left blank).

14.9 Output data

The first thing to consider is how the intended output is to be viewed.

Screen

If the output is not to be retained then the output will be to the screen. The user will select the information from studying the output and then move on.

Printer

If a permanent copy – for example, a report – is required then the output will be sent to the printer. The output will make full use of the printing features available such as font size, style, layout and possible use of colour.

File

If no on-line printer is available then the output can be sent to a print file in order that it can be printed out at a later date.

Programming language features for formatting output

We saw earlier in the chapter how strings can be concatenated.

A line of text can be mixture of text and variables which are storing values in the program.

In a Console Mode application we are limited to the formatting features available.

Here the output string uses this line of code:

```
Console  .WriteLine(Country(Index) & " " &
      Population(Index))
```

```
Country Summary

Angola 13.068
Anguilla 0.015
Antarctica 0.001
Antigua & Barbuda 0.087
Antilles 0.229
Saudi Arabia 25.732
Argentina 41.343
Armenia 2.967
Austria 8.214
Azerbaijan 8.304
```

Writing Maintainable Programs

15

Revision Objectives

After you have studied this chapter, you should be able to:

☞ define, understand and use the following terms correctly as they apply to programming: variable, constant, identifier, reserved word/keyword

☞ declare variables and constants, understanding the effect of scope and issues concerning the choice of identifier (including the need to avoid reserved words/keywords)

☞ select and use meaningful identifier names
☞ initialise variables appropriately, before using them
☞ annotate the code with comments so that the logic of the solution can be followed
☞ use indentation and formatting to show clearly the control structures within the code.

15.1 Programming terms

Variable

A variable is the representation of a data value which is required by the problem. A memory location is used to store the data value and the variable name or identifier – decided by the programmer – is the label for this memory location.

Constant

A data value used by the problem and whose value will not change.

Identifier

A name chosen by the programmer to represent a variable, constant, procedure or function name or a user-defined data type.

Reserved word/Keywords

These are the words used by the programming language itself such as (in Visual Basic) Dim, If, Then, Do, Loop Until, and hundreds of others.

> ✎ **Note**
>
> Reserved words cannot be used as identifiers.

Scope of Variables

A consequence of this is that a program could use the same variable name within different parts of the program code and – due to their different *scope* – they will be treated by the program as separate variables.

Scope of a variable or constant

The scope of a variable or constant refers to the parts of the program code within which the identifier is recognised.

Global Scope

Describes a variable which is recognised throughout all the program code. If we are programming in Console Mode with the code organised within a Module, then 'global' is taken to mean anywhere within the module.

Local Scope

'Local' means the code where the variable is recognised is restricted. This could be restricted to:

✓ a procedure (including Sub_Main)
✓ a function or procedure
✓ an 'event procedure' if you are using a forms based environment.

15.2 Meaningful identifier names

This is common sense; a meaningful variable name is a way of making the code easier to follow and understand. The particular language used will place some restrictions of the names which can be used. For example, in Visual Basic.Net:

- ✓ Maximum of 64 characters
- ✓ Cannot start with a digit character
- ✓ No punctuation characters allowed.

The choice of identifier name by the programmer will be a compromise between names which are meaningful without being too long, and may follow some style adopted by the programmer. For example, the use of Camel Caps.

Progress Check 15.1

Which of the following identifier names would **not** be allowed in Visual Basic.Net?

```
1Total
NoOfChildren
Number Of Children
Numberofchildren
Number_Of_Children
Number-Of-Children
```

15.3 Initialising variables

Most programming languages will insist that all variables and constants are declared before they are used within the program code. Such languages are said to be ***strongly typed*** languages.

The variable may also be initialised with a value. Languages such as PHP work out from the initialisation value the data type which should be assumed.

15.4 Annotating code with comments

Meaningful variable names go a long way to helping with the understanding of any code. The code may however still require **comments** to help the programmer. This could include a comment to describe the use of a variable, the purpose of a procedure or function or simply mark the end of a loop.

We have already done this in pseudocode with line such as:

```
//This is a comment
```

15.5 Indentation

Most modern ***IDE (Integrated Development Environments)*** such as Visual Basic.Net will automatically use indentation to assist with the readability of the code. Indentation is usually used for:

- ✓ the block of statements inside a loop
- ✓ for the layout of If statements
- ✓ and many others.

> ✎ **Note**
>
> We have already used indentation extensively in our pseudocode throughout this Section.

Progress Check 15.2

Which are these are true statements describing the scope of variables?

(a) The scope will be determined by the data type of the variable.

(b) Global scope means the variable is recognised throughout the main program.

(c) Global scope means the variable is recognised throughout the main program but not including procedures and functions.

(d) A local variable would be typically recognised only inside a function.

Progress Check 15.3

Cars have to pass a roadworthy test called the Vehicle Test (VT). Four categories are tested.

- ✓ Brakes
- ✓ Steering
- ✓ Tyres
- ✓ Bodywork.

For a car to pass the VT, it must pass all the four categories.

Data is entered and stored for a single car typically as "1110".

This would represent a car which has passed for brakes, tyres and steering but failed on bodywork.

The following program code processes the data for a single car.
Comment on this code for all of the points discussed in this chapter.

```
Module Module1
  Sub Main()
    CarFailed = False
    Console.Write("Next car data ..? ") : NextCar = Console.ReadLine
    For Position = 1 To 4
      NextCategory = SingleCharacter(NextCar, Position)
      If NextCategory = "0" Then
          CarFailed = True
      End If
    Next Position
    If CarFailed = True Then
        Console.WriteLine("Car FAILED")
    Else
        Console.WriteLine("Car PASSED")
    End If
    Console.ReadLine()
  End Sub
  Function SingleCharacter(ByVal ThisString As String, ByVal ThisPosition As Integer)
  As Char
    Dim CategoryData As Char
    CategoryData = Mid(ThisString, ThisPosition, 1)
    Return CategoryData
  End Function
End Module
```

Testing and Running a Solution

16

Revision Objectives

After you have studied this chapter, you should be able to:

- ☞ describe types of errors in programs (syntax, logic and run-time errors) and understand how and when these may be detected
- ☞ describe testing strategies including white box testing, black box testing, alpha testing, beta testing and acceptance testing
- ☞ select suitable test data for a given problem, including normal, borderline and invalid data

- ☞ perform a dry run on a given algorithm, using a trace table
- ☞ describe the use of a range of debugging tools and facilities available in program development environments including translator diagnostics, breakpoints, stepping, and variable check/watch.

16.1 Types of errors

It is the task of any programmer to write robust applications – that is code that will continue to operate under adverse conditions.

The most common 'abnormal condition' is when users supply inappropriate data. The bottom line for the programmer is that this must not cause the program to crash.

> ### ✎ Note
>
> The three types of errors are:
>
> ✓ *Syntax errors*
> ✓ *Logical errors*
> ✓ *Run-time errors*

Errors–or 'bugs'-are the necessary evil of programming! Every programmer will have errors in their program code and depending on how sophisticated the programming environment – the programming software will have features which are designed to eliminate errors.

It is estimated that over half the code written by a developer for a real-world application is

designed to identify and trap errors and avoid the program crashing.

Syntax errors

Also called 'design time errors' these are the errors which result from code which does not conform to the rules of the programming language. Syntax errors will be the easiest types of error to fix. This is because the Integrated Development Environment (IDE) will indicate most of these before the program is compiled.

The language is made up of hundreds of keywords or reserved words, and a simple typing error in their use will cause a syntax error.

```
Dem Position As Integer
Dem NextCar As String
Dem NextCategory As Char
Dem CarFailed As Boolean
```

Dim spelt incorrectly triggers two errors. The Visual Basic. Net IDE indicates:

- ✓ an incorrect language keyword
- ✓ the variable which follows has not been declared.

In this next example the programmer has incorrectly used the `Console. Readline` statement.

```
CarFailed = False
Console. Write ("Next car data ..? ")
Console. ReadLine = NextCar
```

This is a syntax error.

Control structures

```
For Position = 1 To 4
    NextCategory = SingleCharacter (NextCar, Position)
    If NextCategory = "θ" Then
        CarFailed = True
    End If
Next Position
```

The IDE tries to help with this by indicating the various parts of the FOR loop. It will do a similar highlighting for other loop structures, If statements, etc.

Logic error

A logic error will only become apparent at run-time and means the program is not doing what the programmer intended it to do. These will not be reported by the IDE since this is an error in the programmer's logic.

Examples

✓ A loop which iterates 21 times, when it should only be 20 iterations
✓ A condition which tests for an exam mark 'greater than 50', when it should be 'greater than or equal to 50'.

Progress Check 16.1

There is a logic error in the program below.

```
Sub Main()
    Dim i As Integer
    i = 1
    Do While i > 0
        i = i + 1000
        Console. WriteLine("i is ..." & i)
    Loop
End Sub
```

What fundamental error is there in this program code?

Run-time error

Run-time errors will only become apparent when the program is executed. Run-time errors may only surface after the software is run on computers away from the programmer's development PC.

Examples

✓ The user enters character data when the program was expecting a number (or vice versa)
✓ An attempted 'division by zero' error
✓ An attempt to open a file which does not exist (see the screenshot which follows)
✓ Accessing a file from a folder to which the user does not have read permissions
✓ An attempt to assign a value to (for example) index position 6 of an array – but the array was declared with an upper bound of 5 (see the screenshot which follows).

16.2 Testing strategies

The purpose of program testing is to discover any errors that might be present in the software.

Testing a program can never adequately prove or demonstrate the correctness of the program. Generally speaking, testing can only reveal the existence of errors.

When is testing done?

✓ Tests done at the development stage
✓ Tests done on the developed system.

Development stage testing includes:

Black box Testing

This is testing that is applied to a module, for example, a procedure.

Black box testing checks that a module is functioning correctly by supplying the required inputs to the procedure and monitoring the outputs. There is effectively a 'black box' around the code and we are only concerned with what goes in and what come out of the procedure. Test cases are devised that provide a module with inputs.

For example, the following procedure requires three different values as inputs.

```
Public Sub Search82 (parBand () As String, parSearch As String, _txtObj As Object)

Do While Found = False And BandNo < 11
    If parBand (BandNo) = parSearch Then
       Found = True
       FoundNo = BandNo
    End If
    BandNo = BandNo + 1
Loop

If Found = True etc .....

End Sub
```

The Black box testing may be summarised as:

✓ the corresponding outputs produced by a module are examined for correctness
✓ the actual code contained in the module is kept hidden
✓ this type of testing is effectively testing the procedure's interface.

White box testing

This is again testing applied to a module, but this time the code inside the procedure is examined and test cases are devised that exercise every possible route through the code.

In this way each logical path through the code is tested.

For example, the procedure above has a loop and a conditional IF statement in the code, so the programmer must test all routes through the code.

Acceptance Testing

This is testing that is specified by a customer for whom the system has been developed. The customer checks that the supplied system meets his/her requirements as specified in the requirements specification document. The client may be asked by the developer to formally 'sign off' the system as proof of acceptance of the software.

Alpha Testing

Alpha testing is the initial stage where all the testing is done for the first time away from the development team, but still 'in-house'.

Beta Testing

An advance copy of software is released to selected customers and participants for trial purposes.

A large company such as Microsoft might invite users to be beta testers for the next release of a software product.

16.3 Test data

We have already made the point that a prime source of program errors could be the user attempting to input incorrect data. This could take a number of forms. It could be data value of the wrong type. It could be a data value which is of the correct type but outside the range of values which – by the nature of the problem – the program is expecting.

This second case can be planned for by the programmer and the formal testing should include choosing a full range of test data:

Normal data

Data values which are to be expected.

Borderline data

Also called '*boundary data*'. A data value which is at the limit of what can be expected.

Invalid data

Also called *erroneous data*. A data value chosen which is not a permitted value.

For example, a number value is input when a string is expected (or vice versa). It could also be a data value which is outside the range of permitted values.

Progress Check 16.2

All players in a basketball team are awarded a match performance rating figure of 1 to 10.

Suggest normal, borderline and invalid data for this data input.

16.4 Perform a dry run on a given algorithm, using a trace table

A dry run is when the programmer checks the execution of a computer program away from the computer. A *trace table* will have a column for each of the variables in the code and then each row will show the changing state of any variables. This way the programmer can confirm or otherwise that the program is doing what was expected.

Example

A firm employees three sales staff and they are each given a target sales figure for the four quarters of the year.

The data is stored in a 2-D array `Target` of type Boolean and shows whether or not each target was meet.

Target				
	1	2	3	4
1	True	False	True	False
2	False	False	True	True
3	False	False	False	False

```
FOR Quarter ← 1 TO 4
  NewArray[Quarter] ← 0
ENDFOR

FOR Person ← 1 TO 3
  FOR Quarter ← 1 TO 4
    IF Target[Person, Quarter] = FALSE
      THEN
        NewArray[Quarter] ← NewArray[Quarter] + 1
    ENDIF
  ENDFOR
ENDFOR
```

The trace gives the completed trace table as shown here.

NewArray						
Person	Quarter	Target[Person, Quarter]	[1]	[2]	[3]	[4]
	1		0			
	2			0		
	3				0	
	4					0
1	1	TRUE				
	2	FALSE		1		
	3	TRUE				
	4	FALSE				1
2	1	FALSE	1			
	2	FALSE		2		
	3	TRUE				
	4	TRUE				
3	1	FALSE	2			
	2	FALSE		3		
	3	FALSE			1	
	4	FALSE				2

Progress Check 16.3

A company makes computer flat-screens and operates seven days a week. Each day a record is made of the number of flat-screens which are rejected at the final quality control stage. An average of one reject each day is considered acceptable. This is investigated at the end of each week using the algorithm which follows.

Variable	Data Type
DayNo	INTEGER
RejectTotal	INTEGER
DailyRejects	ARRAY[7] OF INTEGER

```
RejectTotal ← 0
FOR DayNo ← 1 TO 7
  RejectTotal ← RejectTotal +
    DailyRejects[DayNo]
  OUTPUT RejectTotal
ENDFOR
```

(a) What is the purpose of this program?

Another program is to be developed. The number of rejects per week is recorded over a five week period. This data is stored in array `NoOfRejects`. The array `WeeklySupervisor` records who the supervisor was for week 1, week 2 etc. A third array `SupTotal` will record the total number of unsatisfactory weeks for each of the three supervisors.

The pseudocode which follows makes clear which array position is used for each supervisor.

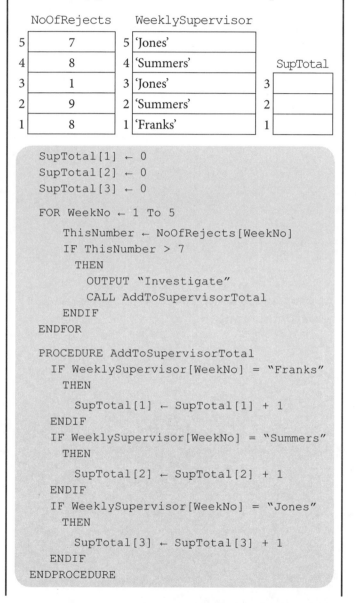

NoOfRejects	
5	7
4	8
3	1
2	9
1	8

WeeklySupervisor	
5	'Jones'
4	'Summers'
3	'Jones'
2	'Summers'
1	'Franks'

SupTotal	
3	
2	
1	

```
SupTotal[1] ← 0
SupTotal[2] ← 0
SupTotal[3] ← 0

FOR WeekNo ← 1 To 5

    ThisNumber ← NoOfRejects[WeekNo]
    IF ThisNumber > 7
      THEN
         OUTPUT "Investigate"
         CALL AddToSupervisorTotal
    ENDIF
ENDFOR

PROCEDURE AddToSupervisorTotal
  IF WeeklySupervisor[WeekNo] = "Franks"
    THEN
       SupTotal[1] ← SupTotal[1] + 1
  ENDIF
  IF WeeklySupervisor[WeekNo] = "Summers"
    THEN
       SupTotal[2] ← SupTotal[2] + 1
  ENDIF
  IF WeeklySupervisor[WeekNo] = "Jones"
    THEN
       SupTotal[3] ← SupTotal[3] + 1
  ENDIF
ENDPROCEDURE
```

(b) Trace the above algorithm using the trace table below.

WeekNo	ThisNumber	OUTPUT	SupTotal		
			1	2	3
1			0	0	0

16.5 Debugging tools and facilities

Visual Basic.NET has a range of software tools as part of the IDE to detect and remove errors in the program. Tracking down and eliminating errors is called **debugging** because the goal is to remove all these program bugs.

Simple in-line error identification

We showed examples of this under the section Syntax errors.

The IDE underlines:

✓ any unrecognised keywords
✓ any variables which are not declared
✓ any declared variables which have not been assigned a value.

Compiler Error report

Once we ask to compile the program, an 'Error List' is produced (See below).

```
Function SingleCharacter(ByVal ThisString As String, ByVal ThisPosition As Integer) As Char
      Dim CategoryData As Char

      CategoryData = Mid(ThisString, ThisPosition, 1)

  End Function

End Module
```

	Description	File	Li...	Column	Project
❌ 1	')' expected.	Module1.vb	10	42	Module 2-5 MOT
⚠ 2	Function 'SingleCharacter' doesn't return a value on all code paths. Are you missing a 'Return' statement?	Module1.vb	34	5	Module 2-5 MOT

Error List — ❌ 1 Error ⚠ 1 Warning ⓘ 0 Messages

This will list all syntax errors which are still present in the code.

Run-time report

Example 1

The program code opens the file, but the file cannot be found.

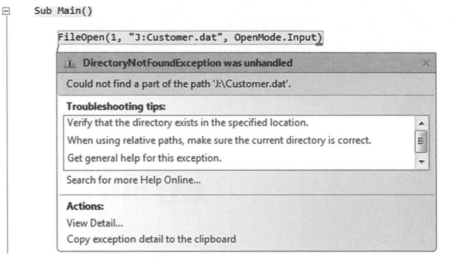

```
Sub Main()

    FileOpen(1, "J:Customer.dat", OpenMode.Input)
```

⚠ DirectoryNotFoundException was unhandled	✕
Could not find a part of the path 'J:\Customer.dat'.	
Troubleshooting tips:	
Verify that the directory exists in the specified location.	
When using relative paths, make sure the current directory is correct.	
Get general help for this exception.	
Search for more Help Online...	
Actions:	
View Detail...	
Copy exception detail to the clipboard	

> ✎ **Note**
>
> The error message and the suggestions as to how the error might be found.

Example 2

The program is using an array subscript outside the permitted range.

```
Sub Main()

    Dim Customer(5) As String

    Customer(1) = "Patel"
    Customer(2) = "Steblyuk"
    Customer(3) = "Saleh"
    Customer(4) = "Mohsen"
    Customer(5) = "Allaf"
    Customer(6) = "Shaaban"

    Console.WriteLine("Custome
    Console.ReadLine()


    'Answer = Number1 / Number

    'Console.WriteLine("Answer
```

⚠ IndexOutOfRangeException was unhandled	✕
Index was outside the bounds of the array.	
Troubleshooting tips:	
Make sure that the maximum index on a list is less than the list size.	
Make sure the index is not a negative number.	
Make sure data column names are correct.	
Get general help for this exception.	
Search for more Help Online...	
Actions:	
View Detail...	
Copy exception detail to the clipboard	

Breakpoints

When we set a breakpoint in a program we are telling Visual Basic to stop executing the program when it reaches this line of code.

Progress Check 16.4

State three examples of run-time errors.

This will then give the programmer the option to:

- ✓ inspect the values of any variables
- ✓ look at the contents of the procedure stack
- ✓ inspect the contents of memory.

Example

We shall use the following 'buggy' code to illustrate how various errors can be identified with the IDE debugging tools which are available.

The program is designed to count the number of vowels in an input string.

```
Sub Main ()
      Dim ThisPhrase As String
      Dim NoOfVowels As Integer

      Console.Write ("Input word or Phrase ...? ")
      ThisPhrase = Console.ReadLine
      NoOfVowels = CountTheVowels (ThisPhrase)
      Console.WriteLine ("Number of vowels is ..." & NoOfVowels)

      Console. ReadLine ()
End Sub

Function CountTheVowels (ByVal ThisString As String) As Integer
      Dim × As Integer = 1
      Dim TotalVowels As Integer = θ
      Dim CharPos As Integer

      Do While × < = Len (ThisString)
          CharPos = Instr ("aeio", LCase (ThisString.Substring (x, 1)))
          If Charpos > θ Then
             TotalVowels = TotalVowels + 1
          End If
      Loop
      Return TotalVowels
End Function
```

If you key-in the code above and attempt to run it you will find it does compile but then appears to be in an infinite loop.

Locals window

The screenshot shows the breakpoint set and the program has paused execution at the breakpoint.

```
  Function CountTheVowels(ByVal ThisString As String) As Integer
        Dim x As Integer = 1
        Dim TotalVowels As Integer = θ
        Dim CharPos As Integer

        Do While x <= Len(ThisString)
            CharPos = InStr("aeio", LCase(ThisString.Substring(x, 1)))
            If CharPos > θ Then
                TotalVowels = TotalVowels + 1
            End If
        Loop
        Return TotalVowels
    End Function
  End Module
```

100 % ▾ ◂

Name	Value
◈ CharPos	0
◈ CountTheVowels	0
◈ ThisString	"the quick fox"
◈ TotalVowels	0
◈ x	1

Visual Basic has a 'Locals Window' which displays the current values of all local variables at this stage in the execution.

This shows up one error in the program code – the index for the substring starts at 0 not 1.

Single stepping

The programmer can also at this point single step through the code <F11> and this will show up the error of the infinite loop.

That is the value of variable is not being incremented and this was used as the condition for the loop.

Watch	
Name	Value
InStr("aeiou", LCase(ThisString.Substring(x, 1)))	0

Watch window

This is similar to the Local window but displays the changing value of an expression.

Progress Check 16.5

This shows the amended code after some errors have been located.

```
Sub Main()
    Dim ThisPhrase As String
    Dim NoOfVowels As Integer

    Console.Write("Input word or phrase ...? ")
    ThisPhrase = Console.ReadLine
    NoOfVowels = CountTheVowels(ThisPhrase)
    Console.WriteLine("Number of vowels is ..." & NoOfVowels)

    Console.ReadLine()
End Sub


Function CountTheVowels(ByVal ThisString As String) As Integer
    Dim x As Integer = 0
    Dim TotalVowels As Integer = 0
    Dim CharPos As Integer

    Do While x <= Len(ThisString) - 1
        CharPos = InStr("aeio", LCase(ThisString.Substring(x, 1)))
        If CharPos > 0 Then
            TotalVowels = TotalVowels + 1
        End If
        x = x + 1
    Loop
    Return TotalVowels
End Function
```

```
Input word or phrase ...? the quick fox
Number of vowels is ...4
```

However the following program run does not report the correct number of vowels. Why?

```
Input word or phrase ...? the quick brown fox jumped over the lazy dog
Number of vowels is ...10
```

1. Anna wants to find out about her fellow students' reading habits. It will be part of her Literature coursework.
   She will ask questions online, so starts by designing a screen layout. The first four questions will ask for:
   ✓ student's first name
   ✓ date of birth
   ✓ type of book they prefer (printed, audio-book or e-book)
   ✓ whether student reads novels (yes/no)

(a) Draw a suitable screen layout.

[4]

(b) Justify the design of your screen layout in **(a)**.

....

....

....

....

....

[3]

(c) The responses from each student will be stored as a record consisting of the following fields:
   ✓ FirstName
   ✓ DateOfBirth
   ✓ BookType
   ✓ ReadsNovels

Complete the following table. Only a single value should be given for the Field Size.

Field Name	Data Type	Field Size (bytes)
FirstName		
DateOfBirth		
BookType		
ReadsNovels		

[8]

Cambridge 9691 Paper 21 Q1(a)(b) & (c) June 2012

2. Nathan is designing a software solution for stock control in a mobile phone shop. He has a colleague, called Andre, who will help him write the program. Nathan decides to modularise the solution.

(a) State why modularisation is a good idea.

....

.... [1]

(b) As the first step in his design he splits the solution into the following main areas:

   Initialisation, PhoneSales, StockOrdering, Accounts.

   Complete the following structure diagram.

```
                          ┌──────────────┐
                          │ Stock Control│
                          └──────┬───────┘
          ┌──────────────┬───────┴───────┬──────────────┐
   ┌──────┴──────┐ ┌─────┴──────┐ ┌──────┴──────┐ ┌──────┴──────┐
   │             │ │ PhoneSales │ │             │ │             │
   └─────────────┘ └────────────┘ └─────────────┘ └─────────────┘
```

[1]

(c) PhoneSales is made up of two modules, ShopSales and OnlineSales. Add them to the structure diagram shown in (b). [2]

(d) Nathan will write the ShopSales module and Andre will write the OnlineSales module.

   Nathan will use the identifier Sale for a sale in the shop, and Andre will use the identifier Sale for an online order. Explain how they can both use the same identifier and not cause a problem when the program is run.

....

....

....

.... [2]

(e) Both programmers need to choose other identifiers that they will use.

   (i) Explain why there are some words that cannot be used as identifiers.

....

....

.... [1]

   (ii) State three other rules of a high-level programming language that restrict the choice of identifiers.

   Language

....

   Rule 1

....

....

   Rule 2

....

....

   Rule 3

....

.... [3]

(iii) Give an example of an invalid identifier.
  Language

....

  Example

....
                                              [1]

(f) One line in the program reads:
ForecastStock = 5*a–b.
(i)   Work out the value of ForecastStock when a is 4 and b is 3.

....

....

....

....

.... [1]

(ii) The programmer has made an error in the code. When a is 4 and b is 3 the expected result is 5.
  Rewrite the line of code with added parentheses to give the expected result.

....

....

.... [1]

(iii) Name the type of testing strategy which identified this error.

....

....

.... [1]

(g) One type of test data is invalid data.
(i) Name the other two types.

 1 ....

  ....

  ....

 2 ....

  ....

  .... [2]

(ii) Andre has written the StockOrdering module, which now needs testing.

 ✓ The StockID is a whole number between 1000 and 9999
 ✓ The ReOrderLevel is between 10% and 20%

Give six different items of test data, other than invalid data, which thoroughly test the two rules given above. Give a reason for each choice.

StockID	ReOrderLevel	Reason
50		Invalid data for Stock ID
	21%	Invalid data for Re Order Level

                                            [6]

(h) When dealing with the Accounts module, an entry, 'y' or 'n' has to be input, indicating whether the accounts should be printed. The variable identifier is PrintAccounts.

  (i) Write a Boolean expression to validate an input for PrintAccounts.

  ....

  .... [2]

  (ii) Write a Boolean expression to validate StockID, as described in (g).

  ....

  .... [2]

  (iii) Describe a possible problem that could occur if the StockID is not validated.

  ....

  .... [2]

Cambridge 9691 Paper 21 Q2 November 2011

3. The following pseudocode is a recursive function where n is an integer.

```
FUNCTION Calc(n)
IF n = 1
  THEN
    Calc ← 1
  ELSE
    Calc ← n * calc(n-1)
ENDIF
RETURN
```

(a) (i) What value is returned by `Calc(1)`?

  ....

  ....

  .... [1]

  (ii) What value is returned by `Calc(3)`?

  ....

  ....

  .... [1]

(b) (i) What happens if the parameter passed is –1?

  ....

  ....

  .... [2]

  (ii) What changes will need to be made to the pseudocode to address the problem in (b) (i)?

  ....

  ....

  .... [2]

(c) Rewrite this function in pseudocode as an iterative function.

  ....

  ....

  ....

  ....

  .... [4]

Cambridge 9691 Paper 23 Q4 June 2011

4. Ahmed is writing a program to record the data for members of the school football squad.
    The input data will be validated. One input is the number of years a member has played for the team. This will be 0, 1 or 2.
    The flowchart for the validation of number of years is shown below.

(a) (i) What is the output when the input is 2?

    .... [1]

    (ii) What is the output when the input is 3?   [1]

    ....

(b) In a high-level language, write the code that will produce the validation process shown in the flowchart.
    Language

    ....

    Code

    ....

    ....

    ....

    .... [5]

(c) The three basic programming constructs used to control the flow of information are:
        sequence, selection and iteration.
        State the two constructs that are used in your code.

    1 ....

    2 ....
                                                                                                                            [1]

(d) Describe what is meant by iteration.

    ....

    ....

    .... [2]

(e) Ahmed thinks it will be a good idea to allow only five attempts at getting the input data correct. If it is not a valid entry
    after five attempts, then a message 'Please check which values are allowed' should be output.

Modify the flowchart to include this additional check.

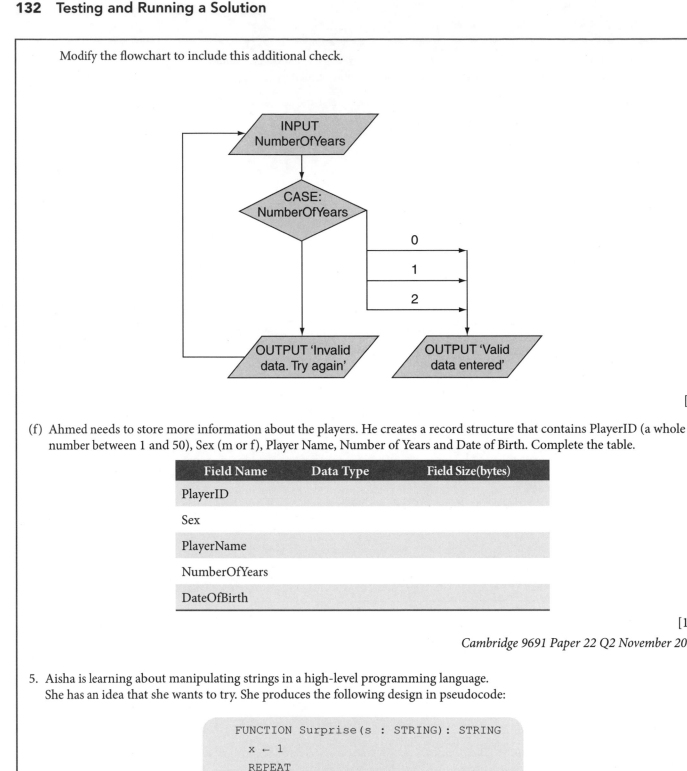

[5]

(f) Ahmed needs to store more information about the players. He creates a record structure that contains PlayerID (a whole number between 1 and 50), Sex (m or f), Player Name, Number of Years and Date of Birth. Complete the table.

Field Name	Data Type	Field Size(bytes)
PlayerID		
Sex		
PlayerName		
NumberOfYears		
DateOfBirth		

[10]

Cambridge 9691 Paper 22 Q2 November 2011

5. Aisha is learning about manipulating strings in a high-level programming language.
She has an idea that she wants to try. She produces the following design in pseudocode:

```
FUNCTION Surprise(s : STRING): STRING
  x ← 1
  REPEAT
    q[x] ← s[x]
    x ← x + 1
  UNTIL s[x] = ' '
  Surprise ← q
ENDFUNCTION
```

(a) Complete the trace of this function for the function call `Surprise('CHO JABA')`.

s	x	q[1]	q[2]	q[3]	q[4]	Surprise
CHO JABA						
	1					

(b) Describe what `Surprise ← q` does.

....

.... [2]

(c) Describe the features of any function.

....

....

.... [3]

(d) Aisha's pseudocode is not easily understood.

(i) She could have annotated her code with suitable comments.
   Write a comment to annotate the line:
   `UNTIL s[x] = '6'`

....

.... [2]

(ii) State **two** techniques, other than annotation, that she should use to improve the understanding of her pseudocode.

1 ....

....

2 ....

.... [2]

(e) Aisha uses an expression:
   `String1 > String2`
   Explain how strings are compared by the processor.

....

....

....

.... [3]

Cambridge 9691 Paper 23 Q3(a) (c) (d) (e) & (f) November 2011

6. A town election is held to elect a new mayor. The people in the town can vote for whoever they prefer from the three candidates A, B, C. The voting is done by each voter pressing one of a set of buttons labelled A, B and C in the voting booth. This acts as input to a computer program.

An early version of the software assumes that there are 1000 people who will be voting. It uses an array, `VOTES()` to store the votes that are cast. `VOTES()` is an array of 1000 characters, A, B or C.

A second array, `CANDIDATE_TOTALS()`, contains three integers and is used with the array,

VOTES() in the following algorithm:

```
01 FOR i ← 1 TO 1000
02   IF VOTES(i)= "A" THEN
03     CANDIDATE TOTALS (1) ← CANDIDATE_TOTALS (1) + 1
04   ELSE
05     IF VOTES(i)= "B" THEN
06       CANDIDATE TOTALS (2) ← CANDIDATE_TOTALS (2) + 1
07     ELSE
08       CANDIDATE TOTALS (3) ← CANDIDATE_TOTALS (3) + 1
09     ENDIF
10   ENDIF
11 ENDFOR
12 OUTPUT A,B,C
```

(a) (i) Explain why it will be necessary to initialise the array CANDIDATE_TOTALS() before the algorithm is run.

....

.... [1]

(ii) Write a FOR loop which can be used to initialise the array CANDIDATE_TOTALS() at the start of the algorithm.

....

....

.... [2]

(iii) Explain what happens when the program based on this algorithm is executed.

....

....

....

.... [4]

(iv) By stating the type of operator in each case, explain why the use of the '=' sign in lines 2 and 3 are different.

....

....

....

.... [3]

(v) Line 12 is meant to output the total votes for A, B and C. It does not work.
Rewrite line 12 to produce the correct result.

....

....

.... [2]

(b) The following algorithm is written to determine which of A, B and C gets the highest vote.
(i) Some people do not vote and the result of a particular vote is that all of A, B and C receive equal votes.
State the line numbers that will be executed by the algorithm and which of A, B or C will be output.

....

.... [4]

```
01 IF CANDIDATE_TOTALS (1) > CANDIDATE_TOTALS (2) THEN
02  IF CANDIDATE_TOTALS (1) > CANDIDATE_TOTALS (3) THEN
03    OUTPUT "A"
04  ELSE
05    OUTPUT "C"
06  ENDIF
07 ELSE
08  IF CANDIDATE_TOTALS (2) > CANDIDATE_TOTALS (3) THEN
09    OUTPUT "B"
10  ELSE
11    OUTPUT "C"
12  ENDIF
13 ENDIF
```

(ii)   Explain how the algorithm would need to be altered to deal correctly with two or three of the candidates receiving equal votes. Do not produce the algorithm.

....

.... [4]

Adapted from Cambridge 9691 Specimen Paper 2 Q3

7. Gina is developing her programming skills in string handling.
   She is going to input two strings.
   Each string is made up of three parts:
   ✓   letters, followed by
   ✓   a single '*' character, followed by
   ✓   letters

   The groups of letters after the '*' characters are joined together to form a new sting which is then output.
   For example, with "DFG*COM" and "B*PUTER" as inputs, the new string output will be "COMPUTER".

(a) Using a high-level programming language, write the code to perform this task. (Ensure that you use meaningful variable names and lay the code out clearly).

   Programming language   ....

   Code   ....

   ....

   ....

   ....

   ....

   ....

   ....

   ....

   ....

   ....

   ....

   ....

....

....

....

....

.... [8]

(b) She writes this code as the function `JoinStrings` because it is to be used several times.

   (i) State the parameters of the function.

....

.... [2]

  (ii) Write the function header in the language you used in part **(a)**

....

.... [2]

 (iii) State why Gina used used a function rather than a procedure.

....

.... [1]

Cambridge 9691 Paper 21 Q3 June 2012

Section 3

Data Representation, Data Structures and Data Manipulation

The Functions of Operating Systems

After you have studied this chapter, you should be able to:

☞ describe the main features of operating systems, including memory management and scheduling algorithms

☞ explain how interrupts are used to obtain processor time and how processing of interrupted jobs may later be resumed (typical sources of interrupts should be identified and any algorithms and data structures should be described)

☞ define and explain the purpose of scheduling, job queues, priorities and how they are used to manage job throughout

☞ explain how memory is managed in a typical modern computer system (virtual memory, paging, partitions and segmentation)

☞ describe spooling, explaining why it is used

☞ describe the main components of a typical PC operating system, including the file allocation table (FAT) and boot file.

17.1 Scheduling

A computer system is a very powerful resource. The prime objective of the operating system is that it manages processing so that the maximum work is done by the computer with an acceptable response time for interactive applications.

Scheduling includes making decisions about which program will get use of the processor and which programs will be loaded next into the main memory to be processed. Some programs will need to be allocated a higher priority than others and this will all be undertaken by various program modules which make up the operating system.

17.2 The main features of operating systems

One of the fundamentals of computing is that all or some of the program instructions when it is executing, are resident in main memory.

← Look Back

To Chapter 2 for more details on the operating system.

Multiprogramming

Multiprogramming is the ability to have more than one program loaded in main memory at the same time. It will then be a task of the operating system to carefully manage the available main memory and the allocation of the processor to the programs in memory.

This module of the operating system is concerned with *memory management*.

Process

A program in execution is called a *process*. So in a multiprogramming environment there will be several active processes and it will be the job of the operating system software to carefully manage these processes.

All these processes will be competing for the use of the processor.

Scheduling

There is only one processor. So at any point in time there will only be one process which is executing and using the processor. Scheduling the use of the processor is called *process management*.

Since we shall use the term 'scheduling' for other issues we shall use the term *low-level scheduling* to describe how the operating system allocates the use of the processor between the various processes in memory.

Progress Check 17.1

What is this the definition for?
   'The ability to have more than one process loaded in main memory.'

Memory management

When a program is compiled the memory addresses will be expressed as relative to the address used for the first instruction in the program. It will be a task of the *loader* software to allocate memory for each program. A key role of the memory manager will be to track where in main memory the program and its data are currently stored. This is all the more important as we shall suggest later that a program could well be moved in memory during the course of its execution.

The memory manager must continually map all relative addresses in a program to their physical memory address.

Operating system + One process

This is the simplest possible scenario. Remember, the operating system is itself a set of program modules and so main memory will be needed for them. If we then load the application program at the first available memory location after the OS modules then the physical address for the process is easily calculated as 'Start address' + each 'Relative address'.

A key role of the memory manager will be to ensure the security of any process. That is a process must not reference any memory locations used by other processes.

This strategy however of Operating system + One process only is wasteful on memory and we hope we have sufficient memory available to load several processes into memory at the same time.

Partitioned memory

A partition (such like a partition in a room) divides up the available memory space.

Fixed partitions

The partitions could be fixed. They could be of different sizes but are set when the operating system boots up.

The operating system must keep a table showing the start address of each partition and its size.

Processes – depending on their size – are then loaded into a partition which is of an appropriate size.

Dynamic partitions

Partitions are created to best fit the needs of the programs which are waiting to be loaded to memory.

Initially after the operating system is loaded the memory can be thought of as one large partition. As further processes are loaded new partitions are created. The operating system must carefully manage these partitions – i.e. their start address and size, and which processes are resident in each partition. Since the partitions are created dynamically and constantly changing so will the partition data.

Dynamic partitions can be changed whenever a process finished execution.

Address management is no different here using partitions. The OS must also know the start address for a process and can then calculate all physical addresses as before (physical address = start address + each instruction's relative address).

High-level scheduling

Since there is only a finite amount of main memory there are likely to be processes waiting to be loaded. The operating system module which decides which process will be loaded next is called the *high-level scheduler*.

Possible strategies for high-level scheduling

That is how the operating system decides which waiting process will be loaded into which partition.

Possible algorithms the OS could use are:

✓ *'First fit'* – load the process into the first partition which is sufficiently large
✓ *'Best fit'* – load the process into the partition which minimises wasted space
✓ *'Worse fit'* – load the process into the largest available free partition.

The arguments for and against each strategy should be considered for both fixed and dynamic partitions.

Paged memory management

Called 'paging'. Programs are divided into fixed sized units called **pages**. The main memory is divided into the same sized units called **page frames**. The implication of this is that:

- ✓ the program's pages may be scattered throughout the available page frames
- ✓ the OS must manage which page frames are allocated to which pages of a process and this is done by maintaining a **page-map (or page-frame) table**
- ✓ the logical address of a program instruction is expressed as (PageNumber, Offset) typically (2 518) which represent the 518th byte from the start address of page 2.

Another implication of paging is that not all the pages of the program need to be loaded to start execution and the strategy which does this is called **demand paging**. This is a fundamental difference to the earlier technique of using partitions where the entire program was loaded into memory before execution. This gives rise to the idea of **virtual memory** where there is now no restriction on the size of a process which can be scheduled before it can start execution.

The program will continue to execute until an instruction is referenced which is in a page which is not currently loaded. The page must then be swapped into memory (at the expense of another page). This is called **page swapping**. Too much page swapping will lead to degradation in the performance and this is called **thrashing**.

> ### Progress Check 17.2
>
> Name three different strategies that could be used by the memory manager of the operating system.

Ready, Suspended and Running state

All processes which are loaded in memory will be in one of the three states.

Running

The process which has current use of the processor is said to be **running**.

Ready

A process which is capable of use of the processor, but is having to wait is said to be **runnable.**

Suspended

A process may not be capable of the use of the processor for some reason and is said to be **suspended**. Reasons for a suspended process include:

- ✓ the process does not have available various resources in order to continue
- ✓ it could be waiting for a signal from some other process (multi-tasking) before it can move to the runnable state
- ✓ (a paging system) is waiting for new pages to be loaded from secondary storage.

Managing the state of all processes

This is a major task for the operating system and is done by storing the data about the current state of each process in a **Process Control Block (PCB)**. The state of all loaded processes must be managed by the operating system and so if there are one or more processes waiting in a runnable state, what is to be the algorithm used by the low-level scheduler to decide which process will get the next use of the processor?

> ### Progress Check 17.3
>
> During its execution a process will change state many times.
>
> Consider each of the following and state the original state and the new state of the process.
> (a) A process is interrupted as its time slice has expired.
> (b) A process now completes a sequence of disc read operations.
> (c) A process in given the use of the processor.
> (d) A process is executing but now has to wait for some input from the keyboard from the user.

17.3 CPU Scheduling algorithms

Strategy 1 – Round – Robin

Give all the runnable processes a **time-slice**, i.e. a fixed amount of time after which the next runnable process will get a time slice.

Strategy 2 – First come first served

The CPU is given to the process which is at the head of the 'runnable' list and it keeps the processor until it moves to a suspended state.

Strategy 3 – Processes have priorities

When a job is loaded the OS will take note of a priory associated with that job.

The criteria for this could include:

✓ a user priority
✓ priority based on the estimated run-time
✓ a priority which changes and is based on the estimated run-time remaining
✓ priority based on the resources the process will require.

17.4 Interrupt

An interrupt is a signal to the processor to indicate that some event has occurred.

If the processor time is to be allocated to various jobs then the starting of one process and the suspension of another will be controlled by the sending and receiving of interrupts. The operating system module which will do this is the fundamental module of the OS – called the *kernel* – and its prime role is to act as a *low level interrupt handler*.

Interrupts and multiprogramming

We shall consider the case where PROCESS-LOW is currently executing. An interrupt is then sent by PROCESS-HIGH.

The sequence of steps taken by the interrupt handler will be:
PROCESS-LOW is currently executing ...

✓ Save the contents of all general-purpose and special-purpose registers for PROCESS-LOW in its PCB
✓ Note this will include the program Counter contents
✓ Load from PROCESS-HIGH's PCB the contents of all registers

✓ Mask out interrupts of a lower priority
✓ Execute PROCESS-HIGH, until an interrupt is received
✓ When PROCESS-HIGH moves to the runnable or suspended state
✓ Restore the contents of the PCB for PROCESS-LOW
✓ Enable interrupts

Continue execution of PROCESS-LOW
If the low-level CPU allocation is a round-robin with a time-slice for each process the above algorithm is simplified and the scheduler will recognise the next process to be given the processor is the process at the head of the runnable queue.

Interrupts from a device

Consider PROCESS-PRINT which at some point sends output to a printer which is 'off-line'. This will require the process to be interrupted and some appropriate software run to deal with the unavailability of the printer. Software programs written to deal with interrupts of this kind are called an *Interrupt Service Routine (ISR)*. Interrupts of the kind will also have a priority. For example the user pressing the <Reset> button will have a higher priority than any other interrupt request!

The sequence of steps now becomes: PROCESS-PRINT is executing...

✓ Receive interrupt
✓ Identify the source of the interrupt
✓ It's the printer
✓ Mask out interrupts of a lower priority
✓ Save the register contents to the PCB for PROCSS-PRINT
✓ Load the ISR program for the 'printer off-line' event
✓ Execute the ISR and on completion...
✓ Restore the registers from PCB for PROCESS_PRINT
✓ Enable all interrupts

Continue with the execution of PROCESS-PRINT.

17.5   Spooling

Spooling (the acronym 'SPOOL' comes from 'Simultaneous Peripheral Output On Line') came about as a technique designed to counter the mismatch in speed between the processor and the speed at which output could be sent to a printer. Spooling saves the output as a 'print file' so that it could then be later output from a device such as a hard disk which has access speeds much quicker that a printer. All of this is transparent to the user.

On a modern network – where typically 20 students will all be sending printer output at the end of their lesson – the print output is controlled by a *print server*. The obvious needs of the spooling system are that no outputs must be lost and they must be self-contained. Users must be able to send their printouts at the same time and the output file is temporarily stored on the hard disk.

The print server will manage print jobs with a queue data structure; first job received will be the first to be printed (i.e. 'first in-first out'). Users may be allowed to allocate a priority to their print job in which case the data structure used by the print server is a *priority queue*. The data structure will only store a reference to each print job and not the entire print file. This job reference data will indicate where on the hard disk each print file is stored.

17.6   The main components of a typical PC operating system

When the power to the PC is turned on, the computer goes through a process called *booting-up* (earlier called bootstrapping). Switching on the power triggers the running of a small program stored in ROM called the *BIOS (Basic Input-Output System)*. The BIOS will identify all the peripheral input and output devices and then run the boot loader software. This program will contain the start address of the operating system stored on the hard disk, so the boot process will effectively load the operating system from secondary storage.

File Allocation Table (FAT)

A key task for the operating system is management of all the files on the hard disk and other storage devices.

We are already familiar with the idea of the surface of a magnetic disk divided into tracks and sectors. A block (some books use the term 'cluster') is the amount of data which can be read/written in a single write/read operation and a block will consist typically of four contiguous sectors. A block forms the basic *file allocation unit* which is allocated to files. A typical block size is 2048 4096 or 8192 bytes. Earlier versions of Windows used a system called FAT32 meaning the size of each file allocation unit is 32 bits. This has now been replaced by a filing system called NTFS.

When the user gives the instruction to save a word processor document the operating system has to decide which file allocation units are to be used to store this file.

The OS will mange this by:

- ✓ maintaining a linked list of all the unused file allocation units
- ✓ recording which allocation units have been used to store each file on the hard disk. This is done with a linked list of the allocation units for every file.

> **Note**
>
> These allocation units will not be in contiguous blocks.

- ✓ when the user deletes a file, the allocation units for that file are returned to the list of available allocation units.
- ✓ Makes a new entry in the file directory.

The FAT is effectively forming a map of the usage of all the file allocation units.

A large video file may well use blocks which are scattered all over the surface of the disk and the result will be that the file takes a long time to load – as many read operations are required. The result is the file is *fragmented* across the disk. Hence the need to periodically run a system program called 'de-frag' which will attempt to re-organise the allocation units used so that they occupy more contiguous blocks.

The Boot sector, the FAT and the directory form the three important reserved areas on the hard disk which the operating system will use. If the hard disk has been set up with more than one *partition*, each partition will have its own FAT.

Exam-style Questions

1. Describe the following components of a typical PC operating system and explain how they are used.

(a) File Allocation Table (FAT)

....

....

....

.... [3]

(b) Boot file

....

....

....

.... [3]

Cambridge 9691 Paper 31 Q1 November 2011

2. (a) Describe what is meant by the spooling of files.

....

....

.... [2]

(b) (i) State why files which are sent to a shared printer on a local network will be spooled.

....

....

(ii) Explain how this spooling is carried out.

....

....

.... [5]

Cambridge 9691 Paper 31 Q5 June 2011

3. Explain how the following memory management techniques may be used:

(i) Paging

....

....

....

(ii) Segmentation

....

....

....

.... [6]

Cambridge 9691 Paper 33 Q8 November 2011

The Functions and Purposes of Translators

18

Revision Objectives

After you have studied this chapter, you should be able to:

☞ understand the relationship between assembly language and machine code
☞ describe how an assembler produces machine code from assembly language
☞ describe the difference between interpretation and compilation
☞ describe what happens during lexical analysis
☞ describe what happens during syntax analysis
☞ explain the code generation phase, and understand the need for optimisation
☞ explain the purpose of linkers and loaders, and describe the use of library program routines
☞ explain how errors are recognised and handled during compilation.

18.1 The relationship between assembly language and machine code

Machine code is the set of basic machine operations which make up the processor's **instruction set**.

Programming in machine code would have been extremely tedious and prone to errors. The big breakthrough in program writing came with the introduction of **assembly languages**. This allowed any machine code instruction to be written using **mnemonics**, for example, 0101000 (which represents 'load') would be written with the assembly language mnemonic LDD.

Consider the following subset of a typical set of assembly language instructions (Table 18.1).

> 📖 **Later**
>
> Different modes of addressing are covered later in Chapter 22.

Each of these instructions has two parts – the **operation code** (or op code) and the **operand**.

In machine code both the op code and operand are written in binary. Assume the op codes are as shown in Table 18.2.

Table 18.1

Assembly language instructions		
Instruction		**Explanation**
Op Code	**Operand**	
LDD	<address>	Load using direct addressing
STO	<address>	Store the contents of the Accumulator at the given address
LDI	<address>	Load using indirect addressing
LDX	<address>	Load using indexed addressing
INC		Add 1 to the contents of the Accumulator
END		End the program and return to the operating system

Table 18.2

Op code	
Assembly language mnemonic	Machine code
LDD	0000 0001
STO	0000 1111
LDI	0000 0010
LDX	0000 0011
INC	0000 1000
END	1111 1111

Table 18.3	
A simple assembly language program	
LDD	70
INC	
STO	70
LDD	71
INC	
STO	71
END	

A simple assembly language program is shown in Table 18.3.

Assembler program

The ***assembler*** is software which translates a program written in assembly language into machine code.

The CPU will not be able to execute this program in its assembly language form. This assembly language 'source program' must be translated into its machine code equivalent using the processor's table of op codes.

So following translation of the above program, the assembler software would produce the following ***object file*** (Table 18.4).

18.2 How an assembler produces machine code from assembly language

How is this translation done by the assembler?

A fundamental relationship between assembly language and machine code is 'Every one assembly language instruction translates into exactly one machine code instruction'.

How is the translation done?

✓ The assembler will look at each assembly language instruction in sequence
✓ Isolate the op code and look up the machine code from the ***Op Code*** Table
✓ Isolate the operand
✓ Convert the denary address or immediate value into a binary value.

Table 18.4	
Object file for the assembly language program in Table 18.3	
00000001	01000110
00001000	
00001111	01000110
00000001	01000111
00001000	
00001111	01000111
11111111	

This is the binary for address value 70

This is the machine code for the opcode END

> **Note**
>
> Some instructions do not have an operand.

The final binary machine code version of the file is called the ***object file***.

This is a simplifying version of what the assembler must do. Further issues will be if the programmer has used symbolic addressing. Then a table must be compiled – called the ***symbol table*** – mapping each symbolic address used to its actual address value.

The sequence of writing and then translating an assembly language program is shown in Figure 18.1.

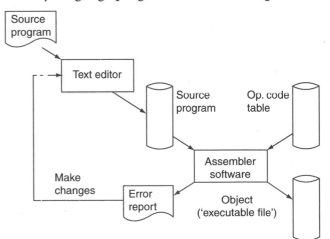

Figure 18.1 The assembly translation process

Progress Check 18.1

Which instructions in the table of instructions – Table 18.1 – shown do not require an operand?

18.3 The difference between interpretation and compilation

The term assembler is used only for an assembly language translator.

High-level language programs will be translated either by:

✓ a *compiler*, or
✓ an *interpreter*.

Both translation methods will provide error reports to help the developer identify any errors in the program code.

Compiler

A *compiler* is a translator for a high-level language program into machine code.

A compiler translates all the source code, finds the errors, and only produces the executable version when all the errors have been found and fixed.

Compilation can therefore be a repetitive process, until all errors are eliminated.

Figure 18.2 shows the compilation process for the translation of a Pascal source code program.

The compiler software will be different for each different programming language. That is to program in Pascal we must have a Pascal compiler available etc.

The issue of translation becomes clouded by the features provided by a modern programming language Integrated Development Environment (IDE) where all aspects of the program development cycle – i.e. write the code, eliminate syntax errors and compile the program – are all done within the one piece of software. Traditionally the source code would have been produced using text editor software, then the compiler was a separate software program as shown below the Figure 18.2.

Interpreter

Using a programming language *interpreter*, the programmer will write the code and is then able to attempt to execute the code at any stage. The interpreter will translate each statement in the program in sequence and execute these program statements until an error is found. When the first error is found execution of the program will terminate and indicate to the programmar the statement which has triggered the error.

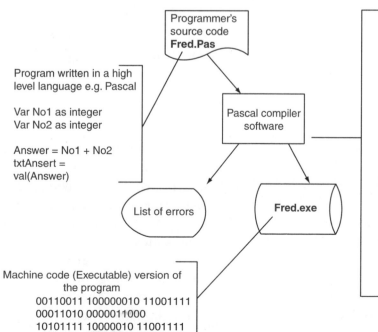

Figure 18.2   The compilation process for the translation of a Pascal source code program

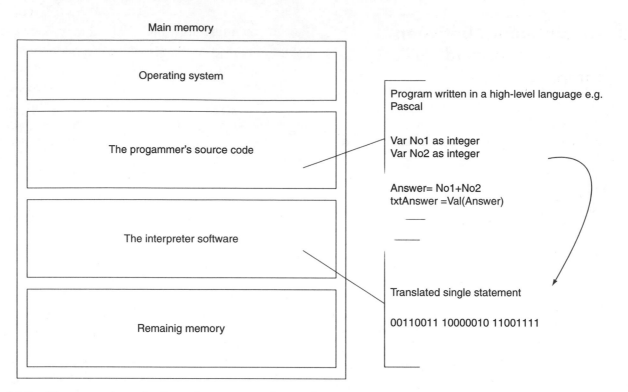

Figure 18.3 The execution of a Pascal program using an interpreter

Figure 18.3 shows the execution of a Pascal program using an interpreter.

Benefits, similarities and differences

Using a compiler the programmer can only attempt to execute the program when all syntax errors have been fixed.

The compiler produces:

✓ an error report
✓ the final executable object file.

Successfully compiling the source program means the Fred.exe file produced by the compiler can now be executed without reference to the compiler software.

This is the key difference between a compiler and an interpreter.

Using an interpreter, the interpreter software must be loaded in main memory whenever we attempt to execute our source program.

Which is best – compiler or interpreter?

✓ Once translated the compiler software does not need to be used with the final executable file

➤ Therefore less resources, i.e. main memory needed to run the program.

✓ The interpreter software must always be present whenever we attempt to run the program

➤ Therefore uses up more main memory and every user of the software must have the interpreter software available.

✓ The final executable file produced by a compiler can be widely distributed without the user having sight of the source code

➤ Using a compiler makes the source code more secure.

✓ Interpreted code always requires that the source code is present

✓ Interpreters usually provide better diagnostics

✓ Using an interpreter will allow some parts of the program to be tested and run, without all the program code being available. This generally fits with the strategy of a modular approach to program design and coding.

Progress Check 18.2

Which of these are true statements?
(a) A compiler generally will have better diagnostic facilities than an interpreter.
(b) A compiler must be present in main memory every time we run a program.
(c) An interpreter produces an object file.
(d) Using an interpreter will use more main memory at run-time.
(e) A compiler will attempt to find all errors in the source code.
(f) An interpreter attempts to find all errors in the source code.
(g) An interpreter runs the program until the first error is found.
(h) The same compiler software can be used to translate a Pascal program and a Java program.

18.4 Lexical analysis

Lexical analysis is the first stage of the compilation process.

The lexical analyser will:

✓ remove any whitespace from the source file
✓ remove any comment statements
✓ check for obvious errors in the use of identifier names, i.e. they do not exceed 64 characters
✓ replace all language keywords with a **token,** which is looked up from a **keyword table,** to simplify the code
  ➤ This will be very complex. For example, the sequence of characters P,R,I,N and T will be identified as the keyword PRINT and replaced by a single token to represent PRINT.
✓ all identifier names are replaced in the source code by a pointer value which links to an entry in the **symbol table.**

Symbol table

The analyser will build up a symbol table which contains:

✓ all the identifiers found in the source code and – if applicable – its data type
✓ constants will have their value stored

✓ an array would have its lower and upper bound recorded.

The compiler must make **two passes** through the source code in order to complete the symbol table entries. The first pass inserts each new variable/constant name, then a second pass through can establish the actual memory address to be used for that identifier.

For a large program the symbol table will contain hundreds of entries and it is important that fast access is possible to any identifier entry. This can be done by constructing the symbol table as a **hash table** with a hash key generated for each entry.

Consider the following program statements:

```
// Calculate discount rate
IF Discount = True THEN
   DiscountRate = 5
ELSE
   DiscountRate = 0
END IF
```

What will the lexical analyser produce from this statement?

Symbol Table		
Variable Identifier	Data Type	Memory address
Discount	BOOLEAN	01CD
DiscountRate	INTEGER	01CF

Keyword Table	
Keyword	Token
REPEAT	Δ
UNTIL	ΔΔ
IF	□
THEN	□Δ
ELSE	□ΔΔ
END IF	□ΔΔΔ
True	▲
False	▲▲

The source code is scanned. The lexical analyser produces the following output string.

□Pointer to 01CD = ▲□ΔPointer to 01CD = 5□ΔΔPointer to 01CF = 0□ΔΔΔ

✓ The comment statement has been removed
✓ All 'Whitespace' has been removed
✓ The two variables are added to the Symbol Table
✓ The output string contains pointers to each variable
✓ The keywords have been looked up in the Keyword Table and replaced by the matching token.

18.5 Syntax analysis

Most syntax errors will be identified in the IDE by careful checking by the developer and using the various aids which the IDE provides. However some syntax errors may not be identified. Then it is the task of the compiler's syntax analyser to identify any remaining errors.

> ← **Look Back**
>
> To Chapter 16 for discussion on Syntax errors.

Syntax checking is to establish whether a sequence of input characters matches with the rules of the language. The rules must be available to the compiler and these would be in the form of a large number of **Backus Naur Form (BNF)** sentences or rules. Alternatively, the rules can be shown visually using a **Syntax Diagram**.

> 📖 **Later**
>
> BNF and syntax diagrams will be covered in Chapter 21.

For example the compiler will check the statement:

Console.Writeline ("My best score was …" & MyScore

and report that the statement has a missing closing bracket.

All syntax errors will be reported by the compiler and then require the developer to return to the source code, make the changes and re-compile the code.

Progress Check 18.3

The three line Visual Basic.Net program is scanned by the lexical analyser of the compiler. Show:

✓ the contents of the Symbol Table
✓ The output character string produced.

```
FOR Index = 1 To 20
   Product = Index * Index
NEXT
```

Symbol Table		
Variable Identifier	Data Type	Memory address

Keyword Table	
Key word	Token
REPEAT	Δ
UNTIL	ΔΔ
FOR	■
TO	■■
NEXT	■■■
IF	□
THEN	□Δ
ELSE	□ΔΔ
END IF	□ΔΔΔ
True	□
False	□□

18.6 The code generation phase, and the need for optimisation

Once the source code is compiled and no errors are found, the compiler will generate the object file or 'executable' file.

This is the third stage of the compilation process called the *code generation* stage.

Consider this statement in a high-level program.

> TriangleArea = Base * Height /2

This will – following lexical analysis – have created the following entries in the symbol table.

Symbol Table		
Variable Identifier	Data Type	Memory address
Base	Single	0F03
Height	Single	0F04
TriangleArea	Single	0F05

The code translation then produces the equivalent of:

```
LOAD    0F03
MULT    0F04
DIV     2
STORE   0F05
```

This would actually be in machine code. It is shown above as assembly language instructions simply for 'readability'.

The code illustrates that any *one* high-level language statement will be translated into *several* machine code instructions.

The code generation process will need to make reference to:

✓ the information stored in the Symbol Table as illustrated above

✓ code contained in various program libraries, for example, when a source code statement uses a built-in function of the language.

Code Optimisation

Optimisation is the process of taking the final executable code produced by the compiler and changing it in some way in order that it will use fewer resources – i.e. less memory or it will execute faster.

The range of these techniques are many and varied but can be illustrated by three simple examples: A statement which multiplies a number by 2, we could replace the statement by a simple left shift operation or by a calculation which adds the number to itself.

Loops are a prime target for optimisation as a loop is a very common construct in high-level programming and the type of loop structure used by the programmer may not be the most efficient.

Generally a high-level (for example) Python program, once complied is 'machine independent'. That is we would expect the complied code to run on any computer system with the same processor architecture.

However, a processor may have slight variations, for example, an additional register – which means that certain parts of the code can be optimised; that is a 'machine dependant' optimisation change.

18.7 The purpose of linkers and loaders, and the use of library routines

Object files output by the compiler may be for a variety of different routines.

Large scale program development is done by breaking down the task; hence programs are designed as modules which are written and compiled separately.

In addition the built-in language routines will be compiled as a module, for example, the object code for the statement Console.Writeline; and this code needs to be available to the final application.

However, this linking process could be delayed until the object code is loaded.

Linker

It is the function of the *linker* software to put the appropriate call and return addresses into the various program modules to ensure successful execution.

Loader

The software which loads the object file(s) from secondary storage into main memory is called the *loader*. If the linking is not done at the compilation stage but delayed until run-time, the software is called a *linking-loader*.

The most useful type of loader will be one which uses re-locatable code. This means the code produced by the compiler can be loaded anywhere in main memory as all address values are not absolute addresses, but addresses relative to the start address of the program.

> 📖 **Later**
>
> Relative addressing is covered in Chapter 21.

> **Progress Check 18.4**
>
> When we say code should be 'optimised' what do we mean in practice?

18.8 How errors are recognised and handled during compilation

The following should act as a summary of what has already been covered.

At the lexical analysis stage

Invalid identifier names will be found.

A keyword may have been spelt incorrectly, for example, `consle` - the lexical analyser will fail to find this as an entry in the keyword table. The analyser could interpret it as an identifier and (wrongly) insert it as an identifier entry in the Symbol Table. However, for a strongly typed language, the compiler would then realise that there was not a matching declaration statement for this identifier.

At the syntax analysis stage

Statements which are incorrectly formed will be identified. That is the statements which do not conform to the rules of the language.

When an error is found the compiler will continue – unlike an interpreter – and all errors will be reported either on-screen or shown in a *listing file*.

Exam-style Questions

1. (a) Explain why an interpreter may be preferred to a compiler as a translator when writing a high-level language program.

   ....

   ....

   ....

   .... [5]

   (b) Describe how the code is checked during the syntax analysis stage of compilation.

   ....

   ....

   .... [3]

   Cambridge 9691 Specimen Paper 3 Q3(a) & (b)

2. (a) Explain differences between using an interpreter and a compiler when translating and executing a source code program.

   ....

   ....

   ....

   ....

   ....

   .... [6]

(b) Explain the lexical analysis phase of compilation.

....

....

....

....

.... [5]

Cambridge 9691 Paper 31 Q4 November 2010

3.   A program is to be run on a computer system.
      Explain the purpose of the following in preparing the program to be run:

   (i) linkers

....

....

   (ii) loaders.

....

.... [4]

Cambridge 9691 Paper 33 Q2(a) June 2011

4. (a) (i) Describe what happens during the lexical analysis phase of compilation.

....

....

....

....

.... [4]

   (ii) Explain how syntax errors are identified during compilation.

....

....

.... [3]

(b) (i) Explain the value of using library routines when writing new programs.

....

....

.... [2]

   (ii) Describe how linkers and loaders are used to make the use of library routines possible.

....

....

.... [2]

Cambridge 9691 Paper 31 Q9 November 2011

Computer Architecture and the Fetch-execute Cycle

19

19.1 Basic Von Neumann architecture

Von Neumann in 1946 proposed the fundamental model for most modern computer systems.

- ✓ A program is a sequence of instructions stored in memory together with the data the program process
- ✓ An *Arithmetic Logic Unit* (ALU) performs calculation on the data
- ✓ A control unit is used to process and then execute each instruction held in main memory
- ✓ The computer system will have various input and output devices connected.

19.2 The fetch/decode/execute cycle

The Von Neumann computer model gives rise to the *fetch-execute cycle*.

The typical microprocessor will consist of:

- ✓ a number of *special purpose registers*
- ✓ one or more *general purpose registers*
- ✓ a number of *buses* which connect the components.

Before we study the detail of the special purpose registers and the buses and what they each do, we need a design for a typical modern microprocessor architecture.

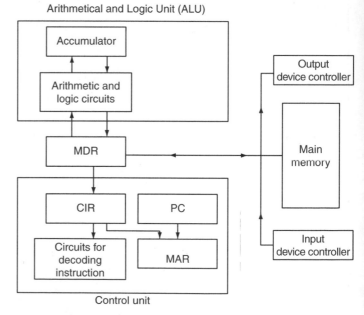

Arithmetical and Logic Unit (ALU)

Control unit

General purpose registers

A typical modern microprocessor will have around 8 general purpose registers. These will be used to store data values which have been read from memory or the results of some processing. These registers can be used by the assembly language programmer.

Accumulator

When we consider some simple assembly language instructions in Chapter 21 we shall assume a single general purpose register called the *accumulator*.

Special purpose registers

Program Counter (PC)

The Program Counter stores the address of the next instruction to be fetched.

Memory Address Register (MAR)

The Memory Address Register is loaded with the address which is about to be used for the fetching of an instruction or data. It could be a main memory address or the address of some input or output device.

Memory Data Register (MDR)

Also called the Memory Buffer Register. This bus connects the data bus to the processor. When a value is to be read from memory, the address is set up on the address bus, the value at this location copied to the MDR and then sent along the data bus to the processor.

Current Instruction Register (CIR)

When a program instruction is copied from main memory it will be copied first to the MDR and then copied to CIR. At this point the instruction is waiting to be *decoded* and then *executed*.

Index register

When in use, the index register will contain a number which acts as an 'index' to be added to some address value.

📖 Later

Using the Index Register in Chapter 21.

The Fetch-execute cycle

All these special purpose registers are involved in the processing of a sequence of program instructions stored in main memory.

The sequence is:

✓ The Program Counter is loaded with the address of the next instruction to be fetched
✓ The contents of the PC are copied to the Memory Address Register
✓ The contents of the PC are incremented (ready for the next fetch)
✓ The address given by MAR is located, and the contents of this address copied to the Memory Data Register
✓ The contents of MDR are copied to the Current Instruction Register
✓ The op code part of the instruction is identified and the instruction executed.

These steps can be expressed in a shorthand form called *Register Transfer Notation.*

$$MAR \leftarrow [PC]$$
$$PC \;\; \leftarrow [PC] + 1$$
$$MDR \leftarrow [[MAR]]$$
$$CIR \;\; \leftarrow [MDR]$$

✍ Note

[PC] denotes 'the contents of' the PC register.

The 'assign' operator denotes the register on the left is 'given the value of what follows'.

Once the final stage decodes the op code and establishes the type of instruction, then this may require a further access of the main memory. The address bus is loaded with the address and the data bus is used to transport the data value found at this address.

Progress Check 19.1

Registers are grouped as either general purpose registers or special purpose registers.

Which are the following?

(a) Accumulator
(b) Memory Address Register (MAR)
(c) Current Instruction Register (CIR)

Explain in words each of the stages – shown in register transfer notation – of the fetch stages of the fetch-execute cycle:

   (a) MAR ← [PC]
   (b) PC   ← [PC] + 1
   (c) MDR ← [[MAR]]
   (d) CIR   ← [MDR]

19.3 Data, Address and Control Buses

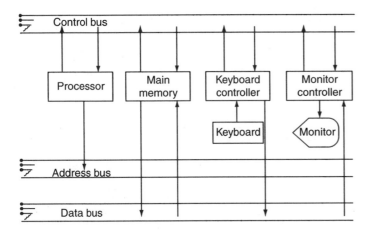

Figure 19.2 shows the buses which connect the various components and how input and output devices would be connected to the computer system.

The number of lines in the address and data bus will determine the size of the binary number which can be transmitted.

Binary arithmetic shows that a bus with 8 lines would give numbers which range from

0000 0000 to 1111 1111

i.e. 256 different numbers.

Hence an address bus with 8 lines would only be able to address 256 different memory locations.

Address bus

The **address bus** carries address values. Typically when a value is to be read from memory, the address bus must first be loaded with the correct address. Then the program instruction to perform the 'read' operation can be performed.

Data bus

When a read operation takes place the **data bus** is used to transport the value from the memory location addressed to the processor. In fact the Memory Data Register is involved in this transfer – more about this later.

The data bus is bi-directional. For example, it will be used to perform both memory read and memory write operations.

> **📖 Later**
>
> At this point you might want to read further about the use of assembly language instructions in the execution of a simple program. Refer to Chapter 21.

Control bus

The **control bus** is made up of a number of lines which are each dedicated to sending or receiving a signal. In the data transfer example above, one of the control bus lines would be used to send a signal to the control unit in the processor to indicate that the 'read operation has now completed'.

Other control signals include:

  ✓   user presses the 'reset' button
  ✓   memory write operation has completed
  ✓   an input/output operating has completed
  ✓   an interrupt has been received.

> **✎ Note**
>
> For both the data bus and address bus, all the lines are used when the bus is in action – unlike the control bus.

Progress Check 19.3

Which of the following statements are True/False?
(a) The data bus is connected to the Memory Data Register (MDR).
(b) The data bus is connected to the Memory Address Register (MAR).
(c) Data values are loaded onto the data bus; these can represent numbers, text characters or a memory address.
(d) The address bus is bi-directional.

19.4 Parallel processing systems

Co-processor

This is an additional processing unit that assists the CPU in performing a certain type of operation. This would typically be a *math coprocessor* to perform floating-point calculations.

Most modern computers will now come with a math coprocessor.

Another example is a graphics coprocessor for the fast rendering of 3-D graphics for a gaming application.

A coprocessor is not a processor in its own right but will have its architecture designed to work with a existing processor.

The benefit of the use of a coprocessor is that they are designed to speed up the execution of program instructions.

Parallel processing

The Von Neumann machine was designed on the principle that each program instruction was fetched in sequence. The vast increase in the speed of operation of processors has lead to a re-think of this design and we now have the following architectures.

The computer system allows several streams for instructions and data. To do this the architecture must have:

✓ several ALUs
✓ several control units.

A major application of the use of parallel processing is neural networks where computers designed for the this application have thousands of processors.

Array processing

The basic architecture here is a single control unit which is processing one instruction only but this instruction is applied simultaneously to an array of data values.

Their application is therefore suitable for any real-world application which requires the processing of array data.

Exam-style Questions

1. When a program is run the processor uses special purpose registers. Describe how the contents of each of the following registers changes during the fetch-execute cycle:
   (i) Memory Address Register (MAR)

   ....

   ....

   .... [2]

   (ii) Memory Data Register (MDR)

   ....

   .... [2]

   ....

   Cambridge 9691 Paper 32 Q11(b) June 2011

2. (i) Explain what the accumulator holds and how the contents change during the fetch-execute cycle

....

.... [2]

   (ii) Explain what the program counter (PC) holds and how the contents change during the fetch-execute cycle.

....

.... [3]

Cambridge 9691 Paper 32 Q3(b)(i) & (ii) November 2010

3. (a) Explain what is meant by Von Neumann architecture.

....

....

....

.... [3]

   (b) Describe the use of the following special purpose registers and how they change during the fetch-execute cycle.

   (i) Program Counter (PC)

....

....

....

.... [3]

   (ii) Current Instruction Register (CIR)

....

....

....

.... [3]

Cambridge 9691 Paper 31 Q2 November 2011

Data Representation, Data Structures and Data Manipulation

20

Revision Objectives

After you have studied this chapter, you should be able to:

☞ express numbers in binary coded decimal (BCD) and hexadecimal

☞ describe and use two's complement and sign-and-magnitude to represent positive and negative integers

☞ perform integer binary addition

☞ demonstrate an understanding of binary floating point representation of a real number

☞ normalise the floating point representation of a number

☞ discuss the trade-off between accuracy and range when representing numbers in floating point form

☞ describe algorithms for the insertion, retrieval and deletion of data items stored in linked-list, binary tree, stack and queue structures

☞ explain the difference between static and dynamic implementation of data structures, highlighting the benefits and drawbacks of each

☞ explain the difference between a binary search and a sequential search, highlighting the advantages and disadvantages of each

☞ use algorithms for implementing insertion sort and quick sort methods, and be able to explain the difference between them

☞ describe the use of a binary tree to sort data

☞ describe how data files are merged.

20.1 Express numbers in Binary Coded Decimal (BCD) and hexadecimal

Using BCD each digit in the denary number is represented as a 4-bit string.

The codes used are:

Denary	BCD
0	0000
1	0001
2	0010
3	0011
4	0100

Denary	BCD
5	0101
6	0110
7	0111
8	1000
9	1001

✎ Note

This means that some 4-bit patterns which are possible, for example, are never used in BCD.

Example

Represent the denary number 83 in BCD.

8 is coded as 1000
3 is coded as: 0011
83 = 1000 0011 BCD

Example

What denary number is the BCD number 0001 1000 1001?

0001 = 1
1000 = 8
1001 = 9

Therefore 0001 1000 1001 BCD = 189 denary.

Progress Check 20.1

1. What is the BCD representation for these denary numbers?
   (a) 36
   (b) 109

2. What are these denary numbers?
   (a) 0100 0111 0101 BCD
   (b) 0100 0000 1001 BCD

Hexadecimal

Hexadecimal (often shortened to 'Hex') is the number system which uses base 16.

If we consider the two fundamentals for any number system, base 16 will require:

✓ the possible digits 0, 1, 2, 3, 4, ... 8, 9, 10, 11, 12, 13, 14 and 15

✓ the first three place values for a hex number will be as shown below:

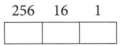

256   16   1

The problem is that if we write 13, this could be confused with 13 units, or 1 lot of 16 and 3 units, i.e. the denary number 19.

The solution is to code the digits for 10 and above with letters as follows:

Denary	1	2	3	4	5	6	7	8	9	10	11	12	13	14	15
Hex	1	2	3	4	5	6	7	8	9	A	B	C	D	E	F

Example

2A hex – What denary number is this?

2 lots of 16
A i.e. 10 units
Which gives: 42 denary

Example

1EF hex – What denary number is this?

1 lot of 256
E (i.e. 14) lots of 16 = 224
F units i.e. 15
Which gives: 256 + 224 + 15 = 495

Example

Convert the denary number 78 to hexadecimal.

4 lots of 16, with a remainder 12 gives:
4C hex

Progress Check 20.2

1. What is the hexadecimal for these denary numbers?
   (a) 90
   (b) 13
   (c) 259

2. What are these denary numbers?
   (a) 36 hex
   (b) FC hex

20.2 Representing positive and negative integers using two's complement, and sign-and-magnitude

Computer programs will need to work with integers – both positive and negative.

There are two possible ways of representing a signed integer:

✓ sign-and-magnitude
✓ two's complement.

Sign-and-magnitude

Assume the integer is to be stored with eight bits.

The most significant bit is used to represent the sign of the integer:

✓ 0 = positive
✓ 1 = negative

The remaining seven bits are used to represent the 'magnitude' or size of the number.

Examples

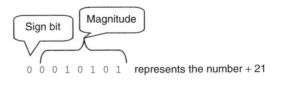

0 0 0 1 0 1 0 1   represents the number + 21

1 0 0 1 0 1 0 1   represents the integer – 21

Two's complement

Using 2's complement, all the bits have a 'place value'. Again consider eight bits available: the place value of the most significant bit is −128.

−128	64	32	16	8	4	2	1

Examples

−128	64	32	16	8	4	2	1
0	1	0	0	1	0	0	1

Denary integer = 64 + 8 + 1 = 73

−128	64	32	16	8	4	2	1
1	1	1	0	0	1	0	0

Denary integer = −128 + 64 + 32 + 4 = −128 + 100 = −28

Note, the range of possible integers is different for each representation and is summarised below for eight bit integers:

	Smallest	Largest
Sign and magnitude	1111 1111 = −127	0111 1111 = +127
Two's complement	1000 0000 = −128	0111 1111 = +127

20.3 Perform integer binary addition

Using two's complement has a major advantage over using sign-and-magnitude when attempting binary arithmetic.

When adding two bits:

✓ 0 + 0 = 0
✓ 0 + 1 = 1, with no carry
✓ 1 + 0 = 1, with no carry
✓ 1 + 1 = 0 and a carry of 1

Example

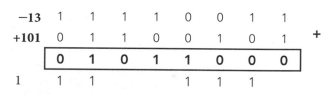

+13	0	0	0	0	1	1	0	1	
+59	0	0	1	1	1	0	1	1	+
	0	**1**	**0**	**0**	**1**	**0**	**0**	**0**	
Carry		1	1	1	1	1	1		

Check carefully the addition and the carry bits which gives the final result + 72.

The example illustrates that using two's complement addition we can expect to compute the correct result as long as the final answer is within the permitted range (i.e. -128 to +127 for eight bits).

Example

Which gives result + 88.

−13	1	1	1	1	0	0	1	1	
+101	0	1	1	0	0	1	0	1	+
	0	**1**	**0**	**1**	**1**	**0**	**0**	**0**	
1	1	1			1	1	1		

20.4 Binary floating point representation of a real number

Computer programs will use, not only integer numbers, but numbers which may have a fraction part, i.e. *real numbers*.

From early math we learnt that a number can be represented in 'standard form'.

Consider 1987.381

This can be expressed as 1.987381×10^3

Or, 0.1987381×10^4

We shall, for our floating point format, express the first part as a fraction and then calculate the appropriate **exponent**.

Very small numbers are also possible.

0.000876 is expressed as 0.876×10^{-3}

Hence for the range of numbers we will want to represent, any number can be expressed as Fraction $\times 10^{\text{Exponent}}$, where both the fraction and the exponent can be both positive and negative.

But, we store numbers in a computer system using base 2 (binary). The same principle can be followed and we conclude:

$$\text{Number} = \text{Fraction} \times 2^{\text{Exponent}}$$

This is called **floating point format** and we label the fraction part the **mantissa**.

$$\text{Number} = \text{Mantissa} \times 2^{\text{Exponent}}$$

Hence we can express any real number in floating point form by stating:

✓ the mantissa (usually in two's complement)
✓ the exponent (usually in two's complement).

The only issue then is how many bits are available for the mantissa and exponent.

Example

A floating point number uses 8 bits for the mantissa and a 4-bit exponent (both in two's complement).

The place values for the mantissa and exponent are as shown below.

−1	1/2	1/4	1/8	1/16	1/32	1/64	1/128		−8	4	2	1

Note carefully the place values for the mantissa.

Example

−1	1/2	1/4	1/8	1/16	1/32	1/64	1/128		−8	4	2	1
0	1	0	1	1	1	0	0		0	1	0	0

Mantissa: $1/2 + 1/8 + 1/16 + 1/32 = -25/32$

Exponent: $+4$

Denary number: $+23/32 \times 2^{+4}$

$= 11.5$

Example

−1	1/2	1/4	1/8	1/16	1/32	1/64	1/128		−8	4	2	1
1	0	0	1	1	1	0	0		1	1	1	0

Mantissa: $-1 + 1/8 + 1/16 + 1/32$

Exponent: -2

Denary number: $-25/32 \times 2^{-2}$

$= -25/128$

20.5 Normalise the floating point representation of a number

An issue that there is more than one possible representation for a number using floating point representation. See one previous example of 1987.381 in base 10.

> **Do not confuse**
>
> The term 'normalised' used here with 'Normal Forms' used in database table design in chapter 22.

Consider

−1	1/2	1/4	1/8	1/16	1/32	1/64	1/128		−8	4	2	1
0	1	0	0	1	0	0	0		0	0	1	1

$+9/16 \times 2^{+3} = 3.5$

Alternatively

−1	1/2	1/4	1/8	1/16	1/32	1/64	1/128		−8	4	2	1
0	0	1	0	0	1	0	0		0	1	0	0

$= (1/4 + 1/32) \times 2^{+4}$

$= +9/32 \times 2^{+4} = 3.5$

In this second representation we have effectively made the mantissa smaller by a factor of 2 but doubled the exponent – which means this mantissa and exponent also represents 3.5.

This begs the question – how do we decide which representation to use?

The first representation above is the one in **normalised form** and is the one which will ensure we preserve the maximum accuracy of the number.

How to recognise a normalised floating point representation?

We look at the mantissa:

- For a positive number, the mantissa must start with the digits 01 ...
- For a negative number, the mantissa must start with the digits 10 ...

Progress Check 20.5

These are three normalised floating-point format numbers which each have an 8-bit mantissa and an 8-bit exponent.

(a) 01110000 01000001
(b) 10001000 00000111
(c) 10100000 10001001

Explain how you recognise that all three numbers are in normalised format.

Calculate each denary number, by showing:
- ✓ the mantissa
- ✓ the exponent
- ✓ the denary number.

20.6 The trade-off between accuracy and range when representing numbers in floating-point form

Consider the scenario where 20 bits are available to store a floating-point number and the software designer must decide how many bits to allocate to the mantissa and how many for the exponent.

We shall discuss first what range of numbers are possible for our 8-bit mantissa and 4-bit exponent used earlier?

The following are four of the extreme values:

Mantissa	Exponent	Denary number
0111 1111	0111	
+1/2	+7	+127

0100 0000	1000	
+1/2	−8	+1/512

1000 0000	0111	
−1	+7	−128

1011 1111	1000	
−65/128	−8	− 65 / 32768

Conclusion

These examples should suggest:

- ✓ more bits given to the mantissa will give for **more accuracy**
- ✓ more bits given to the exponent will allow a **greater range of numbers** to be represented.

20.7 Algorithms for the insertion, retrieval and deletion of data items to data structures

Stack

A stack is a data structure which works on the principle of "last item added to the structure is the first item to leave".

Implement a stack using the following variables.

Variable Identifier	Data Type	Description
MyStack	Array[50] OF STRING	Stores the data values
TopOfStack	INTEGER	Stores the index position of the item currently at the top of MyStack
NewStackItem	STRING	Stores a data value to be added to MyStack

The diagram shows the state of MyStack and TopOfStack after three values were inserted (Golf, Football, Cycling), a value was deleted, then the value Tennis inserted.

Assume we have space for 50 values.

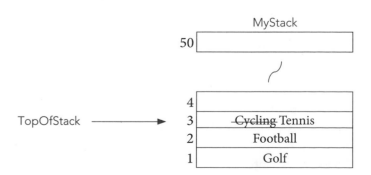

> **Terminology**
>
> Inserting and removing values from the stack is called a 'push' and a 'pop' respectively.

```
PROCEDURE PushToStack
   IF TopOfStack = 50
      THEN
         OUTPUT "Stack is already FULL"
      ELSE
         INPUT NewStackItem
         TopOfStack ← TopOfStack + 1
         MyStack[TopOfStack] ← NewStackItem
   ENDIF
ENDPROCEDURE

PROCEDURE PopFromStack
   IF TopOfStack = 0
      THEN
         OUTPUT "Stack is already EMPTY"
      ELSE
         OUTPUT MyStack[TopOfStack] "is leaving"
         TopOfStack ← TopOfStack - 1
   ENDIF
ENDPROCEDURE
```

Queue

A queue is a data structure which works on the principle of 'first item to join the structure will be the first item to leave'.

A linear queue is to be implemented to store data using the following variables.

Variable Identifier	Data Type	Description
MyQueue	ARRAY[50] OF STRING	Stores the data values
HeadOfQueue	INTEGER	Stores the index position of the item currently at the head of MyQueue
TailOfQueue	INTEGER	Stores the index position of the item currently at the tail of MyQueue
NewQueueItem	STRING	Stores a data value to be added to MyQueue

The diagram shows the state of MyQueue, HeadOfQueue and TailOfQueue after four values (Golf, Football, Cycling and Tennis) have been inserted and one value (Golf) has been removed from the queue.

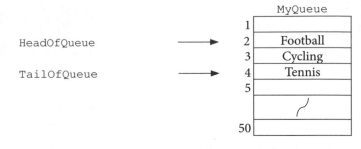

Algorithms to insert and delete a single item to/ from the queue are shown below.

```
PROCEDURE InsertItemToQueue
   IF TailOfQueue = 50
      THEN
         OUTPUT "Refused - No space available"
      ELSE
         INPUT NewQueueItem
         TailOfQueue ← TailOfQueue + 1
         MyQueue[TailOfQueue] ← NewQueueItem
   ENDIF
ENDPROCEDURE

PROCEDURE RemoveItemFromQueue
   IF HeadOfQueue + 1 = TailOfQueue
      THEN
         OUTPUT "Refused - Queue is already
         EMPTY"
      ELSE
         OUTPUT MyQueue[HeadOfQueue]
         HeadOfQueue ← HeadOfQueue + 1
   ENDIF
ENDPROCEDURE
```

There is a major problem with this queue implementation. There is no way in which the array cells which are used can have the same cell used later for another new value. Eventually the head pointer will move to 51 and the entire space becomes un-useable.

The solution is to implement a **circular queue**. Where the head pointer cycles back to the start of the array. You will not be expected to produce the algorithm for a circular queue for this syllabus.

Linked list

A linked list can be implemented using arrays. The array will contain the data values. The list is ordered in some way using a second array of pointer values; using the pointers, the data items are linked alphabetically.

Variable Identifier	Data Type	Description
LinkedList	ARRAY [100] OF STRING	Stores the data values
Pointer	ARRAY [100] OF INTEGER	Stores the pointer values
Start	INTEGER	Stores the index position of the item currently at the start of the list.

Start: 3

	LinkedList		Pointer
1	Golf	1	4
2	Football	2	1
3	Cricket	3	5
4	Tennis	4	0
5	Cycling	5	2
100		100	

These pointers give the following conceptual picture of the current state of the linked list.

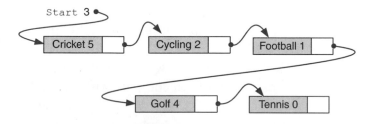

The following values join a linked list data structure in the order shown.

LONDON, AMSTERDAM, NEW DELHI, DHAKA, SINGAPORE and NEW YORK.

Data values are store in array `City` with link pointers is array `Link` and pointer `Start` to the first node in the list.

Shown the contents of the two arrays and the current state of the linked list.

Insert a new item to the linked list

The following additional variables will be used.

Variable Identifier	Data Type	Description
NewListItem	STRING	The item joining the linked list
NextFreePosition	INTEGER	Index of the next free array cell
Previous	INTEGER	Previous array position visited in a traversal
Current	INTEGER	Current value visited in a traversal

```
PROCEDURE InsertItemToList
  IF 'List full'
    THEN
      OUTPUT "REFUSED - list is full"
    ELSE
      IF 'List empty'
        THEN
          Start ← NextFreePosition
          LinkedList[NextFreePosition] ←
          NewListItem
        ELSE
          // traverse the list - starting at
            Start to find
          // the position at which to insert
            the new item
      ENDIF
  ENDIF
ENDPROCEDURE
// the traversal algorithm
IF NewListItem < LinkedList[Start]
  THEN
    Pointer[NextFreePosition] ← Start
    Start ← NextFreePosition
  ELSE
    // the new item is not at the start of
      the list ...
    Previous ← 0
    Current ← Start
    Found ← False
    REPEAT
      IF NewListItem = LinkedList[Current]
        THEN
          Pointer[Previous] ← NextFreePosition
          Pointer[NextFreePosition] ← Current
          Found ← True
        ELSE
          Previous ← Current
          Current ← Pointer[Current]
      ENDIF
    UNTIL Found = True
ENDIF
```

You should study the algorithm and make sure you understand what pointer changes take place to effectively insert a new item to the list.

Delete an item from the linked list

To delete an item, one of the pointers is changed as shown in the example below. Changing the pointer value of Football effectively removes Golf from the list.

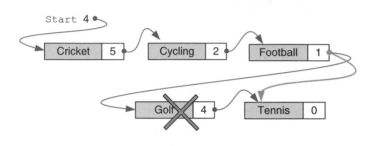

To delete Golf, we would traverse the tree until Golf is found.

`Current` would point to Golf

`Previous` would point to Football

So, the change which takes place is:

The pointer of `Previous` changes to the pointer of `Current`

The algorithm will be very similar to that for the insert routine.

We will need to test for the special cases:

✓ the list is empty
✓ the item to delete is at position `Start`.

Progress Check 20.7

Write the algorithm using pseudocode to describe the output of all the linked list values in order.

Binary tree

A binary tree – similar to a linked list – links the data values together. The tree structure requires two pointers; one to point to a left descendant, the second to a right descendant.

Tree terminology

The tree shown has five nodes and the values were inserted to the tree in the order:

COURGETTE, SWEDE, PARSNIP, ARTICHOKE AND TURNIP.

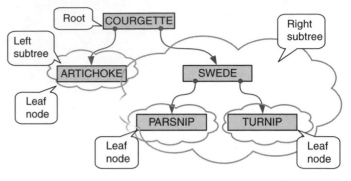

Root – the first item to join the tree is the root value

Left subtree – all values to the left of the root form a subtree

Right subtree – ditto – all values to the right of the root form a subtree

Leaf node – a node value which has no descendants

The tree has been formed as follows:

✓ COURGETTE is the first item so becomes the root
✓ SWEDE – compare SWEDE with COURGETTE and place to the right; link from COURGETTE
✓ PARSNIP – compare with COURGETTE and move right then compare with SWEDE and place to the left of SWEDE by linking from SWEDE.
✓ Etc…

We shall use a similar set of data structures to those used to implement our linked list. An array for the data values, and two set of pointers to point 'left' and 'right'.

Variable Identifier	Data Type	Description
TreeData	ARRAY [100] OF STRING	Stores the data values
LeftPointer	ARRAY [100] OF INTEGER	Stores the left index pointer
RightPointer	ARRAY [100] OF INTEGER	Stores the right index pointer
Root	INTEGER	Stores the index position of the root value

For the earlier tree the array contents would be:

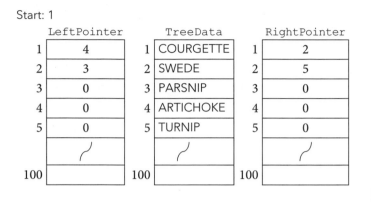

Start: 1

	LeftPointer			TreeData			RightPointer
1	4		1	COURGETTE		1	2
2	3		2	SWEDE		2	5
3	0		3	PARSNIP		3	0
4	0		4	ARTICHOKE		4	0
5	0		5	TURNIP		5	0
100			100			100	

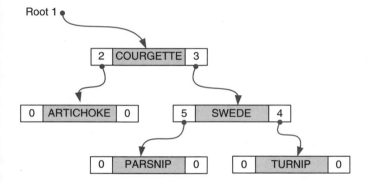

Root 1

This array data gives the conceptual binary tree shown.

Insert a value to the binary tree

This is straightforward.

We shall need to check for the special cases:

✓ the tree is not empty
✓ there is space available for a new item.

Then the algorithm will traverse the tree to locate the right or left position at which to insert the new value.

The following additional variables will be used.

Variable Identifier	Data Type	Description
NewTreeItem	STRING	The item joining the binary tree
NextFree Position	INTEGER	Index of the next free array cell
Previous	INTEGER	Previous array position visited in a traversal
Current	INTEGER	Current value visited in a traversal
LastMove	CHAR	Indicates the last move in the traversal: ✓ L – left ✓ R – right ✓ X – no previous move

```
PROCEDURE AddItemToBinaryTree
  IF NextFreePosition >100
    THEN
      OUTPUT "No more values can be added"
    ELSE
      INPUT NewTreeItem

      IF Root = 0
        THEN
          Root ← NextFreePosition
        ELSE
          //traverse the tree to find the position for the new value
          CurrentPosition ← Root
          LastMove ← 'X'
          REPEAT
            PreviousPosition ← CurrentPosition
            IF NewTreeItem < TreeData[CurrentPosition]
              THEN
                //move left
                LastMove ← 'L'
              CurrentPosition ← LeftPointer[CurrentPosition]
```

```
            ELSE
                // move right
                LastMove ← 'R'
                CurrentPosition ← RightPointer[CurrentPosition]
            ENDIF
        UNTIL CurrentPosition = 0
      ENDIF

  IF LastMove = 'R'
    THEN
      RightPointer[PreviousPosition] ← NextFreePosition
    ELSE
      IF LastMove ← 'L'
        THEN
          LeftPointer[PreviousPosition] ← NextFreePosition
      ENDIF
    ENDIF
    NextFreePosition ← NextFreePosition + 1
  ENDIF
ENDPROCEDURE
```

Progress Check 20.8

The following cities are inserted to a binary tree structure in the order shown.
  Draw the conceptual state of the tree.
  NEW YORK, ISTANBUL, SINGAPORE, LONDON, PARIS, CANBERRA, MOSCOW

Deleting a value from the binary tree

Consider our original tree.

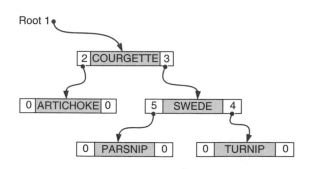

Consider the changes which would need to take place to delete each of the nodes in this tree.

Your conclusions should be:

✓ deleting a leaf node will be straightforward
  ➢ Traverse the tree until found – set the link pointer from the previous node to zero
✓ deleting any node which has descendants is complex.

For this reason the complete 'delete item' algorithm is considered outside the scope of the syllabus.

20.8 The use of a binary tree to sort data

What the tree pointers have done is effectively sort the data values. The major benefit of a tree structure is that – for a tree of (about) some 2000 nodes, searching for a particular value is highly efficient.

The math says that for a tree with 1024 nodes, the average number of comparisons to find a particular value is 11. Compare this with a sequential search through an array list and the average number of comparisons for the same size list would be 512.

Tree traversal algorithms

To output all the values in order from a tree required that we visit the nodes in some defined order. The order of the procedure calls is illustrated with the following diagram.

Consider following tree (used for Progress Check 20.8).

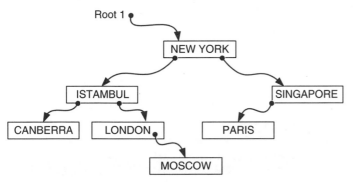

The thinking would be as follows:

✓ go to the root
✓ if there is a left node – move left

✓ repeat moving left until the left pointer is Null
✓ OUTPUT the current value
✓ move back to the Root – OUTPUT the root of this subtree
✓ if there is a right node – move right.

We can visualise this as moving through a sequence of subtrees. Each subtree is dealt with in the order:

✓ move left (if possible)
✓ OUTPUT the root
✓ move right (if possible).

The algorithm is *recursive* as we are continually dealing with a tree, and often have to leave the completion of the current tree (left – root – right) until later when we return to this tree.

The algorithm for this different order of tree traversal is:

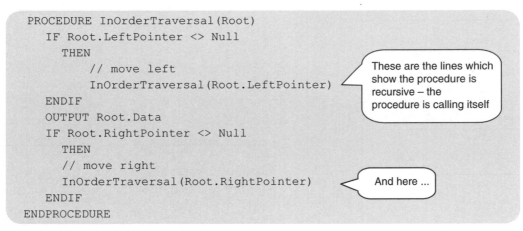

```
PROCEDURE InOrderTraversal(Root)
   IF Root.LeftPointer <> Null
      THEN
         // move left
         InOrderTraversal(Root.LeftPointer)
   ENDIF
   OUTPUT Root.Data
   IF Root.RightPointer <> Null
      THEN
      // move right
      InOrderTraversal(Root.RightPointer)
   ENDIF
ENDPROCEDURE
```

These are the lines which show the procedure is recursive – the procedure is calling itself

And here …

The algorithm is very elegant requiring very few statements.

Traversing which outputs the data values in order is called an *in-order tree traversal*. The order of the procedure calls is illustrated with the diagram which follows. The arrows show when a call is completed and the algorithm returns to a previous call. This process is called *unwinding*.

This is not the only possible order. If the algorithm was changed to read:

Move Left – Move right – then output the root.

This is called a *post-order* traversal.

📖 **Later**

A 'post-order traversal' has a practical application when we study reverse Polish notation in Chapter 21.

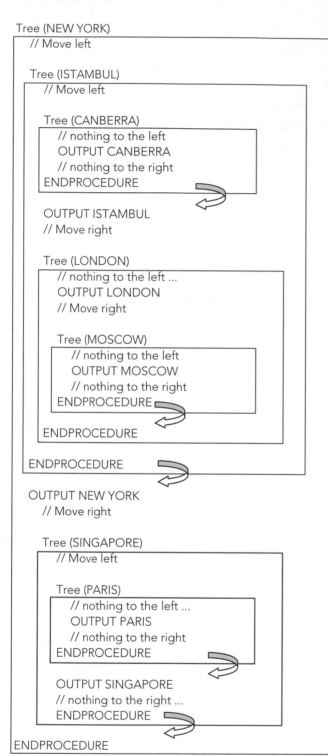

20.9 Difference between binary searching and serial searching

Binary tree search

✓ Input the value required then
✓ Start at the root

REPEAT
✓   compare ...
✓   IF the value is found then OUTPUT 'found'
✓   ELSE, IF the value is before the current one then move left – else move right
✓   UNTIL value found OR pointer is zero.

> **← Look Back**
>
> To Chapter 3 for a 'sequential search'.

The detailed algorithm is set as the progress check exercise which follows.

Progress Check 20.9

Variable	Data Type	Description
TreeData	ARRAY [100] OF STRING	Stores the data values
LeftPointer	ARRAY [100] OF INTEGER	Stores the left index pointer
RightPointer	ARRAY [100] OF INTEGER	Stores the right index pointer
Root	INTEGER	Stores the index position of the root value
ThisTreeItem	STRING	The item we are searching for
Current	INTEGER	Current value visited in the traversal

Use these variables to design the algorithm for a binary tree search of the `TreeData` array for the value `ThisTreeItem`.

Binary search

This method assumes that no attempt has been made to use a linked list or a binary tree. The values are stored in an array, **BUT *the algorithm requires that the values are sorted*.**

The algorithm will search the array `ThisArray` (upper bound N) for the value `ThisValue`.

The algorithm finds the middle value and compares the required value with this middle value. If not found then either the top half or bottom half of the list is discarded. The new middle is calculated and another comparison made.

A variable table is not shown.

```
PROCEDURE BinarySearch
  INPUT ThisValue
  Found ← FALSE                    [Flags if the required
  NotInList ← FALSE                 value is not found]

  Top ← N
  Bottom ← 1
  REPEAT
   Middle ← Integer value of (Top + Bottom)/2 )
   If ThisArray[Middle] = ThisValue
     THEN
       Found ← TRUE
       OUTPUT "Value is FOUND"
     ELSE
      IF Bottom > Top        [Test for value not found]
        THEN
          NotInList ← TRUE
        ELSE
         IF ThisArray[Middle] < ThisItem
           THEN
           // Retain the top half of the list ...
```

```
         Bottom ← Middle + 1
       ELSE
         // Retain the bottom half of the list ...
         Top ← Middle - 1
       ENDIF
     ENDIF
   ENDIF
  UNTIL (Found = TRUE) OR (NotInList = TRUE)

  IF NotInList = TRUE
    THEN
      OUTPUT "Requested item was NOT FOUND"
  ENDIF
ENDPROCEDURE
```

An alternative algorithm

The binary search is an interesting problem. The algorithm shown is an *iterative* one. Each iteration (loop) works with a new list of half the size.

There is an alternative algorithm which **is recursive**. The Visual Basic code for this is shown below. Study the function `Binarysearch` – it is considerably less code than the iterative solution.

```vbnet
Dim ThisArray(50) As Integer

Sub Main()
    Dim IndexPosition As String
    Dim ThisValue As Integer

    Console.Write("Value to find ...? ") : ThisValue = Console.ReadLine
    Call InitialiseArray()
    IndexPosition = BinarySearch(ThisArray, ThisValue, 1, 32)
    Console.WriteLine("Search results ... FOUND at index " & IndexPosition)

    Console.ReadLine()
End Sub

Function BinarySearch(ByVal TheArray() As Integer, ByVal ThisValue As Integer, _
                      ByVal Bottom As Integer, ByVal Top As Integer) As Integer
    Dim Middle As Integer

    If (Top < Bottom) Then
        Return -1 ' not found
    Else
        Middle = Bottom + (Top - Bottom) / 2
        If TheArray(Middle) > ThisValue Then
            Return BinarySearch(TheArray, ThisValue, Bottom, Middle - 1)
        ElseIf TheArray(Middle) < ThisValue Then
            Return BinarySearch(TheArray, ThisValue, Middle + 1, Top)
        Else
            Return Middle ' found
        End If
    End If
End Function

Sub InitialiseArray()
    ThisArray(1) = 12
    ThisArray(2) = 13
    ...
    ThisArray(31) = 129
    ThisArray(32) = 136
End Sub
```

```
Value to find ...? 39
Search results ... FOUND at index 11
```

← Look Back

To Chapter 12. Recursion was covered there. We stated there that a binary search is a problem which can have either an iterative or a recursive algorithm solution.

Progress Check 20.10

Study the function `BinarySearch` in the given code.

Write the pseudocode for the coded recursive solution.

20.10 Difference between static and dynamic implementation of data structures

The terms 'static' and 'dynamic' are often used in computer science. Static generally means 'does not change' – dynamic means 'changing'. Hence we would describe the stack, queue etc., data structures we have studied in this chapter as dynamic as there are values continually joining and leaving the data structure.

The usual example to give for a static data structure is an array. Once the array has been declared and its size or upper bound stated, the data structure will not change. That is we have reserved or allocated memory before the data structure is used.

This use of static data structures is inflexible and is likely to lead to wasted memory.

 Top tip   In the examination use an 'array' as an example of a static data structure.

Pointers

Some programmer languages – including Pascal and C++ – support a data structure called a pointer. This is not the same as the way we have implemented a set of pointer values using an array. A pointer is a variable which stores the address of some other variable.

 Top tip   In the examination, use a pointer as an example of a dynamic data structure.

Pointers allow for dynamic memory allocation; that is, we define and use memory as the program needs it.

The key difference is that for dynamic memory allocation, memory is assigned at run-time not (as with static allocation) at compile time.

20.11 Algorithms for implementing insertion sort and quick sort

There will be many applications which require a list of data items to be sorted. The binary search algorithm we studied earlier in the chapter can only be used on a list of items which are in order.

There are whole textbooks written on different sorting algorithms and the algorithm will be measured by its efficiency. In practice this will mean:

✓ the number of comparisons which are made in order to sort the list
✓ the time taken to complete the sort.

✎ Note

The syllabus required you to understand two of the algorithms:
✓ an *insertion sort*
✓ a *quick sort*.

Insertion sort

The diagram shows the list half way through the insertion sort algorithm.

✓ The value currently considered is 19
✓ The values to the left of 19 form the sorted list (so far ...)
✓ Values to the right of 19 have still to be considered.

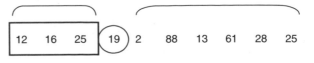

| 12 | 16 | 25 | 19 | 2 | 88 | 13 | 61 | 28 | 25 |

The action required is:

- ✓ 19 must be placed at index position 3
- ✓ values to the right of the insert position will move right one place (that's 25)
- ✓ start again by considering the next value 2.

| 12 | 16 | 19 | 25 | (2) | 88 | 13 | 61 | 28 | 25 |

Selection sort

Variable	Data Type	Description
TheList	ARRAY[N] OF INTEGER	Stores the data values
Index	INTEGER	Index position of the current value considered
CurrentValue	INTEGER	Current value considered
Sorted-ListPosn	INTEGER	Loop counter for moving through the sorted list
ListPosnFound	BOOLEAN	Flags when the insert position in the sorted list is found
InsertPosn	INTEGER	Index of the insert position in the sorted list
ShufflePosn	INTEGER	Loop counter for the sorted list when values to the right have to all be moved up one place

```
//     consider all numbers starting with
the second
  FOR Index 2 TO N
    CurrentValue ← TheList[Index]
    // find the position in the sorted list to
insert
    SortedListPosn ← 1
    InsertPosnFound ← False
    REPEAT
     IF CurrentValue > TheList[SortedListPosn]
      THEN
        SortedListPosn ← SortedListPosn + 1
      ELSE
        InsertPosn ← SortedListPosn
        InsertPosnFound ← True
      ENDIF
    UNTIL InsertPosnFound = True
    // current value is to move to InsertPosn
    // current value moves to InsertPosn and
    all others to
```

```
// the right shuffle right one place
FOR ShufflePosn ← Index TO [InsertPosn + 1] STEP –1
  TheList[ShufflePosn] ← TheList[ShufflePosn – 1]
ENDFOR
  TheList[InsertPosn] ← CurrentValue
ENDNFOR
```

Progress Check 20.11

The array shows a data set in the process of a selection sort.

The next value to be considered is circled.

| 17 | 69 | 71 | 82 | (24) | 19 | 114 | 61 | 28 | 25 |

Show the next **two changes** which take place to the list.

Quick sort

It is also called a *partition-sort* algorithm as the method recursively uses a 'pivot value' to divide the list into two partitions. Quick sort is an example of a general principle of algorithm design called 'divide and conquer' because the partitioning of the list is effectively 'dividing' the problem into simpler ones, then the movement of data items is the 'conquer' stage. The method divides the data list into two lists and then 'quick sorts' each one. Each subsequent list is again divided into two lists and 'quick sorted', and so on.

1. Choose an element, called the pivot, from the list (This can be any value, but in the algorithm which follows is taken to be the middle of the list).
2. Re-order the list so that all elements with values less than the pivot come before the pivot, while all elements with values greater than the pivot come after it.

   This is done by using two pointers; the left pointer (Low) points to the pivot value and the right pointer to the end of the list (High).

   After this partitioning, the pivot is in its final position. This completes the first phase of the algorithm called the partitioning.

3. Then recursively sort the sub-list of values to the left of the pivot value.
4. Recursively sort the sub-list of values to the right of the pivot value.

In common with many recursive solutions the algorithm – although complex to describe – is very concise.

```
FUNCTION Quicksort(a[]: STRING, Lo :
INTEGER, High : INTEGER)
   // Low is the lower index, High is
   the upper index of the array

   i ← Low
   j ← High
   // the pivot position is the middle
     item in the list/sub-list
   X ← a [(Low + High)/2]

   // partition
   REPEAT
     WHILE a[i] < x
       i ← i+1
       WHILE a[j] > x
         j ← j-1
         IF i <= j
       THEN
         // swap values
         // h is a temporary storage variable
         h ← a[i]
         a[i] ← a[j]
         a[j] ← h
         i ← i + 1
         j ← j - 1
       ENDIF
   UNTIL i > j

   // recursion
   IF Low < j Quicksort(a, Low, j);
   IF i < High Quicksort(a, i, High);
ENDFUNCTION
```

Remember the syllabus explicitly states that you will not be expected to produce the algorithms for these sorting methods in the exam. You should however be able to give a description of the algorithms, and it would be a worth while programming exercise.

```
Sub SelectionSort()
    Dim SortedListPosn, InsertPosn As Integer
    Dim Index, ShufflePosn As Integer
    Dim CurrentValue As Integer
    Dim InsertPosnFound As Boolean

    For Index = 2 To 9
        CurrentValue = TheList(Index)
```

```
        SortedListPosn = 1
        InsertPosnFound = False
        Do
            If CurrentValue > TheList(SortedListPosn) Then
                SortedListPosn = SortedListPosn + 1
            Else
                InsertPosn = SortedListPosn
                InsertPosnFound = True
            End If
        Loop Until InsertPosnFound = True

        For ShufflePosn = Index To (InsertPosn + 1) Step -1
            TheList(ShufflePosn) = TheList(ShufflePosn - 1)
        Next
        TheList(InsertPosn) = CurrentValue
    Next
    Call DisplayList()

End Sub

Sub DisplayList()
    Dim Index As Integer

    Console.WriteLine()
    For Index = 1 To 20
        Console.Write(TheList(Index) & "  ")
    Next
End Sub
```

20.12 Merging data files

It does not have to be data from two files which are to be merged. It could be that data is read from two arrays and the values 'merged' and stored in a third array.

We shall assume that the data from two sources is sorted. If not, the algorithm will be complex and involve several passes through each data set.

The following algorithm merges two sets of data that are held in two one-dimensional arrays called `Array1[M]` and `Array2[N]` into a third array `Array3`. `Array1` and `Array2` have been sorted into ascending order.

Variable Identifier	Data Type	Description
Array1	ARRAY[N] OF INTEGER	The first list of values
Array2	ARRAY[M] OF INTEGER	The second list of values
Array3	ARRAY[M+N] OF INTEGER	Contains the merged list
Posn1	INTEGER	Index to Array1
Posn2	INTEGER	Index to Array2
Posn2	INTEGER	Index to Array3
i	INTEGER	Loop counter

```
PROCEDURE MergeList1andList2
    Posn1 ← 1 : Posn2 ← 1 : Posn3 ← 1
    WHILE Posn1 <= M AND Posn2 <= N DO
        IF List1[Posn1] < List2[Posn2]
        THEN
            List3[Posn3] ← List1[Posn1]
            Posn1 ← Posn1 + 1
            Posn3 ← Posn3 + 1
        ELSE
            IF List1[Posn1] >List2[Posn2]
            THEN
                List3[Posn3] ← List2[Posn2]
                Posn2 ← Posn2 + 1
                Posn3 ← Posn3 + 1
            ELSE
                List3[Posn3] ← List1[Posn1]
                Posn1 ← Posn1 + 1
                Posn2 ← Posn2 + 1
                Posn3 ← Posn3 + 1
            ENDIF
        ENDIF
        FinalPosn1 = Posn1
        inalPosn2 = Posn2
    ENDWHILE
    IF Posn1 > M THEN
        // there are remaining items in Array2
        LOOP FOR i ← FinalPosn2 TO N
            List3[Posn3] ← List2[i]
            Posn3 ← Posn3 + 1
        ENDFOR
    ELSE
        // there are remaining items in Array1
        LOOP FOR i ← FinalPosn1 TO M
            List3[Posn3] ← List1[i]
            Posn3 ← Posn3 + 1
        ENDFOR
    ENDIF
ENDPROCEDURE
```

```
Dim Array1(30) As Integer
Dim Array2(30) As Integer
Dim Array3(60) As Integer
Dim M, N As Integer

Sub Main()
    M = 18 : N = 14
    Call InitialiseArrays()
    Call DoMerge()
    Call DisplayMerge()
    Console.ReadLine()
End Sub

Sub DoMerge() ...

Sub DisplayMerge()
    Dim i As Integer
    Dim Count As Integer
    Count = 0
        For i = 1 To 32
            Console.Write(Array3(i) & "  ")
            Count = Count + 1
        Next
        Console.WriteLine()
        Console.Write(Count)
End Sub

Sub InitialiseArrays()
    Array1(1) = 12
    Array1(2) = 13

    Array1(17) = 52
    Array1(18) = 53

    Array2(1) = 60
    Array2(2) = 65

    Array2(14) = 136
End Sub

Sub DoMerge()
    Dim Posn1, Posn2, Posn3 As Integer
    Dim FinalPosn1, FinalPosn2 As Integer
    Dim i As Integer

    Posn1 = 1 : Posn2 = 1 : Posn3 = 1
    While Posn1 <= M And Posn2 <= N
        If Array1(Posn1) < Array2(Posn2) Then
            Array3(Posn3) = Array1(Posn1)
            Posn1 = Posn1 + 1
            Posn3 = Posn3 + 1
        Else
            If Array1(Posn1) > Array2(Posn2) Then
                Array3(Posn3) = Array2(Posn2)
                Posn2 = Posn2 + 1
                Posn3 = Posn3 + 1
            Else
                Array3(Posn3) = Array1(Posn1)
                Posn1 = Posn1 + 1
                Posn2 = Posn2 + 1
                Posn3 = Posn3 + 1
            End If
        End If
        FinalPosn1 = Posn1
        FinalPosn2 = Posn2
    End While

    If Posn1 > M Then
        ' there items remaining in Array2
        For i = FinalPosn2 To N
            Array3(Posn3) = Array2(i)
            Posn3 = Posn3 + 1
        Next
    Else
        ' there are items remaining in Array1
        For i = Posn1 To M
            Array3(Posn3) = Array1(i)
            Posn3 = Posn3 + 1
        Next
    End If
End Sub
```

1. Data is held about the following cities:

     Paris, Cairo, Singapore, Durban, Amman, Sydney

(a) Draw a binary tree of the cities by taking Paris as the root and reading through the list sequentially. Your tree should use an algorithm which will create a suitable tree for reading the data in alphabetical order.

[2]

(b) Describe an algorithm that will read your tree, producing a list of the cities in alphabetical order.

     ....

     ....

     ....

     .... [3]

(c) Explain how the original list can be sorted into alphabetical order using an insertion sort method.

     ....

     ....

     ....

     ....

     .... [6]

Cambridge 9691 Specimen Paper 3 Q5

2. A binary pattern can be used to represent different data used in a computer system.

   (a) Consider the binary pattern: **0101 0011**

       The pattern represents an integer.

       What number is this in denary?

       .... [1]

   (b) Consider the binary pattern: **0001 0101 0011**

       The pattern represents a Binary Coded Decimal (BCD) number.

       What number is this in denary?

       .... [1]

(c) Consider the binary pattern: **1001 0010**

This represents a two's complement integer.

What number is this in denary?

.... [1]

Cambridge 9691 Paper 32 Q2(a) (b) & (c) June 2012

3. Part of the information stored in the data dictionary describes the type of data which is being stored.

A particular piece of data is 10010110.

State what the data stands or if the data dictionary describes it as:

(i) a two's complement binary number;

....

.... [1]

(ii) a sign and magnitude binary number;

....

.... [1]

(iii) a binary coded decimal number.

....

.... [2]

Cambridge 9691 Paper 31 Q7 June 2011

4. (a) Convert the following denary numbers into 8-bit, sign and magnitude, binary numbers:

(i) +39

....

(ii) −47

.... [3]

(b) Convert the following denary numbers into 8-bit, two's complement, binary numbers:

(i) −3

.... [2]

(ii) −47

.... [2]

(c) A particular computer uses a single 10-bit word to store a floating-point representation of a number.

The first 6 bits are used to store the mantissa and the remaining 4 bits are used to store the exponent.

(i) Explain why 000101 0100 = 2 using this notation.

....

.... [2]

(ii) Rewrite the binary value of this floating-point representation so that it is in normalised form.

....

.... [2]

(iii) 011001 0011 is a normalised floating-point number.
By converting each of the mantissa and the exponent into a denary number first, write this number in denary.

....

....

.... [3]

Cambridge 9691 Paper 33 Q3 November 2011

Programming Paradigms

21.1 Characteristics of a variety of programming paradigms

Low-level programming

Low-level describes both programming in *machine code* or *assembly language*.

The programmer is writing code using the basic machine operations which the particular processor provides.

In machine code the programmer must use the actual binary values for each machine instruction and the binary for any addresses or immediate values used.

In assembly language the programmer will use the mnemonic code which represents the instruction (for example, LDD – 'load direct') followed by the address or immediate value. The programmer may

use symbols for addresses, i.e. symbolic addressing, which is designed to make the assembly language code more readable.

Procedural programming languages

All modern high-level languages are procedural. This means the language supports:

✓ the use of functions and procedures
✓ code will take on a 'block like' structure
  ➤ for example, all the statements inside a procedure definition or loop are viewed as a block of program statements.

Procedural languages are also *imperative languages*; the program statements describe what the program must do. An imperative program has statements which must be executed in sequence.

Declarative programming

This is the opposite of an imperative programming paradigm.

The program will state some outcome which is required, but without any code or statements which describe how the processing is to be done.

Declarative programming is the paradigm used for **logic programming languages** (such as Prolog) and **functional programming languages** (such as Lisp).

Progress Check 21.1

1. What is meant by low-level programming languages?
2. State two features of a procedural high-level language.

Object-oriented programming

These terms – procedural, declarative and object-oriented – are not mutually-exclusive. Many languages which are procedural also support the use of objects (for example, Visual Basic.Net, C++, Python and many more).

An OOP language uses the data structure an **object** to model a problem. Objects will have defined **properties** (like attributes in database design) and **methods** which act upon an object.

21.2 The terms object-oriented, declarative and procedural as applied to high-level languages

The definition of a real-world object is first defined as a **class**. The class will have an identifier name and describe the properties and methods for that class. A program can then create many objects of this type and store data about each object. The class is the definition or 'blueprint' from which all objects of that type are created.

You should already have some idea about the use of objects if you have attempted to created a forms-based Windows application in Visual Basic.Net.

The form will typically contain a number of ActiveX controls – such as a text box and a set of radio buttons – and these behave as 'objects'. Hence the .Net programming environment has a class definition of the properties and methods defined for each of these ActiveX controls.

Other objects take the form of abstract objects such as a 'connection' object or a 'recordset' object.

The third kind of objects are those which are used by the programmer to model some real-world problem. It is this third application of object-oriented programming we shall focus on.

Properties

Think of these as like the attributes in database modelling.

The following code shows the class definition for the two properties associated with a RESOURCE object.

✎ Note

The member variables are private to the class and hence will be effectively hidden from the programmer. The way in which the program will assign values to an object and read the current property value of an object is using 'set' and 'get' methods (Visual Basic.Net implements these methods as 'property procedures').

Encapsulation

Means the combining together of an object's properties and the methods which access that data. Encapsulation will restrict the programmer's access to the object's data. Encapsulation means an object's properties can only be read and written using the 'get' and 'set' methods provided with the class definition.

Data hiding is a very important concept of OOP and is a feature of data encapsulation. This provides a structure for the validation of data which can be hidden away from the programmer who will use an existing class definition.

Methods

Think of a method as something we can **do** with an object. ActiveX controls such as a textbox have events which are associated with that object type.

When we model real-world objects such as a 'product' or 'customer' object, methods will be needed for every action required on that object.

The two most basic methods are for example:

✓ A `Set_CustomerName` method to assign a particular name property to a customer object

✓ A `Get_CustomerName` method to access and use the object's `CustomerName` property.

Classes and objects

Class

A class is the definition of what an object will look like – the object specification. The class acts as the template from which an *instance* of an object is created.

The class defines the properties of the object and the methods used to control the object's behaviour.

A class is given an identifier name, for example, `Customer`.

Example

Consider the scenario of a lending library which has a large number of resources which include books (both for lending and reference use), audio-books, DVDs and CDs.

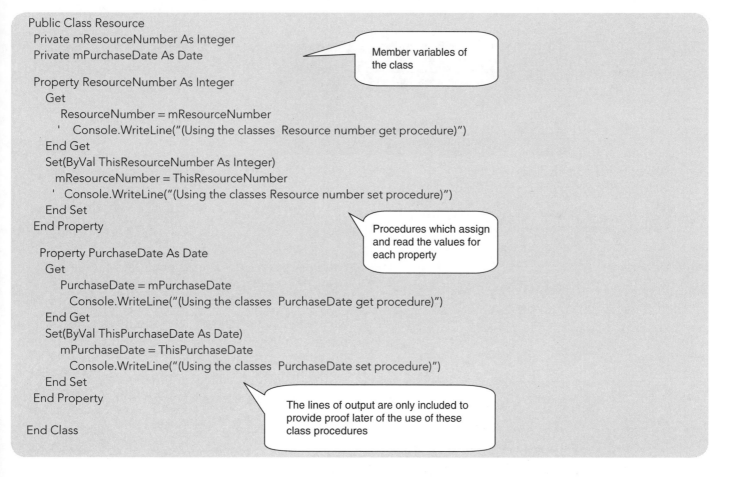

```
Public Class Resource
    Private mResourceNumber As Integer
    Private mPurchaseDate As Date              Member variables of
                                               the class

    Property ResourceNumber As Integer
        Get
            ResourceNumber = mResourceNumber
    '       Console.WriteLine("(Using the classes  Resource number get procedure)")
        End Get
        Set(ByVal ThisResourceNumber As Integer)
            mResourceNumber = ThisResourceNumber
    '       Console.WriteLine("(Using the classes Resource number set procedure)")
        End Set
    End Property
                                               Procedures which assign
                                               and read the values for
                                               each property
    Property PurchaseDate As Date
        Get
            PurchaseDate = mPurchaseDate
            Console.WriteLine("(Using the classes  PurchaseDate get procedure)")
        End Get
        Set(ByVal ThisPurchaseDate As Date)
            mPurchaseDate = ThisPurchaseDate
            Console.WriteLine("(Using the classes  PurchaseDate set procedure)")
        End Set
    End Property
                                               The lines of output are only included to
                                               provide proof later of the use of these
    End Class                                  class procedures
```

Object

An object is an occurrence or instance of the class definition.

An instance will be identified by an identifier name.

The class could define a customer object, for example, the `MyCustomer` object which is an instance of the `Customer` class.

The following code illustrates the creation of an object and the various procedures which are used to assign and access the object's property values.

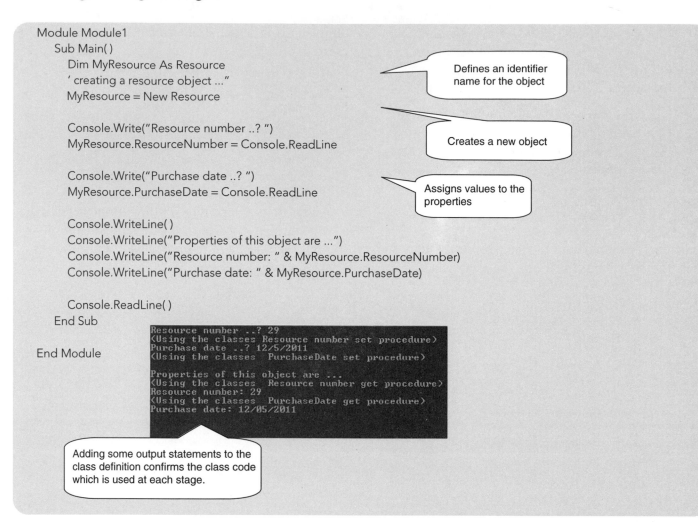

```
Module Module1
   Sub Main( )
      Dim MyResource As Resource
      ' creating a resource object ..."
      MyResource = New Resource

      Console.Write("Resource number ..? ")
      MyResource.ResourceNumber = Console.ReadLine

      Console.Write("Purchase date ..? ")
      MyResource.PurchaseDate = Console.ReadLine

      Console.WriteLine( )
      Console.WriteLine("Properties of this object are ...")
      Console.WriteLine("Resource number: " & MyResource.ResourceNumber)
      Console.WriteLine("Purchase date: " & MyResource.PurchaseDate)

      Console.ReadLine( )
   End Sub

End Module
```

Defines an identifier name for the object

Creates a new object

Assigns values to the properties

```
Resource number ..? 29
<Using the classes Resource number set procedure>
Purchase date ..? 12/5/2011
<Using the classes  PurchaseDate set procedure>

Properties of this object are ...
<Using the classes  Resource number get procedure>
Resource number: 29
<Using the classes  PurchaseDate get procedure>
Purchase date: 12/05/2011
```

Adding some output statements to the class definition confirms the class code which is used at each stage.

Inheritance

Since the library has several types of resource, the detailed class design could be:

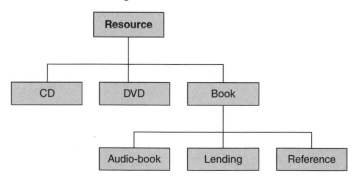

Each of the boxes represents a class in the *object-oriented design (OOD)*.

Various properties and methods will be defined for the RESOURCE class. RESOURCE is the *parent* *class* or *superclass*. The other classes then inherit from this parent class.

In practice this means that, for example, the CD class will have properties and methods of its own, but it also inherits the properties and methods from the RESOURCE parent class.

The diagram is called an *inheritance diagram*. Inheritance can always be clarified by labelling each branch with the term 'is a'.

✓ a DVD is a resource
✓ an audio-book is a book
✓ and several others.

Inheritance is defining a class and then using it to build a hierarchy of descendant classes. Each *descendant subclass* will inherit the properties and methods of a parent class.

21.3 Interpret and create class and object diagrams

A formal diagram showing the class name, its properties and methods is called a *class diagram*.

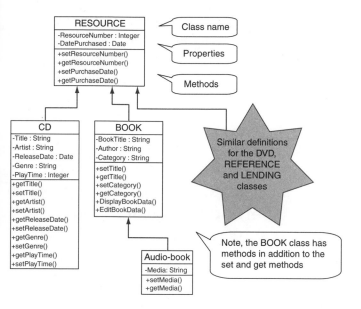

Object diagram

An *object diagram* shows the data values for an actual *instance* of an object.

The diagram shows the properties of the object CD Rubber Sole by the Beatles.

The syllabus has covered some of the fundamentals of the Unified Modelling Language (UML) which has become an industry standard for object-oriented design.

A full coverage of UML is outside the scope of this syllabus but is a topic a student would expect to cover in any Higher Education Computer Science course.

21.4 Declarative languages

Prolog is a declarative language, or a 'logic programming' language.

Given the necessary facts and rules, Prolog will use deductive reasoning to solve programming problems.

Note

Do not confuse declarative languages with 'declaring' variables in a high-level procedural program.

This is in contrast to traditional computer languages, such as Pascal or Visual Basic which are procedural languages. In procedural languages, the programmer must provide step-by-step statements that tell the computer exactly how to solve a given problem. In other words, the programmer must know how to solve the problem before the computer can do it.

Compare this to the Prolog programmer, who only needs to supply a description of the problem and the ground rules for solving it. From there Prolog is left to determine how to go about finding a solution.

A Prolog program for a given application will typically require only one tenth as many program lines as the corresponding high-level language program.

Prolog is a very important tool in programming *artificial intelligence* applications and in the development of *expert systems*.

Prolog stands for Programming in Logic. With Prolog you arrive at solutions by logically inferring one thing from something already known. Typically, a Prolog program is not a sequence of actions, it is:

- ✓ a collection of *facts*
- ✓ with *rules* for drawing conclusions from those facts.

Prolog is based on a formal system called *predicate logic*. Predicate logic is a way of making it clear how reasoning is done. Predicate logic was developed to easily convey logic-based ideas into a written form. In predicate logic, you first eliminate all unnecessary words from your sentences. You then transform the sentence, placing the relationship first and grouping the objects after the relationship. The objects then become arguments that the relationship acts upon.

For example the following sentences are transformed into predicate logic syntax:

Natural Language	Predicate Logic
An open-top car is fun	fun(open_top_car).
An orange is healthy food	healthy_food(orange).

Facts

The above two statements are facts.

Rules enable you to infer one fact from other facts.

Here are some rules concerning a "likes" relation:
Cindy likes everything that Bill likes.
Hilary likes everything that is green.

Rules

To encode these same two rules above in Prolog, you only need to change the syntax:

```
likes(cindy, Something) :-likes(bill,Something)
likes(hilary, Something):- green(Something)
```

The :- symbol is read as 'if', and it serves to separate the two parts of a rule.

Example 2

As a little more complicated and general question,
What does Bill like?
In Prolog syntax, we ask:

```
likes(bill, What).
```

You can also think of a rule as a procedure. In other words, these rules

```
likes(cindy, Something):- likes(bill,Something)
likes(hilary, Something):- green(Something).
```

also mean "To prove that Cindy likes something, prove that Bill likes that same thing" and "To prove that Hilary likes something, prove that it is green".

The use of Something is like using a *variable* in a procedural high-level language.

21.5 Showing an understanding of backtracking, instantiation and satisfying goals when referring to declarative languages

Queries or Setting a goal

Once we give Prolog a set of facts, we can proceed to ask questions concerning these facts; this is known as querying the Prolog program, or setting a *goal*.

The Prolog environment will include an *inference engine*, which is a process for reasoning logically about information. The inference engine includes a pattern matcher, which retrieves stored (known) information by matching answers to questions. Prolog tries to infer that a goal is true (in other words, answer a question) by questioning the set of facts and rules that are given in the program.

Example 1

In natural language we might ask:
Does Bill like Cindy?
In Prolog syntax, we ask Prolog:

```
likes(bill, cindy).
```

> In Prolog syntax What is effectively a variable …
>
> Variables in Prolog always begin with an upper-case letter or an underscore.

Given this query, Prolog would answer – 'Yes', because Prolog can find the fact that states this.

Prolog always looks for an answer to a query by starting at the top of the fact list. It looks at each fact until it reaches the bottom, where there are no more. Given the query about 'what bill likes' Prolog will return:

> What=cindy
> What=dog
> 2 solutions

This is because Prolog knows
likes(bill,cindy).
and,
likes(bill,dog).

Example 3

What does Cindy like?
  In Prolog:

> likes(cindy,What).

Prolog would answer:

> What=bill
> What=cindy
> What=dogs
> 3 solutions

This is because Prolog knows that Cindy likes Bill, and that Cindy likes what Bill likes, and that Bill likes Cindy and dogs.

Example 4

A knowledge base is designed to give advice on whether a person may legally drive a certain class of vehicle. The following partially completed knowledge base has some of these facts and rules. (They have been numbered for easy reference.)

> 1 age(edward,20)
> 2 age(robert,19)
> 3 age(flora,17)
> 4 age(emma,17)
> 5 age(andrew,16)
> 6 minimum_age(motor_cycle,16)
> 7 minimum_age(car,17)
> 8 minimum_age(heavy_goods_vehicle 20)
> 9 passed_test(edward, heavy_goods_vehicle)

Consider these queries:

> ? permitted_to_drive (robert, motor_cycle)

Returns the answer 'yes' using rule 15 and facts 2, 6 and 13.

> ? permitted_to_drive (emma, V)

Returns 'car' using rule 14 and fact 11.

> 10 passed_test(andrew,motor_cycle)
> 11 passed_test(emma, car)
> 12 hasprovisional_licence(andrew)
> 13 hasprovisional licence(robert)
> 14 permitted_to_drive(X,V) If passed_test(X,V)
> 15 permitted_to_drive(X,V) If hasprovisional_licence (X)
>   And age(X,A)
>   And minimum_age (V,L) And A >= L

Facts

✓ Fact 1 means that Edward is 20 years old
✓ Fact 6 means the minimum age for driving a motor-cycle is 16
✓ Fact 10 means Andrew has passed the driving test for a motor-cycle
✓ Fact 12 means that Andrew has a provisional driving licence.

Rules

✓ Rule 14 means that person X may drive a vehicle V if person X has passed the test for a vehicle of class V
✓ Rule 15 means that person X may drive a vehicle V if person X has a provisional licence and is old enough to drive a vehicle of class V.

> ? permitted_to_drive (flora, car)

Consider the query:
  Means, is Flora permitted to drive a car?
  The program would first look at rule 14 and then scan the facts to see if Flora has passed the test for a car. The answer is 'no', so rule 15 is examined. The facts are scanned again to check if Flora has a provisional licence. No relevant fact is found so the program returns 'no'.

Backtracking

Backtracking is a technique for solving a problem which is not restricted to computation. If you have even attempted a crossword or Suduko puzzle then at some point you have applied the technique of backtracking to test a possible solution based on data (words or numbers) which you already have or are suggested as possible solutions.

Consider the following knowledge base:

```
birthday(tom)
birthday(mai)
birthday(sami)
happy(jane)
happy(sami)
happy(terry)
```

with the rule:

```
hold_party(X) :- birthday(X) ,
happy(X)
```

Consider the goal: `hold_party(Who)`

Prolog will consider the first part of the `hold_party` rule and find the clause `birthday(tom)`. It must then search for a clause `happy(tom)` which it fails to find.

The inference engine must then backtrack (i.e. start again) with the clause `birthday(mai)`.

It searched the remaining clauses and fails to find `happy(mai)` so again the goal is not meet.

Backtracking to `birthday(smai)` and searching it now finds `happy(smai)` and so the goal is meet.

Attempting to backtrack again fails to find any other `birthday()` clauses.

So the query/goal has one solution: `Who = sami`

Progress Check 21.3

Study the following knowledge base.

```
1    male(kai).
2    male(john).
3    male(ken).
4    female(tansy).
5    female(tadi).
6    female(natene).
```

```
7     female(yenene).
8     plays(yenene, tennis).
9     plays(tadi, tennis).
10    plays(tadi, golf).
11    plays(ken, rugby).
12    plays(natene, hockey).
13    plays(natene, golf).
14    plays(tansy, golf).
15    plays(ken, football).
16    plays(natene,tennis).
12    likes(yenene, X) :- female(X), plays(X, golf).
18    likes(natene, X) :- male(X), plays(X, rugby).
19    likes(tansy, X) :- male(X), plays(X, tennis).
```

The comma is read as 'and'

(a)   Explain in words 16.
(b)   What is the output from the following goals?

✓   plays(tansy, Y)
✓   likes(yenene, A)

(c)   Write a new rule which states:

"Ken likes all females and males who like golf".

Progress Check 21.4

Study the following knowledge base.

```
1     male(adan).
2     male(alano).
3     male(emidio).
4     male(gael).
5     female(celia).
6     female(chelo).
7     female(malona).
8     male(xavier)
9     male(angel)
10    female(sofia)
11    parents(chelo, celia, adan).
12    parents(emidio, celia, gael).
13    parents(alano, malona, angel).
14    parents(adan, malona, sofia).
15    parents(emidio, chelo, xavier).
16    sister_of(X,Y) :- female(X), parents(A,B,X),
      parents(A,B,Y).
17    brother_of(X,Y) :- male(X), parents(A,B,X),
      parents(A,B,Y).
18    siblings(X,Y) :- sister_of(X,Y), brother_of(Y,X).
19    siblings(X,Y) :- brother_of(X,Y), sister_of(Y,X).
```

(a)   Explain fact 7.
(b)   Explain fact 11.
(c)   Is 17 a fact or a rule?
(d)   Explain rule 19.
(e)   What is the output for the following queries?

✓   parents(Who, malona, angel)
✓   parents(sofia, X, Y)

21.6 Procedural programming

Consider the following task. We are to write a program to demonstrate two different sort algorithms.

This is a simple demonstration program designed to carry out a selection sort or quick sort. The design is shown below.

The program solution is designed as a series of modules and these modules will match exactly with the procedures coded.

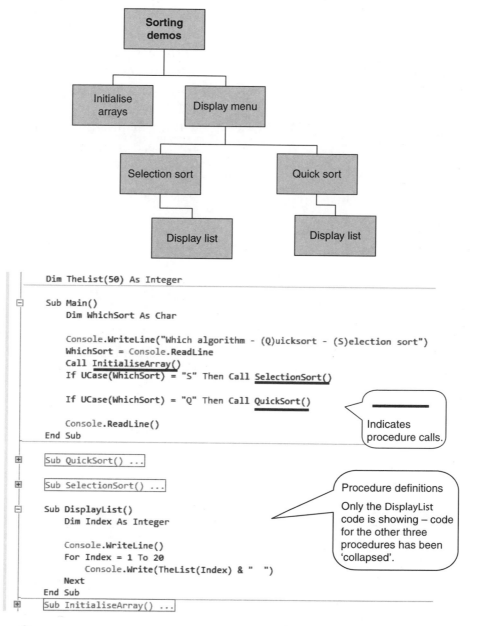

21.7 Stepwise refinement

In the sort demonstration task the solution was designed with procedures and demonstrates some good code efficiency. The procedure `DisplayList` is called from both the `SelectionSort` and `QuickSort` procedures.

```
Sub SelectionSort()
    Dim SortedListPosn, InsertPosn As Integer
    Dim Index, ShufflePosn As Integer
    Dim CurrentValue As Integer
    Dim InsertPosnFound As Boolean

    For Index = 2 To 9
        CurrentValue = TheList(Index)
    ...
End Sub
```

This shows the first few lines of the SelectionSort procedure.

21.8 Standard programming techniques

The procedure code above has 'hard coded' the name of the array to be sorted, i.e. TheList. Its upper bound is also hard coded.

This would be:

Is it possible that the SelectionSort procedure could be coded so that the procedure could be used for any array and of any size?

> **← Look Back**
>
> To Chapter 12 for procedures and functions that use parameters.

The answer is 'yes' and it requires that the values which will change must be passed into the procedure header as *parameters*.

The design for the procedure header is shown below using pseudocode:

This code now has the major benefit that this SelectionSort procedure could now be used within any program to sort any array of integers of any size.

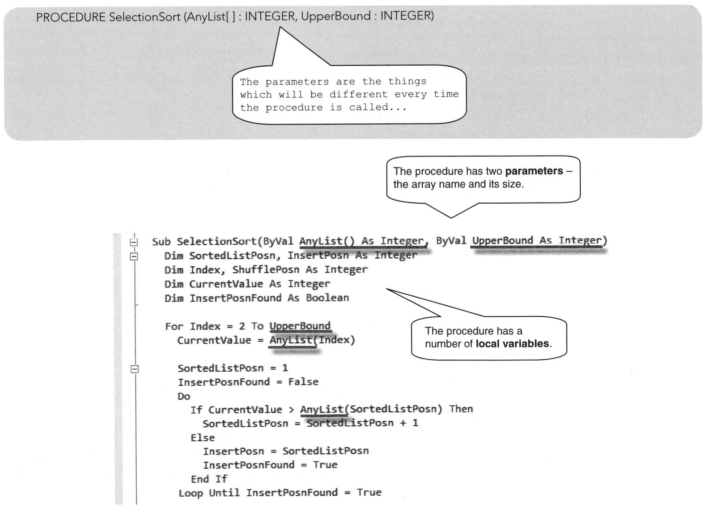

```
PROCEDURE SelectionSort (AnyList[ ] : INTEGER, UpperBound : INTEGER)
```

The parameters are the things which will be different every time the procedure is called...

The procedure has two **parameters** – the array name and its size.

```
Sub SelectionSort(ByVal AnyList() As Integer, ByVal UpperBound As Integer)
    Dim SortedListPosn, InsertPosn As Integer
    Dim Index, ShufflePosn As Integer
    Dim CurrentValue As Integer
    Dim InsertPosnFound As Boolean

    For Index = 2 To UpperBound
        CurrentValue = AnyList(Index)

        SortedListPosn = 1
        InsertPosnFound = False
        Do
            If CurrentValue > AnyList(SortedListPosn) Then
                SortedListPosn = SortedListPosn + 1
            Else
                InsertPosn = SortedListPosn
                InsertPosnFound = True
            End If
        Loop Until InsertPosnFound = True
```

The procedure has a number of **local variables**.

```
        For ShufflePosn = Index To (InsertPosn + 1) Step -1
            AnyList(ShufflePosn) = AnyList(ShufflePosn - 1)
        Next
        AnyList(InsertPosn) = CurrentValue
    Next

    Call DisplayList()

End Sub
```

> These values are the two **arguments** for the procedure call i.e. the actual data values the procedure will use.

The procedure is then called with the statement:

```
If UCase(Choice) = "S" Then Call SelectionSort(TheList, 50)
```

The `DisplayList` procedure must similarly pass into its procedure header the name of the array and the upper bound.

21.9 Stack data structure

The above code example shows that the procedure SelectionSort has itself a call to a procedure DisplayList.

The simplest case will be a procedure call from the main program which – once the procedure code has been executed – must return the flow of control to the next statement in the main program. The key issue here is that the 'point of return' must be remembered.

The case above is more complicated as, before the procedure SelectionSort is completed, a second procedure call is made. Consider the order in which these return points are remembered and the order in which they will later be needed by the execution. This should tell you that they must be managed in the order "the last return point remembered and stored will be the first which it retrieved". That is 'last in – first out'. The return addresses therefore must be managed by a **stack**.

If the procedure calls involved parameter passing then the parameter arguments must also be stored along with the return address.

21.10 The concepts of immediate, direct, indirect, indexed and relative addressing of memory when referring to low-level languages

A typical processor instruction set would support many modes of addressing and there would be assembly language instructions for each. All of these are best illustrated with examples. We shall assume that the architecture has a singe general purpose register – the **Accumulator**.

> ### ← Look Back
>
> To Chapter 18 where machine code and assembly languages were introduced.

Immediate addressing

There is no address as such involved. The operand is an actual number. Consider the assembly language instruction:

LDM #35

This is read as "Load the actual value 35 denary to the accumulator".

The hash symbol is used to clarify that this is an immediate value – although this is already clear from the LDM mnemonic.

Direct addressing

The assembly language instruction LDD 158 means:
   "Copy the contents of memory address 158 to the Accumulator"

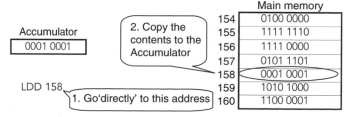

Indirect addressing

The assembly language instruction LDD 158 means:
   "Go to address 158 – the contents of 158 is the address to go to – then copy the contents of this address to the Accumulator".

The address shown as the operand acts as a 'forwarding address'.

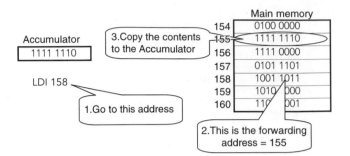

Indexed addressing

This assumes that the processor has a special purpose register called the *Index Register (IR)*.

The assembly language instruction **LDX 158** means:

"Look at the contents of the Index Register. Add this number to the operand address – copy the contents of this calculated address to the Accumulator".

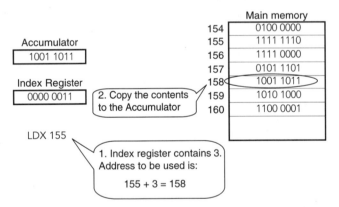

Relative addressing

Appreciate that when a machine code program is executing the program is a sequence of instructions held in main memory.

Hence, if the first instruction was stored at main memory address and a particular instruction (in assembly language) was:

```
LDR +95
```

"Copy of the contents of the memory address 95 locations further on from the location containing this instruction".

> ⬅ **Look Back**
>
> To Chapter 19 for the use of relative addresing by the operating system for memory management.

The use of relative addressing is very important as it makes it possible for programs to be loaded at any particular start address in memory, i.e. provides for re-locatable code.

> **Progress Check 21.5**
>
> Trace the execution of the following assembly language program showing the changing contents of the Accumulator and memory address 500.

LDD	130	130	0000 0011
INC		131	1000 0111
STO	500	132	1111 1111
LDI	131	133	0010 1011
ADD	500	134	1110 1110
STO	500	135	0000 1000
		136	0000 1010
		500	0000 0000

Accumulator	Memory address 500

21.11 Backus-Naur Form (BNF)

Backus-Naur Form is a special language called a *meta-language* which is used to describe the syntax and composition of statements which make up a high-level programming language.

> ⬅ **Look Back**
>
> To Chapter 16 where BNF was mentioned as a tool for describing the syntax of a high-level programming language.

A syntax element is enclosed-between the < > characters and a typical BNF statement would be:

```
<digit> ::= 0 | 1 | 2 | 3 | 4 | 5 | 6 | 7 | 8 | 9
<binarydigit> ::= 0 | 1
```

This first statement reads as <digit> 'is defined as' 0 or 1 or 2 or .... 8 or 9.

Since each of the terms on the right-hand side of each rule cannot be broken down further 0, 1. 2 etc., are called *terminal symbols*.

A rule definition may be recursive.

Consider this definition to describe identifier names for a programming language.

```
<letter> ::= A|B|C .... |Z|a|b|c .... z
<digit>  ::= 0 | 1 | 2 | 3 | 4 | 5 | 6 | 7 | 8 | 9
<identifier> ::= <letter> | <identifier><letter> |
                 <identifier><digit>
```

The third rule states that a valid identifier name can be either:

✓ a single letter character
✓ or, a letter followed by one or many letter characters
✓ or, a letter followed by one or more digit characters.

The process of analysing whether or not a given identifier is valid (following the given rules) is called *parsing* the expression.

Example 1

Consider identifier name She1 – is this valid?

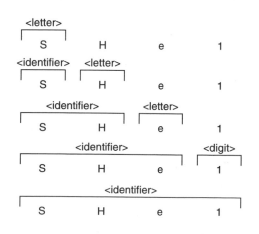

This demonstrates that the expression is a valid identifier name.

Example 2

Consider identifier name 1he – is this valid?

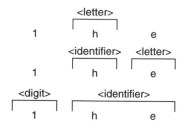

Which is neither of the two permitted identifier formats. Therefore invalid.

Progress Check 21.6

The parsing of BNF expressions is best illustrated by examples:

```
<product_code> ::= <letter> | <letter><letter> |
<letter><letter><letter>
<letter> ::= A | B | C .... | Z | a | b | c .... z
```

Which of the following product codes are valid?
(a) AJA
(b) D5R
(c) SA

Progress Check 21.7

The following set of rules define the format expected for a letter list.

```
<comma> ::= ,
<digit> ::= 0 | 1 | 2 | 3 | 4 | 5 | 6 | 7 | 8 | 9 |
<cap_letter> ::= A | B | C | D | E | ... | X | Y | Z
<lower_letter> ::= a | b | c | d | e | ..... | x | y | z
<valid_character> ::= <digit> | <lower_letter>
<list> ::= <valid_character> | <valid_character>,<list>
```

Which of the following are valid lists ?
(a) S
(b) p
(c) s, y, u,
(d) s, h, y, 4, 6

21.12 Syntax diagrams

Syntax diagrams were used extensively in early books for high-level programming languages.

The following examples illustrate the diagrams needed to define the syntax allowed for an identifier.

First define a digit character.

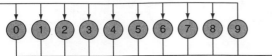

The syntax diagram is always read from left to right and is designed to show here that a digit is always exactly one of the ten characters shown.

The second diagram to define a letter is read in exactly the same way. We conclude a letter is always exactly one of the upper or lower case letters.

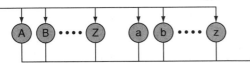

These definitions are then used to define an identifier.

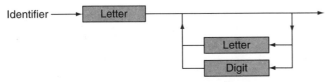

It should be clear from the third diagram that the following identifiers are VALID – INVALID

Suggested Identifier		Explanation
P	VALID	
MyObject	VALID	
8index	INVALID	Must start with at least one letter character
Count	VALID	
My_Object	INVALID	Contains the <underscore> character which has not been defined
Loop5times	VALID	

Progress Check 21.8

Show what new/amended syntax diagrams are need if the language is allow the use of the <underscore> character within an identifier name.

21.13 Reverse Polish notation

When we were taught the fundamentals of math we wrote expressions using infix notation.

Typically:

$$Area = Length \times Width$$

That is the **operator** – the multiply sign – is positioned between the two **operands** (Length and Width).

The meaning for this expression is clear. However some expressions will require the use of brackets to convey the order in which the component parts must be evaluated.

$$Z = (x + y) / 5$$

The brackets are needed here to make it clear that the sum of x+y must be worked out first.

Reverse Polish (or postfix notation)

Here the operand is written following the two operands.

$$Area = Length\ Width \times$$

And for the second expression above:

$$x\ y + 5 /$$

Benefits

Reverse Polish notation has the major advantage over infix in that the meaning for any expression is clear without the use of brackets.

Study carefully these examples:

Infix expression	Postfix expression
$(8 - 4) * 5$	$8\ 4 - 5\ *$
$(3p + 5) / (p - z)$	$3\ p * 5 + p\ z - /$
$2*7 - 8/4$	$2\ 7 * 8\ 4 / -$
$7^4 - 9/3$	$7\ 4 \wedge 9\ 3 / -$

21.14 Convert between reverse Polish notation and the infix form of algebraic expressions using trees and stacks

A binary tree can be used to represent expressions both in infix and reverse Polish notation.

Consider the expression: $(3p + 5) / (p - z)$

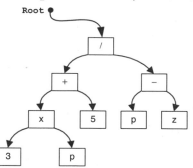

In Chapter 20 we developed a recursive algorithm for traversing a binary tree.

If we use an in-order traversal algorithm, the values in the expression will be output in the order which gives the infix expression.

Progress Check 21.9

Here is the in-order traversal algorithm. Check that the in-order traversal algorithm outputs the infix expression.

```
InOrderTraversal(Root)
  IF Root.LeftPointer <> Null
    THEN
       // move left
       InOrderTraversal(Root.LeftPointer)
  ENDIF
  OUTPUT Root.Data
  IF Root.RightPointer <> Null
    THEN
    // move right
    InOrderTraversal(Root.RightPointer)
  ENDIF
ENDPROCEDURE
```

Post-order traversal

If we simply change the order of doing things for the traversal algorithm, we shall traverse the tree in a different order.

```
PostOrderTraversal(Root)
  IF Root.LeftPointer <> Null
    THEN
       InOrderTraversal(Root.LeftPointer)
  ENDIF
  IF Root.RightPointer <> Null
    THEN
    InOrderTraversal(Root.RightPointer)
  ENDIF
  OUTPUT Root.Data
ENDPROCEDURE
```

We have effectively changed the order to 'left – right – root'. The traversal of the given tree will produce the following traversal and output.

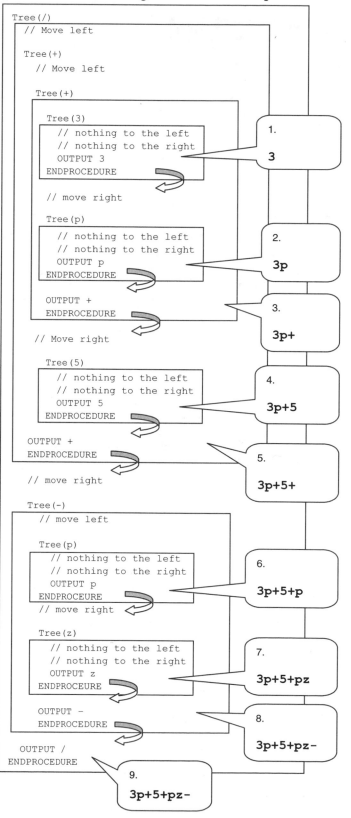

The trace confirms that for the `PostOrderTraversal` algorithm, the expression is output in reverse Polish.

Progress Check 21.10

1. Evaluate the following reverse Polish expressions:
   (a) 11 6 – 5 *
   (b) 3 4 ^ 9 / 3 + 4 /
   (c) 14 6 – 8 *
2. Write these expressions in reverse Polish.
   (a) (a + b) / 6
   (b) (2a + b)³

✎ Note

Use the ^ symbol for 'to the power of'.

Evaluating a reverse Polish expression

This will demonstrate another advantage of the use of reverse Polish. The elements which make up the expression can be processed using a stack.

Consider the evaluation of the expression:
(9 * 7 + 2) / 5
In reverse Polish this becomes: 9 7 * 2 + 5 /
The method will be:

✓ push operands onto the stack in sequence
✓ when an operator is met:
   ➤ pop two values
   ➤ evaluate
   ➤ push the result onto the stack.

Trace the execution of the evaluation of:
9 7 * 2 + 5 / gives:

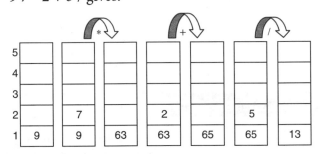

Progress Check 21.11

Trace the changing contents of a stack when it is used to evaluate the reverse Polish expression:
2 4 ^ 5 – 2 /

Exam-style Questions

1. The contents of the Current Instruction Register (CIR) for one instruction are ADD 01011011.
   (Note: The 'ADD' operation would normally be stored as a binary code.)

   (a) Explain what is meant by a mnemonic and why it is used.

   ....

   ....

   ....

   .... [3]

   (b) Describe how this address is used if it is an indirect address.

   ....

   ....

   .... [2]

   (c) Describe how this address is used if it is an indexed address.

   ....

   ....

   .... [2]

   Cambridge 9691 Specimen Paper 3 Q4

2. Describe the characteristics of the following programming paradigms:

(a) Low-level

....

.... [2]

(b) Object-oriented

....

.... [2]

(c) Declarative

....

.... [2]

(d) Procedural

....

.... [2]

Cambridge 9691 Paper 32 Q8 November 2011

3. In a particular object-oriented programming language the classes are defined for use in a payroll program.

```
                    ┌─────────────────────┐
                    │ Employee            │
                    ├─────────────────────┤
                    │ Name                │
                    │ Address             │
                    ├─────────────────────┤
                    │ OutputData()        │
                    │ GetName()           │
                    │ GetAddress()        │
                    └─────────────────────┘

   ┌─────────────────────┐         ┌─────────────────────┐
   │ SalesPerson         │         │ Administrator       │
   ├─────────────────────┤         ├─────────────────────┤
   │ Basicsalary         │         │ Payscale            │
   │ %Commission         │         │ Responsiblity       │
   ├─────────────────────┤         ├─────────────────────┤
   │ OutputData()        │         │ OutputData()        │
   │ GetBasicsalary()    │         │ GetPayscale()       │
   │ Get%Commission()    │         │ GetResponsibility() │
   └─────────────────────┘         └─────────────────────┘
```

With reference to the diagram explain the terms:

(a) data encapsulation

....

.... [2]

(b) inheritance

....

.... [2]

Cambridge 9691 Specimen Paper 3 Q8(a)

Databases

22

22.1 Flat files and relational databases

What is a Database?

A database is a collection of related data. The data could relate to (for example) a firm's customers and each customer data is a *record*. Each record will store the same items of data, for example, customer name, address etc., and these are called *fields*.

Database software has been commercially available for over forty years and early software simply mirrored on the computer what a user would have done using a card index system. The cards would have a header line and the cards would then be filed in some determined order, for example, Customer name.

That was fine if we want to find a particular customer by name but what if we want to find the firm based at 13 The High St or the company with the contact person called Jamie Edwards? The major limitation of a manual card index is that the cards can only be held in one particular order and so can only be searched on one data item.

Look Back

To Chapter 13 for discussion on different types of file organisation and access.

Flat files

Before database software a database application would have been programmed and constructed using one or more *flat files*.

The record structure would first be designed. For example, for our customer database the field structure would be:

✓ CustomerName
✓ ContactPerson
✓ Address
✓ Town
✓ AccountCustomer.

The file organisation could be any of those studied in Section 2-3, i.e. serial, sequential, index sequential or direct access.

A major limitation of any solution based on files is that the record structure is fixed.

If after using the database for (for example) six months, we wanted to add a field this would require a considerable amount of programming to change the original programs.

22.2 Designing a simple relational database to third normal form (3NF)

Relational database

> Relational databases were developed based on the research done by computer scientist Ted Codd.

An *entity* is some thing about which we store data.

Relational database software is based on the approach that the data will consist of entities.

For an order processing scenario the entities could be:

- ✓ customer
- ✓ product
- ✓ order.

Each of these entities will then have its set of fields and we shall again use the term record to describe the data about an entity. Database theory calls the fields *attributes*. The data for each entity is stored in a *table*. Tables can be viewed just like a spreadsheet grid and so each record in a table will be displayed as a row in the table.

Data modelling

Let's decide what fields we need for each entity for the order processing application.

Customer table		
Attribute	Data Type	Comments
CustomerName	STRING	
CustomerAddress	STRING	
CustomerTown	STRING	
ContactPerson	STRING	
AccountCustomer	BOOLEAN	Some customer are given credit and invoiced (i.e. 'pay later') for orders –the attribute is assigned TRUE. Others must 'pay with order' – the attribute is assigned FALSE.

Product table		
Field	Data Type	Comments
ProductID	STRING	Typical code is 0987
Description	STRING	
TypeOfItem	CHAR	E – electrical, C – clothing etc.
RetailPrice	CURRENCY	
InStock	BOOLEAN	

Order table		
Field	Data Type	Comments
OrderNo	STRING	Typically 00987
OrderDate	DATE	
CustomerName	STRING	
ProductID	STRING	Typical code is 0987
Quantity	INTEGER	The amount ordered

> ### ← Look Back
>
> To Chapter 3 as the data types will be exactly the same as you have used for programming.

This design assumes that an order is always for one product only.

22.3 Primary, secondary and foreign keys

Primary key

It is a fundamental rule of relational database design that *every record in a table must be unique*.

Either:

There will be an attribute which will 'do this job' for us – We shall assume that all the customer names are different, hence the `CustomerName` is chosen as the primary key for the `Customer` table.

Or,

We shall allocate a reference number to an entity to ensure all the records are different. `ProductID` is the primary key for table `Product`.

Secondary keys

Part of the table design process will be to decide which attributes are likely to be ones where users will be frequently searching using this attribute. For example in the `Order` table we may frequently search on customer name, but not the quantity.

Hence we would decide to index the `CustomerName` attribute. (As `OrderNo` is the primary key this attribute is already indexed).

The database software will update the list of indexes every time the data in the `Order` table is changed. *Indexing is used make data retrieval faster*.

Any attribute which is indexed (and is not the primary key) is called a *secondary key.*

A table can have any number of secondary keys – but, every index has to be updated when the database data changes, so there is a trade-off between the processing and time taken to keep the

indexes up-to-date and the fast data retrieval times (for example, when running a query).

Table notation

Use the following notation to describe the design for a table. The attribute underlined indicates the primary key.

Customer (<u>CustomerName</u>, CustomerAddress, CustomerTown, ContactPerson, AccountCustomer)

Product (<u>ProductID</u>, Description, TypeOfItem, RetailPrice, InStock)

Order (<u>OrderNo</u>, OrderDate , CustomerName, ProductID, Quantity)

> ### ✎ Note
>
> Some designers will show each relationship as a separate E-R diagram (not all on one diagram as shown).
>
> Each relationship has been given a description
>
> ✓ Places
> ✓ AppearsOn
> ✓ Receives

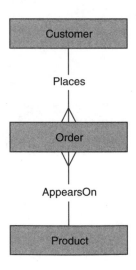

Are the tables related?

Yes, because:

✓ one customer (over a period of time) will place many orders
✓ one product will appear on many orders.

> ### Progress Check 22.1
>
> You are designing a table to store student data for a school admin system.
>
> The table includes the following attributes.
> `PupilNumber, StudentName, Form, Address, YearEntered`
>
> (a) Which attribute will be the primary key?
> (b) Suggest one attribute which should be set up as a secondary index. Why?

Relationships

A link between two tables is called a *relationship*. Relationships are of three kinds:

✓ **1-to-1:** which are rare and probably only because the two tables were created at different times

✓ **1-to-many:** the most common type of relationship

> ### ✎ Note
>
> The two relationships for this order processing scenario are both 1-to-many.

✓ **Many-to-Many:** We could have added a third relationship to our E-R diagram which shows:

"Many customers will receive many products".

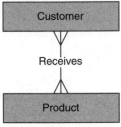

However, it is not possible to implement a many-to-many relationship with relational database software.

Had the designer started with this many-to-many relationship, the strategy must be to re-design by introducing a third table with two 1-to-many relationships (as in the original design).

22.4 Entity-Relationship (E-R) diagrams

The entities and the relationships are shown on an entity-relationship diagram.

✓ The entities have a name

✓ The relationship line shows the degree of the relationship

✓ The relationship is labelled to indicate its purpose.

Foreign key

How are relationships formed?

The primary key attribute in the 'one side' table will link to (the same) attribute in the 'many side' table. This attribute in the 'many side' table is called the *foreign key*.

"One customer (over a period of time) will place many orders".

Primary key `CustomerName` (in the `Customer` table) will link to foreign key `CustomerName` (in the `Order` table).

"One product is present on many orders".

Primary key `ProductID` (in the `Product` table) links to foreign key `ProductID` (in the `Order` table).

Progress Check 22.2

Consider this scenario:

A training agency offers courses in software skills for popular PC software. Courses run for 1 to 5 days. Each course is delivered by one trainer. Courses offered are shown in table `Course`. Each course is available many times throughout the year and this course schedule data is stored in table `CourseDiary`.

Course

CourseCode	CourseTitle	Duration
001	Excel - Beginners	1
002	Excel - Intermediate	2
003	Excel - Advanced	3
004	Access - Beginners	2
005	Access - Intermediate	3
006	Access - Advanced	3
007	Access - Programming with VBA	
008	Word - Beginners	
009	Word - Intermediate	

Trainer

TrainerName	HomePhoneN
Adam Jones	9789 675463
Sarah Jamel	7756 45632
Dave Durrant	7866 54612
Li Chu	0771 33412

CourseDiary

CourseCode	CourseDate	Trainer
001	21/07/2011	Sarah Jamel
001	01/05/2011	Adam Jones
001	13/07/2001	Adam Jones
001	11/06/2001	Adam Jones
002	14/05/2011	Adam Jones
002	01/05/2011	Sarah Jamel
003	14/08/2011	Sarah Jamel
004	06/05/2011	Li Chu
005	17/06/2001	Li Chu
006	27/07/2001	Li Chu
007	14/09/2011	Li Chu

(a) What attribute is used for the primary key of table `Course`?

(b) What data type was used for the `Duration` attribute?

(c) Suggest two other attributes which the company might store about each trainer.

(d) What will be a suitable primary key for the `Trainer` table?

(e) What will be a suitable primary key for `CourseDiary`?

(f) Describe two relationships which exist between the tables `Trainer`, `Course` and `CourseDiary`.

(g) The `CourseDiary` table has two foreign keys. What are they?

(h) Draw the entity-relationship diagram for this scenario.

Duplicated data

Note, we did not have the `CourseName` in the `CourseDiary` table – the `CourseCode` is sufficient for us to be clear what course is referred to. Similarly, the `CourseDiary` table did not store any other data about the trainer – the trainer name is sufficient.

A golden rule of relational database design is to *avoid unnecessary duplicated data.*

If data does become duplicated then some of it will be *redundant*.

22.5 Database Management System (DBMS)

Software products like Microsoft Access are well suited to applications which store thousands of records, but what if the number of records is of a much larger scale?

A registration system in a large College which registers students for every lesson in the day will generate over 1000 records in a day, and that is just for the actual lesson attendance data.

Software used for these applications is called a *Database Management System (DBMS).*

> Examples of DBMS software includes:
> SQLServer from Microsoft – Oracle – MySQL.
> MySQL was developed from the free movement and is available as a free download.

The features we would expect a DBMS to provide are:

✓ basic design of the data model
  ➢ i.e. the tables, relationships

✓ reporting features such as queries and printed reports

✓ the setting of access levels
  ➢ for the College registration system:

♦ students will only be allowed to view their attendance record

♦ a teacher is the only database user allowed to fill in the electronic register – and then for their classes only

♦ a *database administrator (DBA)* is the only user allowed to generate the printed weekly reports

➢ the general rule will be that users have sufficient access to the data in order to 'do their job'

> If you want to use a real DMBS, then start with the (againfree) software XAMPP. It installs the mySQL database server together with the Apache web server which both run as a local server on the PC.

✓ the writing of application programs (in a high-level programming language) which connect to the various databases and then access and use this data

✓ change the data design
  ➢ the basic data table designs can be changed without the need to re-write any of the application program code; this is seen as a major advantage of using a database solution rather than flat files.

> 📖 **Later**
>
> See a summary of the advantages of using a 'database approach' rather than 'flat files' in Section 22.6.

Figure 22.1 illustrates some of these points for a typical business. There are many users each with different access to the data. The different users each uses applications programs – Program 1, Program 2 etc., – which have been developed for the company.

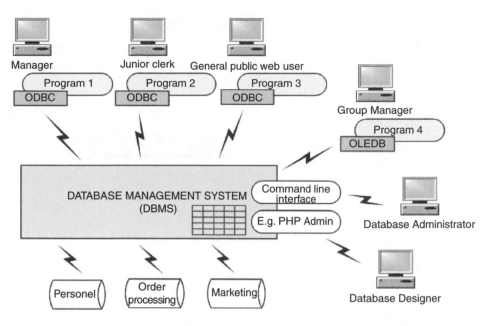

Figure 22.1 A typical DBMS

The administration of a DBMS is a major job role carried out by the *Database Administrator (DBA)*.

> ✎ **Note**
>
> Note, many of the features of a DBMS can be stated as advantages of using a 'database approach' rather than 'using flat files'.

Progress Check 22.3

Describe four features you find in a Database Management System.

22.6 'Database Approach' versus 'File based Approach'

When developing an application from scratch the developer would have to choose between using:

✓ conventional files
  ➢ serial/sequential/direct access files with programs then written which access these data files
✓ or, a Database Management System.

The following are key points to consider and ***all are in favour of using a DBMS.***

Program – Data Independence/Changing Data Requirements

The DBMS software stores not only the data itself but also the definition of the database(s) in a data dictionary (see later). Program-data independence is the separating out of the data definition and the programs which access the data. Changes to the structure of the data can be done quite independently of the programs (Program 1, Program 2 etc.) which access the existing data.

Example

An attribute is to be added to the customer table. Existing programs/queries/reports which access the existing attributes within the table will not require modification following the change(s) to the data structure.

Compare this to a file based approach where the description of the data is defined by 'data types' within the program code. Once a new field is added, all program code must be re-written to take account of the extra attribute(s).

Data integrity

Database Management Systems offer excellent validation support. The DBMS uses its data dictionary to perform validation checks on data entered into database. Validation checks are set up at the table design stage, and are effective every time a reference is made to that item of data. Relational databases are designed to avoid *data duplication*, *data redundancy* and *inconsistent data*.

> ← **Look Back**
>
> To Chapter 8 for discussion on Data validation.

> Compare this to a 'file based approach', where the validation checks have to be coded, and every time that data item is used, the validation checking code must be present as part of the program code.

Security

Since all data is centrally held within the DBMS, strategies for controlling the security of the data are much easier to implement than with a file based approach.

- ✓ Backup is a centralised task administered by the Database Administrator (DBA)
- ✓ Different users will be given different access rights (go back to the earlier discussion for the school registration database).

Concurrent access to data

That is the sharing of data by several terminal users at the same time.

DBMS software will manage the control of 'multi-user access' to the data with techniques such as *record locking* and file/table locking. A record will be locked if (for example) it is being edited by a user; it is not then available to any other users until the edit is completed.

Queries/Reports produced quickly

Since the DBMS has facilities such as queries (written in SQL or visually designed with QBE) and report generators, the time taken to create a new query is minimal.

See the use of a *Data Manipulation Language* which follows.

> Compare this to the time it would take to create a new query program using a file based approach.

Data dictionary

A complicated database may involve hundreds of tables. The data dictionary is a file containing all the data about the database design. It would not be available to users of the database – only the DBA.

> **Progress Check 22.4**
>
> Which of the following would be contained in the database's data dictionary?
>
> (a) The list of attributes used for all tables
> (b) Detail for all attributes; Data type – does it have a secondary index
> (c) The customer data
> (d) The results for all queries
> (e) Query descriptions.

22.7 Data description language (DDL)

The data dictionary contains the description for all the database tables and other components such as queries. What do these descriptions look like?

The standard language used by all modern database software is *Structured Query Language (SQL)*.

The following is the SQL script which would create the database tables `Product` and `Order` and then create the relationship between them.

```
Create Table Product (
  ProductID Char(4) Not Null,
  Description Char(50),
  TypeOfItem Char(1),
  RetailPrice Real,
  InStock Boolean,
Primary Key (ProductID);

Create Table Order (
  OrderNo Char(5) Not Null,
  CustomerName Char(50),
    ProductID Char(4),
    Quantity Int,
Primary Key (OrderNo);

Similar definition for table
  Customer... then,
```

```
Alter Table Order Add Foreign Key (ProductID) References Product (ProductID);
Alter Table Order Add Foreign Key (CustomerName) References
            Customer (CustomerName);
```

Top tip

There are large variations in the data type names used by different versions of SQL.

In the exam use the data types you are familiar with from programming.

For example, don't write int – use integer.

The DDL language keywords have been emboldened.

22.8 Data manipulation language (DML)

What Access is doing behind the scenes is writing a *SQL script* which will carry out the query which the user designed in a visual way.

The usual data manipulation language used by database software is SQL (the same as for DML). If you have used software such as Microsoft Access queries are created with 'point and click' features.

Example

Design a query which displays the dates on which the course with code 001 is offered.

The above screen shows the query being designed with the Query By Example (QBE) feature, i.e. 'point and click'.

When the user creates the database, the tables and the relationships the database software is transforming all the user's 'point and click' actions to generate a SQL script which will be run and perform the task indicated by the user.

```
SELECT CourseDiary.CourseCode, CourseDiary.CourseDate, CourseDiary.Trainer
FROM CourseDiary
WHERE CourseDiary.CourseCode="001";
```

SQL is the Data Manipulation Language (DML) used by Microsoft Access and most database and DBMS software.

22.9 Normalisation

If we return to the original task of designing the database, we must ask the question; "How do we know we have a design which will not result in duplicated data?

There are three formal rules called First, Second and Third Normal form (1NF, 2NF and 3NF) which we must use to check the final design.

Normalisation is the process – using a formal set of rules – which has to be followed to ensure that the data model produced (i.e. the table designs) are such that they will not give rise to duplicated (hence 'redundant') data.

A fully normalised set of tables will contain no redundant data.

Consider this scenario:

A firm encourages its staff to attend training courses. Each course has a unique course title and duration from 1 to 5 days. Some courses are offered more than once on different dates. Employees have a StaffID and their name recorded.

Data is recorded showing all courses attended by each employee.

First Normal Form

States "There should be no repeated groups of attributes".

Example

Consider the following incorrect table design for a staff record storing data for all courses attended by each employee.

```
StaffRecord (StaffID, StaffName, CourseTitle1, Date1, Duration1, CourseTitle2, Date2,
     Duration2, CourseTitle3, Date3, Duration3, etc.)
```

This design has the group of attributes `CourseTitle`, `SessionDate` and `Duration` repeated, and so the table is NOT in 1NF.

Some textbooks will indicate this repeated group of attributes with a table of data as shown below.

StaffID	StaffName	CourseTitle	SessionDate	Duration
037	Polly Earle	Managing People	12/03/2011	2
		Health and Safety 1	19/04/2011	1
		Health and Safety 2	23/12/2011	2
067	Will Harris	Health and Safety 1	19/04/2011	1
		Excel Stage 1	3/3/2011	2
184	Neal King	Marketing Stage 1	5/6/2011	2
		Excel Stage 1	3/3/2011	2
		Customer Care	11/5/2011	1

Solution? Create a second table to store the course attendances separately for each employee, and with a foreign key to link back to the original table.

```
StaffRecord (StaffID, StaffName, CourseTitle1, Date1, Duration1, CourseTitle2,
         Date2,Duration2, CourseTitle3, SessionDate3, etc.)
```

Becomes:

```
Staff (StaffID, StaffName)
StaffRecord (StaffID, CourseTitle,
   Date, Duration)
```

Second Normal Form (2NF)

States "The non-key attributes in the table must be dependent on knowing all of the primary key".

For tables which have a single value primary key, the table MUST be in 2NF.

Table Staff therefore must be in 2NF.

```
StaffRecord (StaffID, CourseTitle,
   Date, Duration)
```

But, consider:
Primary key (is a composite key) of `StaffID + CourseTitle + Date`.

There is one ***non-key attribute*** – Duration.

But, `Duration` will be known from knowing only the `CourseTitle` (i.e. only part of the primary key). Hence the table `StaffRecord` is not 2NF.

Solution? – Remove `Duration` and create a new table `CourseSession`.

```
StaffRecord (StaffID, CourseTitle, Date)
CourseSession (CourseTitle, Date, Duration)
```

Also, the `Duration` will be known by only knowing only the `CourseTitle`, so remove `Duration` to a new table `Course`.

```
Staff (StaffID, StaffName)
StaffRecord (StaffID, CourseTitle, Date)
CourseSession (CourseTitle, Date)
Course (CourseTitle, Duration)
```

Third Normal Form (3NF)

Like 2NF, third normal form is concerned with non-key attributes.

"There must not be a dependency between any non-key attributes".

Example

All three tables above have only one or no non-key attribute – therefore there cannot be two non-key attributes which are dependant. The conclusion is that all four tables are in 3NF.

Consider if we had stored more data items in the `Staff` table because the company has a single location in each of a number of different cities.

```
Staff (StaffID, StaffName, City,
CityAddress, Country)
```

Now we have four non-key attributes and there are dependencies between them.

For example, if we known the city we shall know the country – if we know the city we shall know the address.

Solution: Create a new table `Location`.

```
Location (City, CityAddress, Country)
```

We must then retain a foreign key of City in the Staff table to give:

```
Staff (StaffID, StaffName, City)
```

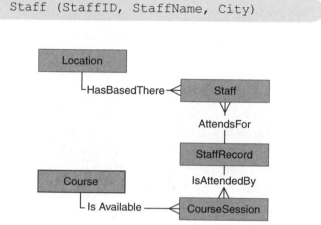

You should now check these final table designs to confirm all four tables are in 1NF, 2NF and 3NF.

```
Course (CourseTitle, Duration)
        1NF – there are no repeated groups.
        2NF – it has a single value primary key so must be in 2NF.
        3NF – it has only one non-key attribute.
    CourseSession (CourseTitle, Date)
        1NF – there are no repeated groups.
        2NF – there are no non-key attributes.
        3NF – there are no non-key attributes.
    Staff (StaffID, StaffName, City)
        1NF – there are no repeated groups.
        2NF – it has a single value primary key so must be in 2NF.
        3NF – there are two non-key attribute but they are not dependant. I.e. if we knew the name we would not know
        the city and vice-versa.
    Location (City, CityAddress, Country)
        1NF – there are no repeated groups.
        2NF – It does not have a composite primary key – therefore must be in 2NF.
        3NF – there are two non-key attributes but they are not dependant.
    StaffRecord (StaffID, CourseTitle, Date)
        1NF – there are no repeated groups.
        2NF – there are no non-key attributes.
        3NF – there are no non-key attributes.
```

Conclusion

All five tables are in Normal Form (1NF and 2NF and 3NF), and so the design will not result in redundant or duplicated data in the database. We conclude that the tables are *fully normalised*.

Progress Check 22.5

1. Which of these are true statements?

   (a) "There must be no repeated group of attributes" – this is Second Normal Form.
   (b) Non-key attributes means those which are not part of the primary key.
   (c) Both 2NF and 3NF are concerned with non-key attributes.
   (d) A table with a composite primary key using two attributes must be in 2NF.
   (e) A table with a single attribute primary key must be in 2NF.

2. Consider this scenario:

   Student (StudentID, StudentName, TutorName, TutorInitials, TutorRoom)

   All students have a tutor. Tutors are referred to by the three initials of their name which are unique. For example, Tutor Will Smythe

---

has initials WSM. All tutors have their own separate tutor room.

Which of these are true statements?

(a) The primary key of student is StudentID.
(b) The table is not in 3NF since TutorName is dependant on TutorInitials.
(c) The table is not in 3NF since TutorRoom is dependant on TutorInitials.
(d) The table is not in 3NF because it has a single attribute primary key.

   Student (StudentID, StudentName, TutorInitials)
   Tutor (TutorInitials, TutorName, TutorRoom)

(e) What attribute in Student acts as a foreign key?
(f) Describe the relationship between these two tables.

✍ Note

These two sample questions on databases are very different.

This question gives you a scenario and asks you to apply your knowledge about database design.

The second question which follows is entirely knowledge recall.

Exam-style Questions

1. A bookshop contains a number of books.
   Each BOOK is about a single SUBJECT. There may be more than one BOOK about each SUBJECT. A BOOK may have more than one AUTHOR and each AUTHOR may have written more than one BOOK.

   (a) Draw an entity relationship (E–R) diagram to represent this data model in third normal form and label the relationships.

[7]

(b) Using examples from this database, explain what is meant by:

(i) a primary key,

....

.... [2]

(ii) a secondary key,

....

.... [2]

(iii) a foreign key.

....

.... [2]

Cambridge 9691 Specimen Paper 3 Q2

Read carefully, each part requires:

♦ an explanation
♦ an example from the Bookshop database

2. (a) Describe the function and purpose of the following parts of a database management system (DBMS):

(i) data dictionary

....

.... [2]

(ii) data description language

....

.... [2]

(iii) data manipulation language

....

.... [2]

(b) Three advantages of using a relational database rather than flat files are:
(i) reduced data duplication
(ii) improved data security
(iii) improved data integrity

Explain what is meant by each of these and why are they features of a relational database.

....

....

....

....

.... [6]

Cambridge 9691 Paper 31 Q8 November 2009

✎ **Note**

For both parts (a) and (b) ...
three parts – 6 marks available, so it must be 2
marks for each part – the key word is 'Explain' so
you will be expected to write sentences and come
up with two separate points for each answer.

Simulation and Real-time Processing 23

Revision Objectives

After you have studied this chapter, you should be able to:

☞ describe real-time applications (process control)
☞ explain the use of sensors for detecting physical signals (temperature, pressure, motion, light intensity)
☞ explain the use of actuators
☞ demonstrate an understanding of the use of robots in a variety of situations such as
the manufacturing process or hazardous environments
☞ explain the reasons for simulation, such as to change time-scales and/or save costs and/or avoid danger
☞ discuss the advantages of simulation in testing the feasibility of a design.

23.1 Real-time applications

A real-time application is one where the response time between receiving some input and producing the response is instantaneous.

Such systems include:

✓ the control of a robot device
✓ control of a nuclear reactor
✓ control of a spaceship
✓ on-line ticket reservation systems.

← Look Back

To Chapter 2 for discussion on real-time operating systems.

For two of these applications safety is an issue.
The other key word here is 'control' – most real-time systems are for a control applications.

Pseudo real-time

On-line reservation systems are an example of a real-time system. Here the results of the processing are captured in a matter of seconds rather than fractions of a second. The reasons are obvious – once a reservation is made, the data must be recorded in the database otherwise there is the risk of making a double-booking.

Progress Check 23.1

Consider each of these applications – are they real-time or pseudo real-time?

(a) You have won an item in an on-line auction. You make an on-line payment for the item.
(b) A car is fitted with sensors in the rear bumper so that a buzzer is heard when the driver reverses too close to another parked car.
(c) A fishing boat has sonar equipment to search for the presence of fish below the boat.
(d) You log-on to the school network for the first time and are required to change your password before your log-on is completed.

23.2 The use of sensors for detecting physical signals

Consider the process control application for the opening and closing of the wing-flaps on an aircraft when the plane is landing or taking off.

Data about the current state of the flaps is collected from a number of sensors.

Data about the speed of the aircraft, its altitude and wind speed will all be received and processed and the results will require an angle change for one or more of the wing-flaps.

For this application the word 'instantaneous' used in our earlier definition of 'real-time' means on a time scale of milliseconds.

Data is collected from the real-world using sensors.

A sensor is a *transducer* which converts some physical phenomena (see below) into electrical signals which are then input to the computer system as digital data.

All the following physical attributes can be 'sensed' and the inputs converted to a digital measurement.

✓ Temperature
✓ Pressure
✓ Force
　➤ Air flow (i.e. wind speed)
　➤ Liquid flow
✓ Light intensity
✓ Motion.

Sensors fall into two types:

✓ ones which capture an analogue signal
✓ or, ones which capture a digital signal.

Example

A set of traffic control lights have a pressure pad (about) 20 metres before the lights so that the pressure caused by the weight of a vehicle driving over the pad is 'sensed'. This input will indicate to the computer system that there will be a car arriving in a couple of seconds (processing) and could trigger a change to the lights (i.e. cause an output). Since the pad is either touched or inactive the signal is *digital*.

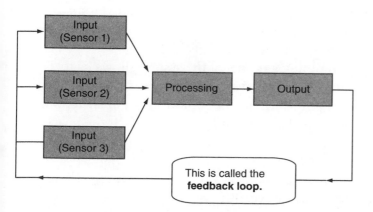

Example

Contrast this with a sensor which is constantly sensing a temperature in (for example) a bakery oven. Here the sensor will record each value as a *voltage* which can change on a continuous scale. Any measurement recorded by a voltage change is an *analogue* signal. Each voltage signal must therefore pass through a piece of hardware called an *analogue-to-digital converter* for it to be stored and processed by a computer.

The traffic lights example and the computer controlled greenhouse which follows each demonstrate the sequence of 'Input-Processing-Output-Feedback'.

23.3 The use of actuators

An actuator is a hardware device which receives a signal from the computer system and then causes some physical movement.

Example

Consider a computer controlled greenhouse where the temperature must be carefully controlled.

A temperature increase is caused by either:

✓ the windows shutting, or
✓ the switching on of a heater.

Temperature decrease is actioned by either:

✓ the switching off of the heater, or
✓ the opening of one or more windows.

The heater control requires only a digital signal. The movement of the windows results from a signal to the actuator to switch on the motor.

Progress Check 23.2

Make a list of the physical attributes in the real-world which can be 'sensed' by a sensor connected to a computer.

23.4 Robots

A robot is a mechanical device which is controlled by a computer program.

Robots can be classified into two types:

- ✓ *Fixed robot* – Typically a robot used for industrial manufacturing on an assembly production line. The robot stays fixed and the cars which are being assembled move.
- ✓ *Mobile robot* – The robot moves about and interacts with its environment. A typical application would be a computer controlled vacuum cleaner which would interact with the environment by sensing when it meets a wall, etc.

A robot is an example of a real-time system and is made up of:

- ✓ *sensors* to capture data about the robot's real-world surroundings
- ✓ *actuators* to drive various motors to perform the robot's movement
- ✓ *microprocessor* to process the various inputs and execute the control program.

Mobile robots generally require programs which are based on *artificial intelligence* techniques to model the environment and produce the required actions.

Benefits of robots

In a production line application these include:

- ✓ the robot can work for long periods of time without the need for maintenance or a break in production
- ✓ the robot is not affected by adverse conditions (which would be unacceptable to a human worker)
- ✓ the robot can be re-programmed to change some aspect of the task
- ✓ produces a consistent performance
- ✓ the long-term production costs should be reduced.

Limitations

- ✓ The 'start up costs' (i.e. capital cost) of buying the equipment may be high and must be justified
- ✓ The robotic equipment will require support in the form of maintenance technicians and computer programmers.

Progress Check 23.3

The UK television programme 'Robot Wars' requires competing teams to build a robot and then compete against other team's robots – the aim is to destroy the competitor!
(a) What sensors might be fitted to a robot?
(b) What actuators would be fitted?

Progress Check 23.4

An Adventure Park has a 'simulator' where customers can sit inside a room and a large display screen then simulates (for example) a fast downhill ski-run.

What sensor equipment would be fitted to the simulator room?

23.5 Simulation

The following are all examples:

- ✓ a pilot will spend many hours training in a *flight simulator* before they attempt a real flight
- ✓ a supermarket will use software to predict how many checkouts are needed for a proposed new store based on the anticipated number of customers
- ✓ a manufacturing firm will simulate a wind tunnel to study the wind-flows for proposed new car body shapes.

These are three examples where simulation is used.

Simulation is the building of a *model* for a complex system and then manipulating the model and measuring the results.

Building a model of the system allows us to understand the system over time as the result of changing parameters. A model is an *abstraction* of the real system and abstraction is at the heart of many of the tasks undertaken by the computer scientist.

There are some key differences with the three examples above.

✓ The wind tunnel is a physical model
✓ The fight simulator is a physical model but under the control of software
✓ The supermarket model is generated entirely by software.

Mathematics or Statistics?

The performance of the modelled system may be predicted and calculated based on mathematics.

Alternatively, statistical data will be collected about previous performance and then modelled based on this data. A new supermarket proposal may collect data about customers shopping habits from a supermarket in a town with a similar size population, location and locality.

Examples

✓ The model for the fight simulator and wind-tunnel examples – although still an abstraction – is real
✓ The modelling of the supermarket checkout operation is abstract and only realised by a computer program.

Producing the model based on mathematics

The task for the computer scientist is to identify the characteristics and features which affect the behaviour of the system. For example the number of checkouts in operation at any time will clearly have an effect.

Example

Consider a simulation of weather forecasting.

The characteristics which influence the weather include:

✓ wind speed
✓ temperature
✓ water vapour
✓ cloud formation.

The effect each of these has on the other and their net effect on the weather can be modelled mathematically by *equations* and so predictions can be made about the weather over a continuous time scale. Weather forecasting results are time critical – there is no point in receiving a prediction for yesterday's weather! The formulae and equations which are used for weather forecasting have been known for some time; it has only been with the advent of parallel high-performance computing that the results can be produced in a timely way.

Producing the model using an object-oriented approach

A different approach has very close similarities with object-oriented design. The model is produced by identifying the various objects and their behaviours which make up the system.

The supermarket example fits with this approach where the objects are checkout and customers. A property we could measure for a checkout is its queue length and behaviours associated with a checkout would include the arrival of a customer, movement of a customer to a different checkout, the serving of a customer and others.

> **← Look Back**
>
> To Chapter 3 where the 'queue' data structure was introduced and to Chapter 20 where it was studied again.

Queuing systems

"All our customers advisers are currently dealing with a client… you are currently number 14 in the queue". This is often what we hear when we try to (for example) book cinema tickets over the telephone.

When we visit the supermarket it is unlikely that we get served immediately when we finally move to the checkouts – we expect to queue.

The objective of any queuing system will be to utilise the available staff to the full whilst maintaining a wait time which is acceptable to customers. Hence we are aiming for a compromise between operating cost and customer satisfaction.

Common sense will tell us that factors which must be known for the supermarket checkout scenario are:

✓ the number of operating checkouts
✓ the distribution of arrival times of customers at the checkout

➤ certain days of the week or times of day will be busier than others

✓ the average time taken to serve a customer.

All of these will determine the average customer wait time.

Changing one of the parameters (for example opening another checkout) will have an effect on the performance of the system and this can be measured.

Queuing systems are modelled as a *time-driven simulation*. The changing state of the system is measured after (about) every one minute. Generating data is done using *random numbers*. For example, previous data collected showed that the number of customers arriving at the checkout every minute was evenly distributed between 0 and 4. This can then be simulated by generating a random number between 0 and 0.99999. A random number under 0.2 would represent 0 customers, between 0.2 and under 0.4 would represent 1 customer arrival etc. The actual number arriving is unlikely to be evenly distributed but will follow a normal distribution curve. This can still be modelled from a generated random number.

The number of customer arrivals over (for example) a three hour period would be simulated by generating 180 random numbers.

Progress Check 23.5

"Some simulators are an 'abstraction' of the real-world problem".

What does this statement mean?

23.6 Advantages of simulation in testing the feasibility of a design

✓ Parameters can be changed and their effect observed
   ➤ The checkout queuing example illustrated this.
   ➤ It provides a tool for doing 'what if' types exercises.

✓ Results can be produced quickly
   ➤ The computer is the perfect tool for producing results quickly. For example, the results for the operation of the checkouts over a day may be produced by the computer programs in (about) five seconds!

✓ Some events are dangerous to carry out for real
   ➤ Some chemical experiments would be safer demonstrated to students with a computer generated simulation.
   ➤ It will be cost-effective. For example, it would cost much less to build a computer model of the wind tunnel than build and use an actual wind-tunnel.

Progress Check 23.6

Medicine training is done by simulators involving a computer connected to a life-size plastic body anatomy. Various parts of the body will move in response to certain inputs.

What features of simulation does this example illustrate?

Exam-style Questions

1. (a) State what is meant by a real-time application.

....

.... [1]

(b) An air conditioning system is a real-time application. Explain how sensors and actuators are used to control an air conditioning system in an apartment.

....

....

....

.... [4]

(c) Give one other example of a real-time application. Justify why your choice is a real-time application.

Example ....

Justification ....

.... [2]

Cambridge 9691 Paper 31 Q4 June 2011

2. A new car is being designed. It is decided that different designs for the braking system should be tested using a computer simulation of each design rather than building prototypes.

(a) Describe three advantages of using computer simulation when testing each design.

....

....

....

....

....

.... [6]

(b) Simulation allows for the braking system to be tested in different conditions.
Describe the variables in the simulation that would need to be changed in order to replicate different driving conditions.

....

....

....

....

.... [5]

Cambridge 9691 Paper 33 Q5 November 2011

Networking 24

Revision Objectives

After you have studied this chapter, you should be able to:

☞ demonstrate awareness of different media for transmitting data and their carrying capabilities

☞ explain the different purposes of network components, including switches, routers, hubs, network interface cards (NIC) and modems

☞ discuss common network environments, such as intranets, the Internet and other open networks, their facilities, structure and ability to exchange information using appropriate software and techniques

☞ discuss the problem of maintaining security of data on an open network and practical techniques to address the issue

☞ explain the need for encryption, authorisation and authentication techniques.

24.1 Different media for transmitting data and their carrying capabilities

The media used will depend upon the nature of the data transmission. This could include:

✓ communication between two computers close to each other
  ➢ for example, we need to transfer a large number of files from one computer to another
✓ communication between devices (for example) in the same building over a network
✓ communication between a large number of devices across a wide area network.

Wired connection

(Several) Single wires

The simplest connection would be either a *serial* or *parallel* cable connecting the two devices

A serial cable (the universal standard is now the *Universal Serial Bus*, i.e. *USB*) which replaced other standards such as RS-232. The cable consists of four shielded wires – one for sending data, a second for receiving data and the other two for various communication signals.

> **← Look Back**
>
> To Chapter 5 for serial and parallel transmission.

Coaxial cable

Coaxial cable is available in a number of specifications. Its uses include:

✓ the connection between a radio or television receiver/sender and the arial
✓ computer network connections
✓ cable television connections.

The cable has a central single strand wire which is insulated from the other multi-strand wire braided around the central insulation.

An advantage of coaxial cable is that the signals are unlikely to be affected by electro-magnetic interference from other metal objects in close proximity.

Twisted Pair

Again available is several specifications – the simplest is made up of two insulated copper wires surrounded by the external insulation.

Alternatively the two wires may have an external copper braid enclosed by the external insulation.

All forms of copper wiring suffer from a loss of signal strength the further the distance. The shielding screen is used either as a return path for the signal or as a form of screening to eliminate forms of electro-magnetic interference.

One of the Ethernet networking standards uses a cable with four twisted-pairs called Cat-5 which supports a maximum cable segment length of 100 metres.

Fibre optic cable

'Wires' consist of very fine glass strands that transmit modulated light beams. A cable is made up of between 1 and 24 separate fibres which allow for the concurrent sending of many signals.

Fibre optic has many advantages over copper wire.

- ✓ The signals will be free of any interference
- ✓ Signals do not suffer from a loss of strength (*attenuation*)
- ✓ The cabling does not suffer from corrosion.

Typical applications include any form of long-distance communication such as:

- ✓ telephone communication
- ✓ Internet communications
- ✓ networking.

Telecommunications

All forms of telecommunications include some form of electro-magnetic wave acting as the *signal carrier* and then a form of *modulation* for the signal when the carrier wave is made to vary. Modulation is the way in which carrier wave is made to change to represent different signals and hence different data.

If two humans communicate by talking, the carrier is a sound wave and the range of frequencies possible with a sound wave will limit the possible signals. The same is true for electro-magnetic communication – each form will have a range of frequencies which are possible and corresponding benefits and drawbacks which make them suited to particular applications.

The Electro-magnetic spectrum

Radio waves

Radio waves have the largest range of wavelengths and include AM-radio (around 400 m), television (40 m) and FM-radio (around 4 m).

Radio waves are used for:

- ✓ receiving television signals by the domestic antennae sent from the TV broadcaster radio mast
- ✓ sending/receiving of mobile phone communication.

Microwaves

Microwaves have wavelengths measured in centimetres.

Microwaves have the benefits that microwave energy can penetrate haze, light rain and snow, clouds and smoke. For this reason *satellites* which capture pictures of the earth use microwave communication.

Infrared waves

Infrared waves occupy the range of wavelengths between microwaves and visible light. The range of wavelengths varies from the size of a pin-head to the size of a cell – measured therefore in a unit called a micron – one millionth of a metre.

The shorter ranges for infrared are the wavelengths used for remote control signals between a controller and a device such as a television.

Satellite communication

Artificial satellites orbiting the earth provide telecommunications between the satellite and receiving/sending stations.

Applications are numerous and varied:

- ✓ satellite radio and television broadcasting
- ✓ photography of the earth (see earlier section on microwaves)
- ✓ satellite based Internet
- ✓ satellite phones
- ✓ military communications.

Wireless

Communication can be using any of the wavelengths radio, microwave or infrared. The term 'wireless' has come to be used to describe any form of data communication which is 'without wires'.

Wi-Fi is the term for the industry standard IEEE.802.11. Wi-fi hotspots are now popular, for example, as a way of attracting custom to a cafe.

The range of applications of wireless communication is now widespread and includes:

✓   communication for a local area network
✓   smartphones and other portable devices

Bluetooth

Bluetooth is an industry standard wireless technology which uses short wavelength microwaves to transmit and then a protocol for the sending and receiving of data. Latest standards use transfer speeds up to 3 Mbps. Bluetooth is designed for communication between devices over a short distance.

Typical application would be sending music MP3 file or picture file from one mobile phone to another. The communication is set up by entered a device PIN on both devices.

Security has been improved and latest Bluetooth standards use highly secure encryption.

24.2 Network components

We already introduced the idea of the bus, star and ring network topology in Section 1.

Depending on the complexity of the topology specialist hardware may be needed.

> **← Look Back**
>
> To Chapter 5 where we introduced networks.

Switch

A switch sets up a temporary dedicated connection between the sending and receiving device and so avoids the problem of data collisions with a single segment bus topology (Figure 24.1).

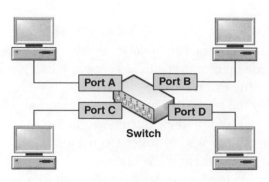

Figure 24.1   A switch

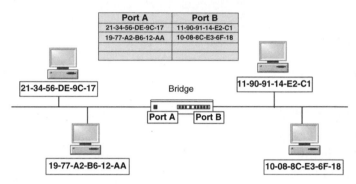

Figure 24.2   A bridge

A switch is more sophisticated than a hub which makes no attempt to route data packets – a hub simply broadcasts packets across all other ports except the port of the sending device.

> **Progress Check 24.1**
>
> Draw a diagram for a bus network with a single switch which connects:
>
> ✓   three computers A, B and C
> ✓   a fourth computer D which acts as a print server.

Router

When a computer sends data to another computer on the Internet, the *data packets* will contain the *IP address* (see later) of that receiving computer. This will not be directly known to the sending computer; what it does know is that the web page it is requesting has a *Universal Resource Locator (URL)* of 213.87.7.64.

Therefore somewhere on the Internet the IP address must be 'looked up' from the URL. This is the role of a **Domain Name Server (DNS).**

Once the IP address is known, it is the function of hardware called routers to route the data packets to their receiving device.

More discussion on the routers in the next section.

24.3 Common network environments

The Internet

The Internet is the hardware infrastructure which forms a global wide area network. The hardware consists of computers, networks, routers and the communications channels. The Internet is a collection of connected **internets** and is a **packet switched network**. Based on the idea that all network traffic is made up of packets of data with a **source address** and **destination address**. There will be a large number of different paths for the transmission of data packets.

The Internet is an **open network**. Access to it is provided by companies called **Internet Service Providers (ISPs)**. The **Internet protocol** used is **TCP/IP** where all devices which connect to the Internet are identified by an IP address; this is a four byte number usually written in denary, for example, 192.168.4.7. IP addresses allow the public access to facilities offered by computers and networks which are connected, for example, email and information stored on **web servers**, i.e. the **World Wide Web**.

Router

A router routes data packets to their IP destination address. A router can be used on a LAN to 'bridge' two **segments** of the network. Each segment is identified by the first three bytes of the IP address (Figure 24.3).

Modem

An Internet connection using the public service telephone network requires a modem. The telephone

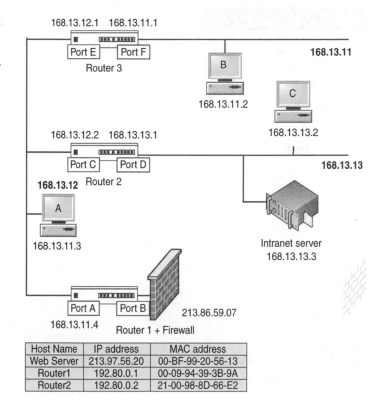

Figure 24.3 Router

Host Name	IP address	MAC address
Web Server	213.97.56.20	00-BF-99-20-56-13
Router1	192.80.0.1	00-09-94-39-3B-9A
Router2	192.80.0.2	21-00-98-8D-66-E2

Progress Check 24.2

Study the network shown.
(a) How many segments are there?
(b) How many devices are connected to Port A of Router 2?
(c) What is the segment address of the segment containing the Intranet server?

network – using copper wire – was designed to carry voice traffic, i.e. analogue signals. Data into and from the computer which is to be transmitted over the telephone network will therefore require either digital to analogue conversion or the reverse analogue to digital conversion. A modem is the hardware which does this conversion.

For a **broadband** or **Integrated Services Digital Network (ISDN)** connection the carrying line has already been enabled to carry digital data hence the sending and receiving data is digital. However, the hardware which makes the connection to the computer is still called a modem and may well be combined with a router as a single piece of hardware.

An Intranet

An *Intranet* is a closed private network available to selected users – probably from the same organisation or company – which provides information and processing of interest to those companies' employees only.

Information is provided as web pages available from an Intranet server which is viewed with browser software. The network will use the normal Internet protocols such as TCP/IP.

24.4 Security of data on an open network

Much of the data stored and processed on computers is sensitive and 'mission critical' for a business and so may well be of interest to third parties with suspect motives.

An *open network* is designed to that all users gain access to the facilities offered – hence confidentiality and security may be a serious concern.

User Ids and passwords

Passwords are a tool for controlling access to particular resources. A community such as Facebook is open to all but we would expect only the subject to have the ability to change their profile.

Firewall

Figure 24.3 shows the use of routers included a firewall to protect the network from unauthorised access from the outside.

The firewall can be hardware or software, or a combination of both, designed to protect a network from unauthorised access.

The firewall will monitor all incoming data traffic by carrying out *packet filtering*. The firewall will monitor domain names and IP addresses which are known to be undesirable.

24.5 Encryption, authorisation and authentication techniques

Encryption

Encryption is not specific to computing. It has been used for thousands of years for the sending and receiving of messages. Encryption is designed – not to stop a third party having access to data – but to ensure that they are unable to understand the data if it is intercepted.

Data which is sent over a communication link is susceptible to interception.

Emails and other data pass through many computers, routers and networks before they reach their destination; therefore the data could be read by a third party.

Encryption is the process whereby a message can be securely stored and transmitted so that it is only understood by the sender and receiver. The encryption process requires the application of an *encryption algorithm* using an *encryption key*.

The terminology used with encryption is explained here.

Plain text

Plain text describes the message before it is encrypted.

Cipher text

Cipher text is the message after it has been encrypted.

Decryption

Decryption is the process of converting the cipher text back to plain text.

Example

Consider a message which is to be sent and received. The user writes the message into a (for example) 5×5 grid and then sends the message (not each row in sequence) but the columns in sequence.

I	L	L	Δ	M
M	E	E	T	Δ
U	Δ	A	T	Δ
6	Δ	O	C	L
O	C	K	Δ	Δ

Δ is used to represent a <Space> character.

✓ The plain text is the message –
ILLΔMEETΔUΔATΔ6ΔOCLOCKΔΔ
✓ The *encryption algorithm* is: "Write the message into a grid starting with the first row"
✓ The *encryption key* is 5 (the number of characters on each row)
✓ The cipher text is:
IMU6OLRΔΔCLEAOKΔTTCΔMΔΔLΔ

A recipient of the cipher text would be able to decrypt this message if they know the encryption algorithm and the key.

Symmetric encryption

The example above uses symmetric encryption.

Symmetric encryption uses the same algorithm and key for the encryption and the decryption process.

Asymmetric encryption

A much more secure technique is to use *asymmetric encryption*. Two keys are used, called the *public key* and *private key*.

The plain text is encrypted with the sender's private key and is then decrypted by the recipient as they are in possession of the sender's public key.

The golden rule is that the public key is widely known, but the private key will only ever be in the possession of its owner.

The tool for sending and receiving encrypted messages is to purchase a *Digital Certificate* from a Certification Authority such as Verisign.

Some clients you communicate with may insist that (for example) all email communication is encrypted and so you must purchase a Digital Certificate and install it on the computer used for sending and receiving messages.

Encrypted email

Once the users each have a digital certificate they must give their public key to the intended correspondent.

The ownership and knowledge about keys is illustrated below.

Figure 24.4 shows the keys which are used to encrypt and decrypt a message when A sends an encrypted email to B.

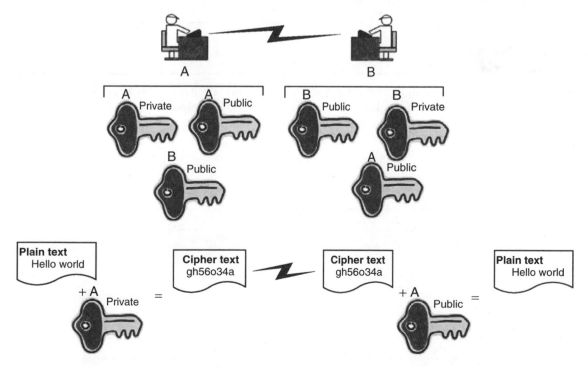

Figure 24.4   Keys which are used to encrypt and decrypt the message

Digital Signature

The sender could add a digital signature to the email. Digital signatures are used to authenticate that the email did indeed come from the sender and has not been tampered with.

The detail of how this is done is considered outside the scope of the syllabus.

Authentication and authorisation

These are general computing terms which describe issues with any computer system.

Authentication

Are we sure that this user is indeed who they say they are?

Authentication is the process of checking that the user of the computer, or some correspondent, is who they claim they are.

The measures taken for this on a network would be to use network accounts where the user ID is publically known but the password is known only to the user. Hence a successful logon should 'authenticate' that user.

Measures used for authentication include:

✓ the use of user accounts each with a password
✓ the use of digital signatures attached to an email

✓ the use of **biometric data** to gain access to the computer system. For example, a thumb print scanner on the keyboard.

Authorisation

Is a user 'authorised' to:

✓ use the network?
✓ have access to certain:
   ➤ programs?
   ➤ data files?
✓ log on:
   ➤ at particular times of the day only?
   ➤ at certain terminals only?

These are just some of the issues of authorisation.

Authorisation is the control of a user's access to computer resources. Measures taken to do this will include:

✓ the use of user accounts
✓ each user account has appropriate **permissions** set by the Network Administrator.

Progress Check 24.4

Explain the difference between authorisation and authentication.

Exam-style Questions

1. An import/export company is based in two offices in London and Lahore. Each office has an accounts department and a warehousing department. Each department has a network of computers. It is important that at each office the accounts and warehousing departments must be able to communicate. The London and Lahore offices must also be able to communicate electronically.

   With reference to this example, explain the use of the following:

   (i) copper cabling,

   ....

   .... [2]

   (ii) wireless communication,

   ....

   .... [2]

   (iii) routers,

   ....

   .... [2]

(iv) bridges,

....

....[2]

(v) modems

....

.... [2]

Cambridge 9691 Specimen Paper 3 Q9

2. A business uses the Internet to communicate with suppliers and to pay bills electronically.

   Discuss the problems of maintaining confidentiality of data on the Internet and techniques that can be used to address these problems.

....

....

....

....

....

.... [6]

Cambridge 9691 Paper 31 Q12 June 2011

3. A health ministry has decided that it would be useful for doctors in that country to communicate using an intranet.

   Patient records could be shared and advice could be given by the doctors.

   (a) Describe what is meant by an intranet.

....

....

....

.... [3]

   (b) Explain why an intranet was used rather than an open network like the World Wide Web.

....

....

....

....

.... [5]

Cambridge 9691 Paper 31 Q4 November 2011

Answers and Tips

SECTION 1

Chapter 1

Progress Check Answers

Progress Check 1.1

Central processing unit
Main memory
Various input and output devices
Secondary storage devices (Example: hard disk, optical devices, etc.).

Progress Check 1.2

Input stage: The user will input the start point and destination, method of travel (Example: walking/car)
Processing stage: The software will calculate alternative routes – List the towns which are intermediary points, distance between towns, total distance, journey time
Output stage: All this information will be displayed to the user either on-screen or as hard copy.

Progress Check 1.3

General purpose applications software – since the use of web pages for the display is used for a wide range of applications.

Answers to Exam-style Questions

1. (i) The physical/electronic parts of a computer system.
   (ii) (Sequence of) instructions/programs.

2. (a)
   ✓ Diagrams used to plan new solution/DFD's/Algorithms
   ✓ Designs of Input and Output screens/user interface
   ✓ Probably as prototypes with nothing behind them
   ✓ Discussion between analyst + client/user
   ✓ Hardware/software requirement considered
   ✓ Data structures will be designed
   ✓ Processing requirements will be decided

   ✓ Objectives agreed with client
   ✓ Design test strategy.

   (b)
   ✓ Purchase and installation of hardware
   ✓ Installation of software on the hardware
   ✓ Creation of data files
   ✓ Producing user manuals
   ✓ Consideration of need for training staff
   ✓ Method of changeover decided
   ✓ Convert/Transfer files
   ✓ Consideration of future maintenance of system
   ✓ Uninstalling the old system
   ✓ Monitoring initial performance of system.

3. (i) A peripheral which can accept data/allows data to be entered to a computer/processor as electrical pulses.
   (ii) A peripheral which allows information to be reported by a computer after data has been processed/in human readable form (or in form suitable for reprocessing by the computer at a later data)
   To give information from the computer/after processing.

Chapter 2

Progress Check Answers

Progress Check 2.1

1. The OS is system software.
2. The OS is the software which makes the hardware usable. Or, the OS provides the user interface between the computer and the user.

Progress Check 2.2

Data entered as a batch – **YES**
The payroll program will run without any user involvement? –**YES**
   ✓ it just reads the monthly data from the transaction file, updates the payroll master file and produces the payslips and other output.

Output produced as a 'batch'? – **YES**

✓ All the payslips are produced at the same time

Acceptable time delay? – **YES**

✓ The employees must complete their claim by the 14th of the month. The payroll program runs on the 25th of each month and the employees receive their payslip and pay on the 26th of the month. This period from data capture to final output is acceptable to the employees.

Progress Check 2.3

Continuous cycle of inputs-processing-output? – **YES**

✓ Temperature sensors send readings – readings are processed – may/may not send signal to the windows to open/close

Latest input affect outputs? – **YES**

✓ Example: Big drop in temperature will result in windows closed

Events occur in parallel – intermittent intervals? – **YES**

✓ Several sensors would send reading at the same time. Sensors may not send data overnight

Progress Check 2.4

Application which needs multi-user access.

The ticketing example (used as an example of pseudo real-time) would require that the bookings database is available at the same time to (about) hundreds of ticket agencies or even globally available to web users who can book concert tickets online.

Progress Check 2.5

Check boxes or radio buttons?

✓ Radio buttons are used for a response where only one (of about the five possible) is selected. For example, five radio buttons which each show an age range

✓ Check boxes are used for responses where any number (of about the five possible) is selected. For example, do we use regularly the five software packages shown

Answers to Exam-style Questions

1. (a) (i) Controls responses to external requests/controls hardware/makes system work/acts as an interface between the user and the hardware/controls input and output.
   (ii) Program that allows the user to do something useful/ something that would have needed to be done without the computer.
   (b) Batch not time sensitive. Real-time must produce some sort of immediate output.
   (c) Batch processing would be used for the production of utility bills (for example an electricity supplier) at the end of each month.

   ✓ Input is from all the customer meter readings
   ✓ All the input data is organised as a batch
   ✓ The batch is processed at the same time
   ✓ Without any user interaction

✓ The output (i.e. the customer bills) are produced as a batch

✓ There is an acceptable time delay between the final gathering of the input data (for example, the 18th of the month) – the processing run (for example, the 23rd of the month) and the posting of the bills (for example, the 28th of the month)

2. (a) OS will only allow one user at a time to use the computer. Each approved user is identified by a user ID. Provides security for user files/user profiles.
   (b)
   ✓ The manage the main memory available
   ✓ To manage the filing system
   ✓ To manage the use of the peripheral devices available
   ✓ To manage the allocation of the processor between various processes in a multiprogramming/multi-tasking environment.

Note: This fits exactly with our general definition that the purpose of the operating system software is to 'manage the resources of the computer system'.

Chapter 3

Progress Check Answers

Progress Check 3.1

No – 4 will be treated as an integer – '4' will be treated as a character.

Progress Check 3.2

1. Character ('S', 'M', or 'L')
2. Integer
3. Integer
4. Date
5. Boolean (or could be coded as Character with 'S' – single and 'M' – married)

Progress Check 3.3

Another one could be – record whether or not a person has passed their driving test.

Progress Check 3.4

1. (a) 65
   (b) 170
   (c) 255
2. (a) 0000 0011
   (b) 0101 1001
   (c) Not possible – the largest integer which can be represented with a single byte is 255

Progress Check 3.5

When the loop terminates ...
```
IF Found = False
   THEN
      OUTPUT "There were no months with
         sales below 10"
ENDIF
```

Progress Check 3.6

Final state is HORSE – GIRAFFE.
HORSE is the next to leave the queue.

Progress Check 3.7

Final state is BAT – GIRAFFE.
GIRAFFE will be the next to leave the stack.

Progress Check 3.8

1. (a) Sequential
   (b) Random
   (c) Indexed sequential (as we need both direct access to individual records and the benefits of sequential access for the price update program.

Answers to Exam-style Questions

1. (a) (i)
   - ✓ The symbols recognised/used by the computer
   - ✓ Often equates to the symbols on the keyboard
   (ii)
   - ✓ Represented by a set of bits
   - ✓ Unique to that character. The number of bits needed is equal to 1 byte/2 bytes. ASCII/Unicode is a common set.
   (b)
   - ✓ Bits are used to store the correct binary representation of the integer
   - ✓ Leading zeroes included to complete required number of bits
   - ✓ Standard number of bits irrespective of size of integer
   - ✓ Concept of short and long integer dependent on sizes of integers
   - ✓ Two's complement used to represent negative numbers.
2. (a) (i)
   - ✓ Set of data items of the same type
   - ✓ Stored together, physically
   - ✓ Under a common name
   - ✓ Using index as reference
   - ✓ One dimensional array is a list.

(ii) INPUT ITEM
```
FOR I = 0 TO END_OF_ARRAY
   IF ARRAY [I] = ITEM THEN 'FOUND', END
ENDFOR I
REPORT 'NOT FOUND'
```
   - ✓ Identify item to be found
   - ✓ Loop with suitable condition
   - ✓ Condition statement correctly structured with suitable condition
   - ✓ Error condition reported.

(b)
   - ✓ Dimension an array
   - ✓ Two pointers/One pointer
   - ✓ One to front, one to rear/to front
   - ✓ Data input is stored at rear pointer and pointer moved/move down queue to last item and link new item
   - ✓ Data read from queue is read at front pointer and pointer moved
   - ✓ Check made for queue full/empty
   - ✓ A FIFO structure
   - ✓ Example of a FIFO structure.

3. (a)
   - ✓ Back-ups are necessary because if original data is corrupted/lost, back-up can be used to replace.

(b)
   - ✓ File copied daily to portable storage
   - ✓ At least one copy kept off site/in fireproof safe
   - ✓ Mention of need for Transaction log
   - ✓ User must be familiar with the 'restore' process.

Chapter 4

Progress Check Answers

Progress Check 4.1

1. (a) True
   (b) False – all data values are transmitted along the data bus (not the address bus)
   (c) True
   (d) True

Progress Check 4.2

(a) True
(b) False
(c) True
(d) True
(e) False

Progress Check 4.3

Optical	Magnetic	Solid state
CD-ROM DVD-R Blu-ray	External hard disk	Flash memory stick

Progress Check 4.4

Application	Media	Typical Capacity
Backup of all files on a PC	External hard drive	250 GB
Distribution of high definition (HD) films	Blu-ray	50 GB
Storage inside a digital camera	Flash memory stick	2 GB
Copying large images from a PC for distribution to other PC users	DVR-RW	13 GB

Progress Check 4.5

(a) Bar code
(b) RFID tag
(c) Scanner
(d) Touch screen

Answers to Exam-style Questions

1. (a) (i)
   - ✓ Contents of RAM can be altered/ROM cannot
   - ✓ RAM usually has a greater capacity than ROM
   - ✓ Data held in ROM, after processing, can only be written to RAM
   - ✓ RAM is volatile/ROM is non-volatile.

   (ii) Example: The boot-strap program/operating system/system data/BIOS

It must be available when power is switched on/to boot up the system/so it cannot be changed.

   (iii) Example: A word processor document/user data
   - ✓ User must be able to alter it. *Or,* Part of the software being used (application/operating system).
   - ✓ The processor needs to fetch the instructions.
   - ✓ Can be replaced by another program at any time.

   (b) (i) Processor works at high speed while peripherals are much slower.
   (ii)
   - ✓ Use of buffer/temporary storage area
   - ✓ Data transferred from primary memory to buffer (or vice versa)
   - ✓ When buffer full, processor can carry on with other tasks
   - ✓ Buffer is emptied to the peripheral
   - ✓ Interrupt
   - ✓ Sent to processor
   - ✓ When buffer empty
   - ✓ Requesting more data to be sent to buffer.

2.
   - ✓ Bar code reader/to input ID number of goods from bar code
   - ✓ Keyboard/key-pad/to input ID number if bar code is damaged
   - ✓ Scales/to weigh produce
   - ✓ Touch screen/to choose items
   - ✓ (Chip + PIN)/bill payment
   - ✓ Magnetic stripe reader/pay bill.

3. (a) Example: Hard drive/tape
      Use: Storing OS/Software/User files/Back up (for tape)/transaction file.
   (b) Example: Pen drive/Memory card
      Use: Copy data from one machine to another/use in camera/mobile phone; use as backup/backing store.

4. (a) Redundant data/Little used data/ancient data removed **not** **copied** to separate, long term storage.
   (b)
   - ✓ To free up space on main storage
   - ✓ Data no longer necessary because order has been met
   - ✓ Kept in case there is a query in future
   - ✓ Legal requirement to keep data
   - ✓ To speed up searches/system.

Chapter 5

Progress Check Answers

Progress Check 5.1

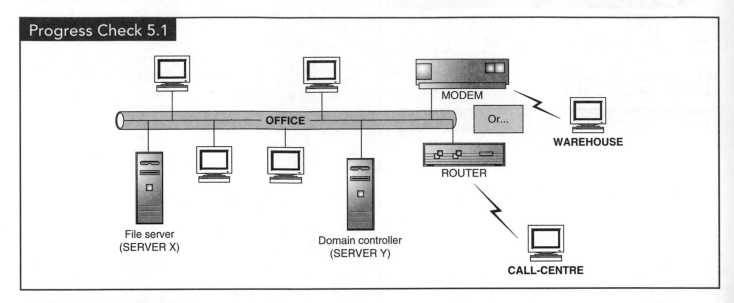

File server
(SERVER X)

Domain controller
(SERVER Y)

MODEM

Or...

WAREHOUSE

ROUTER

CALL-CENTRE

OFFICE

Progress Check 5.2

(a) False	(e) True
(b) True	(f) True
(c) False	(g) False
(d) False	(h) False

Progress Check 5.3

Bytes 2 and 3 will fail.

Progress Check 5.4

1111 1110
1111 0111
1100 1000
1101 1110
1110 0000

Progress Check 5.5

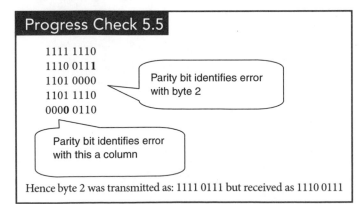

1111 1110
1110 011**1**
1101 0000
1101 1110
000**0** 0110

Parity bit identifies error with byte 2

Parity bit identifies error with this a column

Hence byte 2 was transmitted as: 1111 0111 but received as 1110 0111

Answers to Exam-style Questions

1. (a) A set of rules/instructions to allow communication between devices.

   (b) (i) Circuit switching involves setting up the route for the message before any of it is sent

   As packet switching involves sending the message in segments of equal size, each of which finds a different route to the destination.

   (ii) The message does not have to be reordered at the destination.

   (iii) The message is almost impossible to intercept/large amounts of the communication medium are not idle for other messages until the given message is completed.

2. (a)

   ✓ LAN over short distances/buildings/site//WAN geographically remote

   ✓ LAN uses own communication medium/WAN uses third party

   ✓ LAN more secure/WAN more open to attack.

   (b) (i)

   ✓ Individual bits sent one after another/along single wire.

   ✓ Advantage(s): Can be used over long distances; Less chance of corruption/less chance of bits having order changed.

   (ii)

   ✓ A byte is sent simultaneously/at the same time along eight wires

   ✓ Advantage: Much faster transmission rate.

   (c) Corrupted byte: 01101101/First byte
   Reason: The other three all have an even number of ones/ even parity. This byte has an odd number of ones.

3. (a) Hardware: 2 from: Router/Gateway/Modem/Cables
   Software: Browser/Communications software/Modem driver/Firewall.

   (b) Video files contain large volumes of data. If watched at a later time then it does not matter how long download takes. Therefore bit rate can be low. However, if watched as it is downloaded then the bit rate must be high or the video will not run without jerking/losing quality.

4. (a)

   ✓ Printer/to print till receipt
   ✓ Beeper/to indicate correctly read barcode/error reading barcode

   ✓ Speakers/to give instructions to customer
   ✓ LED/LCD screen to show information about purchase.

   (b)

   ✓ Sound/indicates barcode properly read without operator diverting attention from job
   ✓ Sound to indicate terminal is free
   ✓ Video image or screen output or soft copy/to allow shopper to check goods and prices as they are input to system
   ✓ Receipt or printout or hard copy/to allow shopper to check payments and shopping at home, proof of purchase.

Chapter 6

Progress Check Answers

Progress Check 6.1

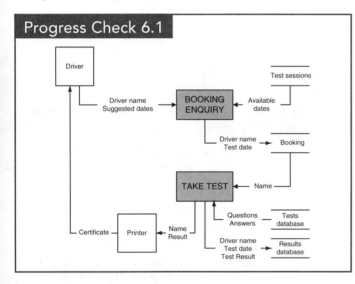

Progress Check 6.2

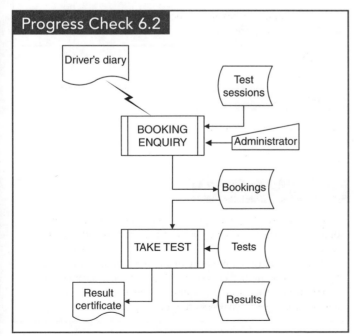

Progress Check 6.3

Phased – introduce the system initially for a few subjects only or use by only some examiners.

Progress Check 6.4

See the list of contents 'User Support'. All of these could be included.

Progress Check 6.5

Document	Timing
Project brief	Before a feasibility study can start
Requirements specification	Following completion of the analysis
Design specification	Once the Requirements Specification is available
Program specifications	Once the design specification is completed
Maintenance documentation	Following all the development and testing
User manual	At installation time

Progress Check 6.6

(a) Adaptive
(b) Perfective
(c) Adaptive
(d) (Sorry – this was trick question) – this is not 'maintenance', it is updating the files/database
(e) Adaptive
(f) Corrective

Answers to Exam-style Questions

1. (a) Manager must provide knowledge of and requirements of business as they are expert in how the business works.

    ✓ Analyst provides knowledge of what is possible particularly within confines placed by manager, for example, budget.

    ✓ If not properly defined analyst will solve the wrong problem.

    ✓ Manager's requirements and analyst's understanding must match.

    (b) (i) Evaluation carried out by:

    ✓ functional/black box testing
    ✓ testing against the agreed objectives
    ✓ testing against user requirements/specification
    ✓ testing done by software house/alpha
    ✓ testing done by users/beta.

    (ii) Important to analyst to ensure that there is evidence that all objectives have been met or will not be paid/ruin his reputation.

    Important to manager to ensure that there is evidence that all objectives have been met or system may prove unsatisfactory in the future.

2. (a)

    ✓ Diagrams used to plan new solution/DFD's/Algorithms
    ✓ Designs of Input and Output screens/user interface
    ✓ Probably as prototypes with nothing behind them
    ✓ Discussion between analyst + client/user
    ✓ Hardware/Software requirement considered
    ✓ Data structures will be designed
    ✓ Processing requirements will be decided
    ✓ Design test strategy.

    (b)

    ✓ Purchase and installation of hardware
    ✓ Installation of software on the hardware
    ✓ Creation of data files
    ✓ Producing user manuals
    ✓ Consideration of need for training staff
    ✓ Method of changeover decided
    ✓ Convert/Transfer files
    ✓ Consideration of future maintenance of system
    ✓ Uninstalling the old system
    ✓ Monitoring initial performance of system.

3.

    ✓ Is the technology/hardware available to solve the problem
    ✓ To determine if the new system is visible
    ✓ Is it economically possible to produce the solution
    ✓ Will the end product be so expensive that it bankrupts the company
    ✓ Are the social effects likely to be too damaging
    ✓ Are there enough skilled people available to make the solution operate effectively/for example: is cost of training employees too high

    ✓ Can the new system be created in a time effective manner
    ✓ Is the solution legal
    ✓ Is it operationally feasible.

4.

    (i) Adv: See first hand the system operating/may spot problems actual users do not see
    Dis: People do not act naturally if they are being watched/only see a snapshot.

    (ii) Adv: Detail can be explored/direction of enquiries can be altered
    Dis: Very time consuming.

    (iii) Adv: Shows how data is collected/shows data that needs to be collected/shows information that needs to be output
    Dis: Documentation often difficult for an outsider to understand/Privacy issues/Relevance of files.

Chapter 7

Progress Check Answers

Progress Check 7.1

(a) The final software will have all the features which match exactly what is needed by the company.

(b)

    ✓ Choice – there will be several software houses which can sell you payroll software
    ✓ Cost should be lower as:

    • competition from other suppliers
    • development costs will be minimal as only some tailoring of the software will be needed

    ✓ Software has already been extensively tested – should be bug free

Progress Check 7.2

Refer to the section Point-Of-Sale systems.

Progress Check 7.3

Bitmaps encode the picture data as a sequence of pixels each of a different colour. Each colour is represented by a different number.

Vector graphics are made up of a number of drawing objects (such as a straight line, circle etc.) Objects have properties (i.e. length, width, background colour etc.) The data for each object and its properties is what is stored for the graphic.

Progress Check 7.4

	Rectangle	Circle	Straight line
Line colour	√	√	√
Line thickness	√	√	
Centre coordinates		√	
Radius		√	
Fill (Yes/No)	√	√	
Fill colour	√	√	
Start coordinate	√ *		√
End coordinate	√ *		√
Shading style	√	√	

*A rectangle could store the coordinates for the top-left and bottom-right corners.

Progress Check 7.5

(a) Spreadsheet (one sheet per employee in a workbook with five sheets).
(b) Word processor.
(c) Bitmap graphics software (**Note:** A vector graphics program would not be suitable to edit a photograph as the photograph is encoded as a large number of pixels).
(d) Special purpose software.
(e) Spreadsheet for a simple list of loans – anything more sophisticated will require database software.
(f) Presentation software.

Answers to Exam-style Questions

1. (a) Desktop Publishing (DTP)
   Use: Producing leaflets/Flyers/Brochures/Posters
   Feature: Using frames to divide up content/editing features; combining images and text.
   (b) Presentation software
   Use: Producing a presentation for an audience, perhaps for head office/to produce training materials, for advertisements
   Feature: Use of multi-media to maintain interest in presentation.
2. (a) (i) The systems software which contains the operation of the computer.
      (ii) Software to carry out a task which would need to be done if a computer was not available.
   (b) (i)
   - ✓ Custom-written is software which is written in response to a user's specific requirements
   - ✓ Off-the-shelf software is written to respond to the requirements of a group of problems that are similar/is available to buy/is immediately available.
      (ii)
   - ✓ Immediately available
   - ✓ Tested with a wider range of users/tried and tested

- ✓ Ready trained work force
- ✓ Shared cost of development
- ✓ Greater range of support/help
- ✓ Compatible with other software from same manufacturer/with software of other people/organisations.

Chapter 8

Progress Check Answers

Progress Check 8.1

(a) Take the photograph with a digital camera – then emboss this onto a magnetic strip card.
(b) A web form containing the usual controls. Users will key in most of their personal data.
(c) Attach a barcode to each camera.
(d) Scan the photographs using a flatbed scanner and then import the image files into a word processed report.

Progress Check 8.2

Field	Validation check
Name	Length check – maximum 30 characters
Date of birth	Range check on Day (1 to 31) Month (1 to 12) and Year (1931 to 1994)
Forenames	Length check – maximum 30 characters
Address	Length check – maximum 30 characters
Email address	Format check – must contain exactly one @ character
Membership	From a list – allow A, J or S only
Type of membership	From a list – allow F or L only
Number of times per week?	Range check – number between 1 and 15
Member of gym before?	From a list – allow Y or N only

Progress Check 8.3

(a) Use an interactive presentation. The 'interaction' is the student's answers to the questions which will determine the resulting sequence of slides.
(b) A paper based (or screen based) report which will contain many images.
(c) A written report which will include graphs to summarise sales and make comparisons between different weeks/different stores.
(d) Video – which is then uploaded onto the web site.

Progress Check 8.4

- ✓ Knowledge base – made up of facts and rules
- ✓ Inference engine – which processes a query from the user
- ✓ User interface

Answers to Exam-style Questions

1. Barcode:
   - ✓ Barcode consists of pairs of dark lines of varying thickness which combine to give a (character) code
   - ✓ Used to identify worker.

   OCR:
   - ✓ OCR is a means of computer reading standard characters
   - ✓ Comparing the values with examples in memory
   - ✓ Light reflected off character
   - ✓ Determines shape by reading intensity reflected in small squares
   - ✓ Used for reading times/signatures
   - ✓ Different days signified by different positions of data on the card.

2. Set-up
   - ✓ Data collected from experts in the field and from resource material like books/encyclopaedias
   - ✓ Create user interface
   - ✓ Data stored in the knowledge base
   - ✓ Create inference engine
   - ✓ Rules governing the use of the data are stored in the rules base
   - ✓ Test the system against known outcomes.

   Use
   - ✓ Questions asked about the sample as part of the interface
   - ✓ Knowledge base is searched for answers to questions posed
   - ✓ Inference engine used
   - ✓ Results are presented on screen/given to user along with
   - ✓ Probabilities in percentage form
   - ✓ Reasoning behind the results given/explanation system.

3. (a) Device 1: Portable hard drive
   Justification: To store OS/Software/Files.

   Device 2: Flash/Pen/Solid state pen drive
   Justification: To transport files between home and school/backup/archive.

   (b)
   - ✓ Only one user can use it at any one time
   - ✓ Recognises user and user rights
   - ✓ Able to give impression that more than one thing can be done at a time
   - ✓ Keeps an individual's files more secure
   - ✓ More than one application open at the same time [not in (i) and (ii)].

Chapter 9

Progress Check Answers

Progress Check 9.1

- ✓ Explanatory text
- ✓ Factual text
- ✓ Warning messages
- ✓ Labels used for data entry controls such as a text box
- ✓ Text box content on data entry – Data entry control background colour
- ✓ Use colour to distinguish between data which is entered by the user and other data which is then looked up from a database and displayed on the form.
- ✓ Colour used for button controls

Progress Check 9.2

Intuitive means the user is always clear what has to be done (reading content only, data entry, etc.) and is clear what is required next.

Progress Check 9.3

- ✓ The size of the window
- ✓ Size, colour and font used for the command text
- ✓ Background colour of the window.

Answers to Exam-style Questions

1. (a) Colour
   - ✓ Contrasting colours for background and text otherwise text becomes difficult to read
   - ✓ Colour (red) to highlight items more important than others, needs to be used sparingly
   - ✓ Use of corporate colour scheme
   - ✓ Care with red/green and other colour combinations because of colour blindness.

   (b) Layout
   - ✓ Layout should follow normal reading pattern for eye because less chance of errors or omitting detail
   - ✓ Limit the volume of information because otherwise too daunting
   - ✓ Ensure that all areas of screen are used and that density of information is not dependent on position
   - ✓ Layout should be similar on different types of software so that user gets used to it.

   (c) Content
   - ✓ Content should be similar across pieces of software to enable user to be trained easily
   - ✓ Content must be relevant or user will begin to ignore it

✓ Content type must be accurate (if in red it really must be important)
✓ Help should be available.

2. (a) Colour

✓ Colours should provide suitable contrasts
✓ Should be meaningful, for example, red for danger
✓ Reference to colour blindness/epilepsy.

(b) Layout

✓ Should use whole screen
✓ Important information in top left hand corner/centre of screen
✓ Big buttons for ease of navigation
✓ Similar content grouped together
✓ Consistent layout when moving from screen to screen.

(c) Content

✓ Must be relevant
✓ Must be understandable
✓ Must be restricted so no information overload.

3.

✓ Limit volume of information because of small screen and
✓ Important to remove extraneous information as driver can only glance at screen
✓ Appropriate colour used to show route on map
✓ Sound to provide a commentary of directions/instructions
✓ So that driver does not need to look away from road
✓ buttons/touch screen for input/menu based.

4.

✓ Prompts question to ask
✓ Ensures all details are taken
✓ Allows for ease of validation routines/standard entry of data/reduces entry error
✓ All data is relevant
✓ Allows use of drop-down lists and radio buttons.

Chapter 10

Progress Check Answers

Progress Check 10.1

The number of combinations is increasing by a factor of 2 – therefore 5 inputs has 25 combinations, i.e. 32.

Progress Check 10.2

Inputs					Output
A	B	P	Q	R	X = A NOR B
0	0	0	0	1	1
0	1	0	1	0	0
1	0	0	1	0	0
1	1	1	1	0	0

Progress Check 10.3

Inputs						Output
A	B	C	P	Q	R	X
0	0	0	0	1	0	1
0	0	1	1	0	0	0
0	1	0	1	0	0	0
0	1	1	1	0	0	0
1	0	0	0	1	0	1
1	0	1	1	0	1	1
1	1	0	1	0	0	0
1	1	1	1	0	1	1

Answers to Exam-style Questions

1. (a)

A	B	Output
0	0	0
0	1	1
1	0	1
1	1	1

(b)
(i)

A	B	C	S
0	0	0	0
0	1	0	1
1	0	0	1
1	1	1	0

(ii)

✓ Adds together two single bits
✓ Part of an accumulator/half adder.

2.

A	B	C	D	Y
0	0	0	1	0
0	1	1	0	0
1	0	1	1	1
1	1	1	0	0

3.

A	B	C	D	OUT
0	0	1	0	0
0	1	1	1	1
1	0	0	1	0
1	1	0	1	0

4. (a)

C	S
0	0
0	1
0	1
1	0

(b) Adds together two single bits/A half adder.

SECTION 2

Chapter 11–16

Progress Check Answers

Progress Check 11.1

Forms-based interface would use:
   Text boxes – drop-down lists – radio buttons – check
   boxes – buttons

Progress Check 11.2

Consistency – layout – choice of fonts – use of colour – use of icons

---

Progress Check 11.3

Decision boxes need labels as shown below:

Progress Check 11.4

```
NoOfAttempts ← 0
INPUT ThisNumber
// now start guessing ...
REPEAT
  INPUT NextGuess
  IF NextGuess = ThisNumber
    THEN
      OUTPUT "CORRECT"
    ELSE
      NoOfAttempts ← NoOfAttempts + 1
  ENDIF
UNTIL NoOfAttempts = 6

IF NoOfAttempts = 6
  THEN
    OUTPUT "You did not guess the number"
ENDIF
```

Note the use of the integer
variable NoOfAttempts
to total some value

Progress Check 12.1

```
FOR Index = 1 TO 6 DO
   INPUT Description [Index]
ENDFOR
```

Progress Check 12.2

```
REPEAT
  INPUT NextReg
  IF NextReg <> "XXX
    THEN
       Registration[Index] ← NextReg
       Index ← Index + 1
  ENDIF

UNTIL NextReg = "XXX"
```

Progress Check 12.3

```
FUNCTION CountVehicleByType( ....Type : CHAR) : RETURNS INTEGER
```

The data type returned by the function was not stated

Progress Check 12.4

```
FUNCTION ISCharacterPresent(ThisString : STRING,
                    ThisChar : CHAR) RETURNS BOOLEAN
```

The data types from the two parameters were not stated

Progress Check 13.1

```
Surname : STRING
Initials : STRING
EmployeeCode : STRING
YearsService : INTEGER or BYTE
FullTimeEmployee : BOOLEAN
```

Progress Check 13.2

Use five one-dimensional arrays.
```
Surname[20]            : STRING
Initials[20]           : STRING
EmployeeCode[20]       : STRING
YearsService[20]       : INTEGER (or BYTE)
FullTimeEmployee[20]   : BOOLEAN
```

Progress Check 13.3

```
(a)  4
(b)  Sales[2,8]
```

Progress Check 13.4

(a) Design a record type structure to describe the product data.
```
   TYPE ProductRecord
     ProductCode       : STRING
     QuantityInStock   : INTEGER or BYTE
     RetailPrice       : CURRENCY
     WholesalePrice    : CURRENCY
   ENDTYPE
```
(b) `DECLARE MyProducts[200] : ProductRecord`
(c) (i) `MyProducts[57].ProductCode`
    (ii) `MyProducts[57].WholesalePrice`

Progress Check 13.5

(a) To delete a record from a serial/sequential file:

```
OPEN the file for input- FILE
OPEN a new file for output - NEWFILE
INPUT the name to delete
REPEAT
   READ next record (from FILE)
   IF name matches one to delete
     THEN
        // do nothing
        Flag record is found
     ELSE
        Write this record to NEWFILE
   ENDIF
UNTIL required name is found
WHILE NOT EOF(FILE)
   DO
     READ from FILE
     WRITE this record to NEWFILE
ENDWHILE
Close both files
DELETE FILE
RENAME NEWFILE as FILE
```

(b) To amend a record in a serial/sequential file (the algorithm is very similar to the 'delete record' algorithm above.

```
OPEN the original file for input- FILE
OPEN a new file for output - NEWFILE
INPUT the name to amend
REPEAT
   READ next record (from FILE)
   IF name matches one to amend
     THEN
        INPUT new data
        Flag record is found
            WRITE the data to NEWFILE
     ELSE
        FILEWRITE the current record to
   NEWFILE
   ENDIF
UNTIL required name is found
WHILE NOT EOF(FILE)
   DO
     READ from FILE
     WRITE this record to NEWFILE
ENDWHILE
Close both files
DELETE FILE
RENAME NEWFILE as FILE
```

NOTE: Both algorithms above assume that the required name/ record is found in the original file.

Answers to Exam-style Questions

1. (a)

You need to be a bit inventive!	Data Type	Thinking ...	Field Size (bytes)
Name	STRING	Sensible guess	20 characters (bytes)
NumberOf Bedrooms	INTEGER	Number of Bedrooms is a integer less than 255.	1 byte
Date	STRING	Assume the format will be NN/NN/ NNNN	10 characters (bytes)
Details Requested	BOOLEAN	TRUE/FALSE	A single byte

(b) One query record uses 20 + 1 + 10 + 1 = 32 bytes
A file of 100 query records needs 32 X 100 = 3200 bytes = 3200/1024 i.e. 3.125 kilobytes

(c)
```
INPUT new record
READ first record from file
Compare with record 1
REPEAT
   IF same name
     THEN
        replace record/end
     ELSE
        read next record
   ENDIF
UNTIL record = 100
READ new record to new copy of file
READrecords 1 to 99 to positions 2 to 100
in new file
```

2. (a)
```
PROCEDURE Mean
   OPENFILE STUDENT FOR INPUT
   TotalMark ← 0
   Counter ← 0
   WHILE NOT EOF(STUDENT)
     DO
        READ Mark
        Count ← Count + 1
        TotalMark ← TotalMark + Mark
   ENDWHILE

   AverageMark ← TotalMark/Count
ENDPROCEDURE
```

(b)
```
PROCEDURE Prize
   OPEN FILE STUDENT FOR INPUT
```

```
    INPUT ThisForm
    HighestAverageMark ← 0
    WHILE NOT EOF(SDUENT)
       DO
         READ student record (CurrentName,
CurrentForm and marks)
         IF CurrentForm = ThisForm
            THEN
               CALL PROCEDURE Mean
               IF AverageMark >
HighestAverageMark
                  THEN
                     HighestAverageMark ←
AverageMark
                     TopStudent ← CurrentName
                     PrizeWinner ← TRUE
                  ELSE
                     If AverageMark =
HighestAverageMark
                        THEN
                           PrizeWinner ← FALSE
                     ENDIF
                  ENDIF
       ELSE
          // ignore this student (wrong form
...)
       ENDIF
    ENDWHILE

    IF PrizeWinner = TRUE
       THEN
          OUTPUT 'Problem - Equal highest mark
scorers'
       ELSE
          OPEN FILE PRIZES FOR OUTPUT
          WRITE Form, TopStudent (to PRIZES
file)
    ENDIF
ENDPROCEDURE
```

Progress Check 14.1

(a) (11/2 + 2.5) / 4 = 2
(b) (2^3 + 5) / (3+1) = 3.25

Progress Check 14.2

   a = 6 : b = 3 : c = 2
(a) (a + 2b) +2/c = 13
(b) 3(a+b+c) / (2a – 3b) = 11

Progress Check 14.3

NewString = "FC Liverpool"

Progress Check 14.4

Position = 7

Progress Check 14.5

Final = 76

Progress Check 15.1

1Total	Starts with a digit character	✗
NoOfChildren	✓	✗
Number of children	No <Space> characters allowed	
numberofchildren	✓	
Number_Of_Children	✓	✗
Number-Of-Children	The <dash> character not allowed	

Progress + 15.2

(a) ✗
(b) ✓
(c) ✗
(d) ✓

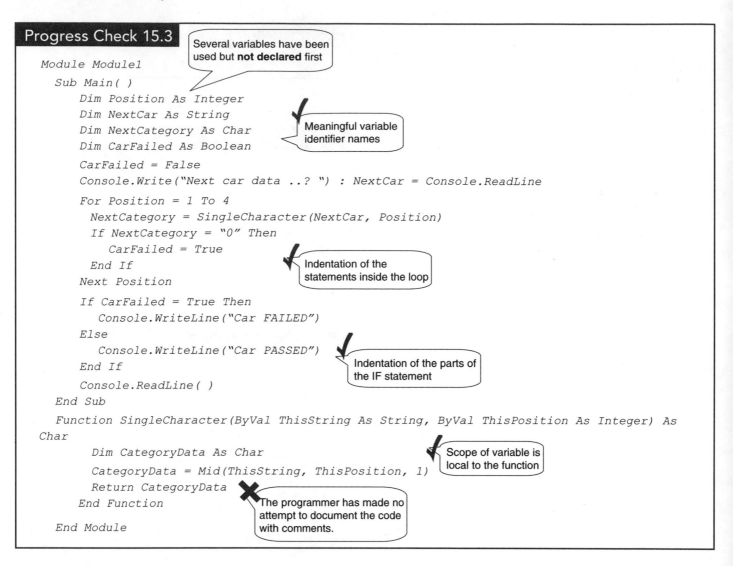

Progress Check 15.3

Several variables have been used but **not declared** first

```
Module Module1
  Sub Main( )
    Dim Position As Integer
    Dim NextCar As String
    Dim NextCategory As Char
    Dim CarFailed As Boolean
    CarFailed = False
    Console.Write("Next car data ..? ") : NextCar = Console.ReadLine

    For Position = 1 To 4
      NextCategory = SingleCharacter(NextCar, Position)
      If NextCategory = "0" Then
        CarFailed = True
      End If
    Next Position

    If CarFailed = True Then
      Console.WriteLine("Car FAILED")
    Else
      Console.WriteLine("Car PASSED")
    End If
    Console.ReadLine( )
  End Sub
  Function SingleCharacter(ByVal ThisString As String, ByVal ThisPosition As Integer) As
Char
    Dim CategoryData As Char
    CategoryData = Mid(ThisString, ThisPosition, 1)
    Return CategoryData
  End Function

  End Module
```

Meaningful variable identifier names

Indentation of the statements inside the loop

Indentation of the parts of the IF statement

Scope of variable is local to the function

The programmer has made no attempt to document the code with comments.

Progress Check 16.1

The example illustrates that although this is a logic error it will become apparent as a run-time error when the size of the number becomes too large to be stored.

```
Sub Main()
    Dim i As Integer
    i = 1
    Do While i > 0
        i = i + 1000
        Console.WriteLi
    Loop
End Sub

End Module
```

⚠ **OverflowException was unhandled**   ✕

Arithmetic operation resulted in an overflow.

Troubleshooting tips:

Make sure you are not dividing by zero.

Get general help for this exception.

Search for more Help Online...

Actions:

View Detail...

Copy exception detail to the clipboard

Progress Check 16.2

Typical data: integer in the range 1 to 10
Borderline data: values 1 to 10
Invalid data: 0, 11 and over, any 'non-integer' data value, i.e. a real number or string

Progress Check 16.3

(a) The program calculates the total number of rejects for the seven days of the week.

(b)

WeekNo	ThisNumber	Output	SupTotal 1	2	3
			0	0	0
1	8	Investigate	1	0	
2	9	Investigate		1	
3	1				
4	8	Investigate		2	
5	9	Investigate			1

Progress Check 16.4

Three examples of run-time errors:
- ✓ Attempt to open a non-existent file
- ✓ A 'division by zero' error
- ✓ Referencing an array subscript which is outside the declared range for the array

Progress Check 16.5

The character 'u' has been omitted from the list of vowels – a logic error by the programmer.

Answers to Exam-style Questions

1. (a)
- ✓ Labelled box for name
- ✓ Calendar for date of birth//drop-down lists for day, month, year//formatted boxes or other indication of how to write the date
- ✓ Drop-down list for type of book//radio buttons
- ✓ Yes/No radio buttons or (drop-down) list
- ✓ Button to move from screen.

(b)
- ✓ Easy to use
- ✓ Clear instructions
- ✓ Appropriate for the purpose
- ✓ Easy to understand
- ✓ To reduce errors.

(c)

Answers to Exam-style Questions

1. (a)
- ✓ Labelled box for name
- ✓ Calendar for date of birth//drop-down lists for day, month, year//formatted boxes or other indication of how to write the date
- ✓ Drop-down list for type of book//radio buttons
- ✓ Yes/No radio buttons or (drop-down) list
- ✓ Button to move from screen.

(b)
- ✓ Easy to use
- ✓ Clear instructions
- ✓ Appropriate for the purpose
- ✓ Easy to understand
- ✓ To reduce errors.

(c)

Field Name	Data Type	Field Size (bytes)
FirstName	String/alphanumeric/text	8–20
DateOfBirth	Date/string/integer	4, 6, 8, 10
BookType	String/alphanumeric/text	10
ReadsNovels	Boolean/chaer	1

2. (a)
- ✓ Each can work on individual modules
- ✓ Modules can be written in parallel.

(b) & (c)

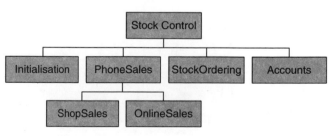

(d)
- ✓ These will be local variables
- ✓ That only have effect in the module they are in //Local scope
- ✓ Stored in different memory locations
- ✓ And have no meaning outside that module.

(e) (i)

   ✓   Keywords/Reserved words
   ✓   A word in the vocabulary of the *language*
   ✓   That can only have the meaning defined in that language.

   (ii)

   ✓   For example, Visual Basic
   ✓   Names must begin with a letter
   ✓   Must not contain a space/punctuation characters/ certain characters
   ✓   Must be unique in their block/scope
   ✓   Can't be more than 64 characters
   ✓   Can't be a keyword.

   (iii) Any keyword//Word breaking a rule given by the candidate.

(f)

   (i) 17
   (ii) 5*(a-b)
   (iii) Black box

(g) (i)

   ✓   Valid/Normal data
   ✓   Extreme/Boundary data.

   (ii)
   6 different types of test data sets + 6 sensible reasons
   Example:
   9999, 1000, 10, 20 all boundary values
   4000 valid data
   Reason must relate to the scenario.

(h) (i)
   (PrintAccounts = 'y') OR (PrintAccounts = 'n')
   PrintAccounts IN ['y','n']

   (ii)
   (StockID >= 1000) AND (StockID <= 9999)
   Alternative: (StockID > 999) AND (StockID < 10000)
   Alternative answer:
   NOT ((StockID < 1000) OR (StockID > 9999))

   (iii)

   ✓   Data outside expected range/Invalid data could be entered
   ✓   The program would not find an associated record/ data.

3. (a) (i) 1
     (ii) 6
   (b) (i)

   ✓   Cannot end
   ✓   Infinite loop
   ✓   Produces error message (heap/stack overflow).

   (ii) Second line needs to be changed to
       if n<=1 (or comparable)

(c)
```
FUNCTION calc(n)
    x ← 1
    FOR i ← 1 TO n
        x ← x * i
        NEXT i
    calc ← x
ENDFUNCTION
```

4. (a)
   (i) Valid data entered
   (ii) Invalid data. Try again.

   (b) Example: Pascal
```
READLN (NumberOfYears);
CASE NumberOfYears OF
   0..2: WRITELN('Valid data entered');
   ELSE WRITELN('Invalid data. Try again');
END
```

   Example: VB6
```
NumberOfYears = txtBox.Text
SELECT CASE NumberOfYears
  CASE 0 TO 2
    MsgBox "Valid data entered"
  CASE ELSE
    MsgBox "Invalid data. Try again"
END SELECT
```

   Example: VB 2005 (Console Mode)
```
NumberOfYears = Console.ReadLine
SELECT CASE NumberOfYears
  Case 0 TO 2
    Console.WriteLine("Valid data
    entered")
  Case Else
    Console.WriteLine("Invalid data.
    Try again")
END SELECT
```

Example: C#
```
numberOfYears = Console.ReadLine();
switch (numberOfYears)
{
  case 0:
  case 1:
  case 2:
    Console.WriteLine("Valid data entered");
    break;
  default:
    Console.WriteLine("Invalid data. Try
    again");
    Break;
}
```

Example: Java
```
numberOfYears = reader.readLine();
switch (numberOfYears)
}
  case 1:
  case 2:
    System.out.println("Valid data entered");
    break;
  default:
    System.out.println("Invalid data. Try
    again");
    break;
}
```

(c) Sequence, selection *(in any order, these words only)*

(d)

✓   A process of repeating
✓   A block of statements/number of steps
✓   Until some condition is met.

Note: NOT loop

(e)

✓   A counter variable
✓   Correctly initialising counter
✓   Incrementing counter
✓   Condition for terminating
✓   Output from decision

(f)

Field Name	Data Type	Field Size (bytes)	
PlayerID	Integer/byte/ shortint	a value within 1-6	*NOT a range*
Sex	Boolean/ character	1	
PlayerName	String/Text	a value within 10 - 50	*NOT a range*
Number Of Years	Integer/byte/ shortint	a value within 1-6	*NOT a range*
DateOfBirth	Date/Integer/ String	2/4/6/8/10	

5. (a)

s	x	q[1]	q[2]	q[3]	q[4]	Surprise
CHO						
	1					
		C				
	2					
			H			
	3					
				O		
	4					
						CHO

Pick out the first word of a sentence/group of words.

(b)

✓   Assigns return value to *Surprise*
✓   That value is returned to the function call
✓   Name of function used as a variable.

(c)

✓   Is a subroutine//Can be called more than once//Can be called from different locations
✓   Given a name/Identifier
✓   May take parameter values from the program
✓   Returns a value to the program.

(d) (i)

✓   Ends the REPEAT loop
✓   By finding an empty space
✓   Indicating end of word.

(ii)

✓   Indentation
✓   Meaningful/Sensible variable names.

(e)

✓   Characters are compared in turn
✓   From the left hand side/Start of each word
✓   The first higher code value determines the largest word
✓   If 2 words are the same when one ends
✓   The other is the larger alphabetically.

6. (a) (i) Algorithm assumes that the start values are 0/May contain values from previous processing.

(ii)
```
FOR i ← 1 TO 3
    CANDIDATE_TOTALS(i) ← 0
ENDFOR
```

(iii)

✓   Algorithm reads each vote from the *CANDIDATE_ TOTALS* array
✓   Decides whether the vote is for *A,B,C*
✓   Keeps a running total of the votes for *A,B,C*
✓   Outputs 0,0,0/meaningless output.

(iv)

✓   Line 2: operator is relational/comparative
✓   Returns a value true or false
✓   Line 3: operator is arithmetic
✓   Changes the value in the stated variable.

(v) OUTPUT CANDIDATE_TOTALS(1), CANDIDATE_TOTALS(2), CANDIDATE_TOTALS(3)

(b) (i) −1, 7
       −8,10
       −11, 12, 13
       C

(ii)

✓   Check if all three are equal
✓   Output suitable message
✓   Check if two are equal and one is different
✓   IF the one different is the smallest
✓   Then output a message that there is a tie
✓   Else declare the winner
✓   Repeat three times.

7. (a)
Key points gaining credit in the code are:

✓   inputing 2 strings
✓   identifying *in each
✓   identifying last part of first word
✓   adding second part of second word
✓   meaningful variable names

✓ output result
✓ indented code
✓ corect use of specified language.

Example: Pascal
```
ReadLn (String1);
ReadLn (String2);
1 ; = 0;
REPEAT
    i : = i + 1
UNTIL String1 [i] = '*' ; {or use i = Pos
    (String1, '*')}
String1 : = RightString1, Length(String1) -
    1);
{or use Delete (String1, 1, i)}
i ; = ;
REPEAT
    i : = i + 1
UNTIL String2 [i] = '*'
String2 : = RightString (String2, Length
    (String2) -i);
NewString ; = Concat(String1, String2);
WriteLn(NewString);
```

Example: VB 2005
```
String1 = Console.ReadLine()
String2 = Console.ReadLine()
i = 0
DO
    i = i + 1
LOOP UNTIL (String1(i) = "*")
String1 = String1.SubString(i+1, String1.
    Length-i)
i = 0
DO
i = i + 1
LOOP UNTIL (String1 (i) = "*" )
String2 = String2.SubString(i+1, String2.
    Lenght-i)
NewString = String.Concat(String1, String2)
Console.WriteLine (NewString)
i = i + 1
}
String2 = String2.SubString(i+1, string2.
    Length-i)
newString = String.Concat (string1, string2)
```

(b) (i) **String1, String2 (their input string names)**
(ii) **Example: Pascal**
```
Function JoinStrings (String1, String2);
String
```

Example: VB 2005
```
Function JoinStrings (ByVal String1,
String2 As String): As String
```

(iii) **The calculation needs to return a single value – a function will do this.**

SECTION 3

Chapter 17

Progress Check Answers

Progress Check 17.1

Multiprogramming

Progress Check 17.2

✓ Use fixed partitions
✓ Use dynamic partitions
✓ Paging.

Progress Check 17.3

(a) *A process is interrupted as its time slice has expired* RUNNING and then changes to RUNNABLE
(b) *A process now completes a sequence of disc read operations* SUSPENDED and changes to RUNNABLE
(c) *A process in given the use of the processor* RUNNABLE and changes to RUNNING
(d) *A process is executing but now has to wait for some input from the keyboard from the user* RUNNING and changes to SUSPENDED

Progress Check 17.4

✓ user priority
✓ estimated run-time
✓ estimated run-time remaining
✓ resources the process will require

Answers to Exam-style Questions

1. (a)

✓ Disk space is organised into allocation units (clusters)
✓ FAT is a map of which clusters are used to store which files//Individual sectors on the disk are organised into clusters which are used to store the files

✓ Details where files are stored on backing store
✓ Acts as an index on the hard drive
✓ Shows unused/unusable clusters.

(b) The boot file contains user-defined information to:

✓ tailor the operating system//contains parameters by which the system will operate
✓ boot file stored on backing store/RAM
✓ read/written to by the boot program (held on ROM).

2. (a) Example:

✓ Touch sensor/Pressure sensor/Infrared sensor/Other sensible
✓ Needed to tell robot when components arrive
✓ To investigate orientation of component
✓ To tell when it has applied enough pressure to pick it up.

Example:

✓ Actuator (electric motor/stepper motor/end effecter) of some sort
✓ Needed to move robot arm/to physically interact with component/to screw the two components together
✓ (Speaker/LCD display) conditional on:
✓ a description of error reporting

(b)

✓ Cheaper, do not need to be paid
✓ Work 24/7
✓ Do not require heat, light, space, ventilation, facilities
✓ Robots can work in hazardous environments
✓ Items
✓ Actions produced are all to a consistent high standard// Fewer errors
✓ Reliable/Workers can be off work/Will never strike
✓ Actions are more accurate than those of human.

(c)

✓ May involve simply changing from one stored program to another
✓ Set new parameters for current program
✓ Edit program/writing new program code
✓ By physically being moved through intermediate positions …
✓ …which the system can then replicate.

3. (a) Paging

✓ Memory is divided into equal-sized units called page frames
✓ Program/Data file is divided into equal-size units called pages
✓ One or more pages may be loaded into memory at any one time
✓ Pages may be discontiguous
✓ Pages swapped in and out as required
✓ Pages not in main memory are stored in virtual memory/Backing store
✓ Page table/Index of pages/Processes maintained

✓ Absolute Address is calculated by adding page address to relative address in instruction
✓ Paging is transparent to the programmer.

(ii) Segmentation

✓ Memory is divided into variable length blocks
✓ Programs can consist of many segments
✓ Segments normally match natural divide in jobs/ logical blocks
✓ Index of segments stored which must store base address and length of segment
✓ Programmer will organise code modules into segments.

Chapter 18

Progress Check Answers

Progress Check 18.1

END and *INC* do not have an operand.

Progress Check 18.2

(a) FALSE – an interpreter has the better diagnostic features
(b) FALSE – once compiled the compiler is not needed to execute the program
(c) FALSE – no object file is produced using an interpreter
(d) TRUE – as both the source program and the interpreter must be in main memory
(e) TRUE (unlike an interpreter which simply stops execution as soon as the first error is found)
(f) FALSE – see previous question
(g) TRUE
(h) FALSE – compiler software is language specific. The compiler for a Pascal program is different software to the compiler used for a program written in any other high-level language

Progress Check 18.3

	Symbol Table	
Variable Identifier	**Data Type**	**Memory address**
Index	*INTEGER*	9873
Product	*INTEGER*	9875

▪Pointer to 987B = 1▪▪20Pointerto 9875 = Pointer to 987B*
Pointer to 987B▪▪▪

> **Progress Check 18.4**
>
> The code is changed so that:
> ✓   It will execute as fast as possible
> ✓   It uses up the minimum amount of main memory.

Answers to Exam-style Questions

1. (a)

   ✓   Whole program not written
   •   So may not compile
   ✓   Testing needs to be done
   •   Diagnostics will be more complete
   ✓   Individual segments can be run
   •   Allowing errors to be isolated
   ✓   Running will be necessary after very minor changes
   •   Continual compilation of whole code is very time consuming.

   (b)

   ✓   Check on grammar of statements
   ✓   Error diagnostics are issued
   ✓   Jump destinations checked for existence
   ✓   Control constructs checked
   ✓   Check that variables have been declared
   ✓   Check for existence of library modules.

2. (a)

   ✓   Interpreter translates one instruction and runs it before translating the next
   •   Complier translates whole program before it is executed
   ✓   Interpreter maintains source code throughout run/program execution
   •   Compiler creates the object code and drops the source code
   ✓   Interpreter must be present in memory during run/program execution
   •   Compiler removed once object code produced
   ✓   Object code larger than source code
   ✓   Complied program runs more quickly once it is translated
   ✓   Interpreter produces error diagnostics as they are met
   •   Complier produces a file of error diagnostics at end of compilation
   ✓   Interpreter makes debugging easier
   •   Compiler needs whole program to be syntax error free to produce object code
   ✓   Interpreter can execute partial programs
   •   Compiler needs a whole block of code to run.

   (b)

   ✓   Puts each statement into form required by the syntax analyser
   ✓   Keywords are tokenized
   ✓   If keyword not in dictionary then error reported
   ✓   Programmer-defined names entered into symbol table//symbol table created
   ✓   Names not following rules create error message
   ✓   Removes unnecessary characters.

3. (i) Linkers:

   ✓   Used to combine already compiled procedures to produce an executable file
   ✓   Deals with external references from the main program to other (pre-compiled) modules.

   (ii) Loaders:

   ✓   Copies object code/executable code into primary memory ready for execution
   ✓   Deals with addressing anomalies/re-locatable addresses.

4. (a) (i) Strings of characters are grouped to form keywords/reserved words

   ✓   Checks reserved words for validity
   ✓   Keywords/reserved words/identifiers replaced by tokens
   ✓   Identifiers placed in symbol table
   ✓   Unnecessary characters/comments/whitespace removed
   ✓   Final output is a token string.

   (ii)

   ✓   The format of instruction/token string is compared to forms for acceptable expressions and statements
   ✓   As defined by the meta-language used
   ✓   Example of a syntax error, for example, IF THEN x = 3.

   (b) (i)

   ✓   Routines are already written and can be inserted with a single command word // Saves time in writing code
   ✓   Many projects require similar code, for example, sorting/searching
   ✓   Routines are already tested
   ✓   Code is robust and reliable
   ✓   Should ensure consistency of standards
   ✓   Routines are already translated / makes translation process faster/simpler.

   (ii)

   ✓   Loader is used to load routine into memory when required
   ✓   Ensures no memory conflicts between different routines
   ✓   Linker links segments/files of code (to produce executable code).

Chapter 19

Progress Check Answers

> **Progress Check 19.1**
>
> (a) Accumulator – General purpose
> (b) Memory Address Register – Special purpose
> (c) Current Instruction Register – Special purpose

Progress Check 19.2

(a) MAR ← [PC]
   The contents of the Program Counter are copied to the Memory Address Register
(b) PC ← [PC] + 1
   The contents of the Program Counter are incremented
(c) MDR ← [[MAR]]
   The Memory Address Register has the address to be used.
   Copy the contents of this address to the Memory Data Register.
(d) CIR ← [MDR]
   The contents of the Memory Data Register are copied to the Current Instruction Register

Progress Check 19.3

(a) True   (b) False
(c) True   (d) False

Answers to Exam-style Questions

1. (i)
   ✓ Contents copied from PC
   ✓ Contents changed to the operand/address part of CIR

   (ii)
   ✓ Instruction copied *from memory/location* to MDR (when contents of MAR are from PC)
   ✓ Data copied *from memory/location* to MDR (when instruction is LOAD)
   ✓ Data copied *from ALU/Accumulator* to MDR (when instruction is STORE).

2. (i)
   ✓ Hold the data currently being processed
   ✓ Result of calculation is held in accumulator…
   ✓ Before being passed to memory unit.

   (ii)
   ✓ The address of the next instruction
   ✓ Contents incremented (after being read)
   ✓ Contents changed by a jump instruction.

3.
   (a)
   ✓ Single processor/control unit
   ✓ Sequential processing of program instructions
   ✓ Instructions and data indistinguishable
   ✓ Can be stored together in same memory unit
   ✓ Programs can be exchanged/reloaded easily to the same memory space.

   (b)
      (i)
   ✓ Contains the address of the next instruction to be fetched
   ✓ Passes address to the MAR
   ✓ And is then incremented
   ✓ Contents altered to the operand if the instruction is a jump instruction.

   (ii)
   ✓ Holds the current instruction
   ✓ Divided into the op code and operand
   ✓ Holds the instruction while the operation code is decoded
   ✓ Sends the address to the MAR
   ✓ Mention of use of address to alter PC/need for other parts of instruction, for example, addressing type used.

Chapter 20

Progress Check Answers

Progress Check 20.1

1. (a) 0011 0110   2. (a) 475
   (b) 0001 0000 1001   (b) 409

Progress Check 20.2

1. (a) 5A   2. (a) 54
   (b) D   (b) 402
   (c) 103

Progress Check 20.3

1. (a) +28   2. (a) +71
   (b) −63   (b) −58

Progress Check 20.4

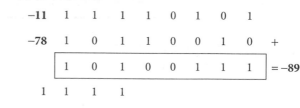

Progress Check 20.5

(a) Mantissa: 7/8
    Exponent: +1
    Number: 1.75
(b) Mantissa: −15/16
    Exponent: +7
    Number: −120
(c) Mantissa: −3/4
    Exponent: −119
    Number: -3×2^{-121}

Progress Check 20.6

LONDON, AMSTERDAM, NEW DELHI, DHAKA, SINGAPORE and NEW YORK.

Start: 5

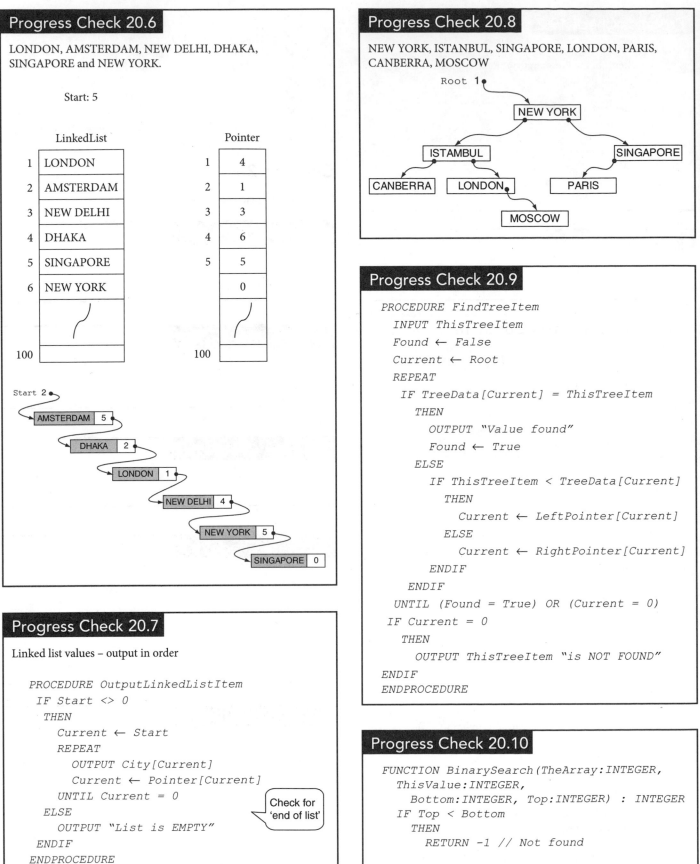

Progress Check 20.7

Linked list values – output in order

```
PROCEDURE OutputLinkedListItem
 IF Start <> 0
  THEN
     Current ← Start
     REPEAT
       OUTPUT City[Current]
       Current ← Pointer[Current]
     UNTIL Current = 0
  ELSE
     OUTPUT "List is EMPTY"
 ENDIF
ENDPROCEDURE
```

Check for 'end of list'

Progress Check 20.8

NEW YORK, ISTANBUL, SINGAPORE, LONDON, PARIS, CANBERRA, MOSCOW

Progress Check 20.9

```
PROCEDURE FindTreeItem
  INPUT ThisTreeItem
  Found ← False
  Current ← Root
  REPEAT
   IF TreeData[Current] = ThisTreeItem
     THEN
       OUTPUT "Value found"
       Found ← True
     ELSE
       IF ThisTreeItem < TreeData[Current]
         THEN
           Current ← LeftPointer[Current]
         ELSE
           Current ← RightPointer[Current]
       ENDIF
     ENDIF
  UNTIL (Found = True) OR (Current = 0)
 IF Current = 0
   THEN
     OUTPUT ThisTreeItem "is NOT FOUND"
 ENDIF
ENDPROCEDURE
```

Progress Check 20.10

```
FUNCTION BinarySearch(TheArray:INTEGER,
  ThisValue:INTEGER,
    Bottom:INTEGER, Top:INTEGER) : INTEGER
 IF Top < Bottom
   THEN
     RETURN -1 // Not found
```

```
ELSE
    Middle = Bottom + (Top - Bottom)/2
    IF TheArray[Middle] > ThisValue
      THEN
        RETURN BinarySearch(TheArray,
          ThisValue, Bottom, Middle - 1)
      ELSE
        IF TheArray[Middle] < ThisValue
          THEN
            RETURN
              BinarySearch(TheArray,
              ThisValue, Middle + 1, Top)
          ELSE
            RETURN Middle
        ENDIF
    ENDIF
  ENDIF
ENDFUNCTION
```

Progress Check 20.11

17	69	71	82	24	19	114	61	28	25
17	24	69	71	82	19	114	61	28	25
17	19	24	69	71	82	114	61	28	25

Answers to Exam-style Questions

1. (a)

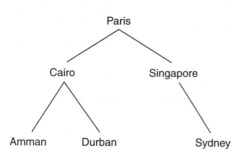

(b)

✓ In-order traversal
✓ Traverse left hand subtree using in-order traversal
✓ Visit root node
✓ Traverse right hand subtree using in-order traversal

(c)

✓ Insert Paris
✓ Compare Cairo and insert Cairo, Paris
✓ Compare Singapore and insert Cairo, Paris, Singapore
✓ Compare Durban and insert Cairo, Durban, Paris, Singapore

✓ Compare Amman and insert Amman, Cairo, Durban, Paris, Singapore
✓ Compare Sydney and insert Amman, Cairo, Durban, Paris, Singapore, Sydney.

2.
(a) 83
(b) 153
(c) −110

3.
(i) −106
(ii) −22
(iii) 96

4. (a) (i) +39 = 00100111
       (ii) −47 = 10101111

   (b) (i) −3 = 1111 1101
       (ii) −47 = 1101 0001

   (c) (i) = (1/8 + 1/32) * 2^4
          = 5/32 *16
          = 2 ½
          Or
          = 0.00101 * 2^4

Hence move point 4 places.
     = 10.1 = 2 1/2
   (ii) 010100 0010
   (iii) M = ½ + ¼ + 1/32 *Or* =25/32
        E = 3
        Number is 25/32 * 8
          = 6 ¼

Chapter 21

Progress Check Answers

Progress Check 21.1

1. Low-level means writing a program in either machine code or assembly language.

Progress Check 21.2

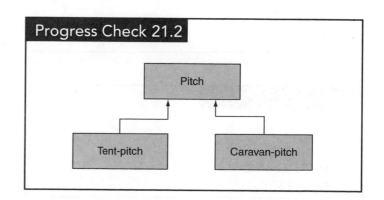

Progress Check 21.3

(a) Natene plays tennis (a 'fact')
(b) Y = golf
(c) A = natene
A = tadi

Progress Check 21.4

(a) Malona is female.
(b) The parents of emidio are celia and adan.
(c) Rule.
(d) X is a sibling of Y if X and Y are brothers or X has a sister Y.
(e) (i) Elano
(ii) X = Null
Y = Null (i.e. there is no fact which states the parents of Sofia)

Progress Check 21.5

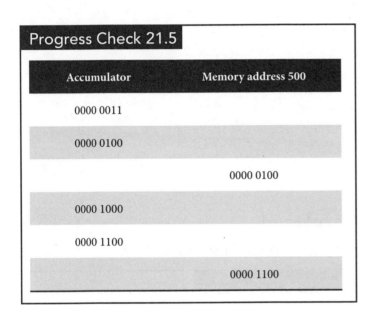

Accumulator	Memory address 500
0000 0011	
0000 0100	
	0000 0100
0000 1000	
0000 1100	
	0000 1100

Progress Check 21.6

(a) Valid
(b) Invalid (there is no definition for digit 5)
(c) Valid

Progress Check 21.7

(a) Valid
(b) Valid
(c) Invalid
(d) Invalid (no definition for the digit 4)

Progress Check 21.8

Identifier → Letter →
Letter
Digit
Underscore
Underscore → ⊖ →

Progress Check 21.9

Tracing the algorithm should give the values output in the order:
$$(3 \times p + 5) / (p - z)$$

Progress Check 21.10

1. (a) 25
   (b) 3
   (c) 64
2. (a) a b + 6 /
   (b) 2 a * b + 3 ^

Progress Check 21.11

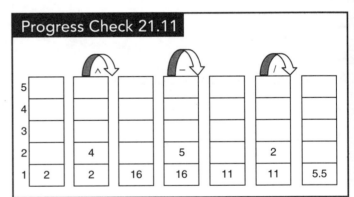

Answers to Exam-style Questions

1.
(a)
   ✓ Short piece of user friendly code to stand for the operation in a low-level language instruction
   ✓ Used to make program code more easy to remember
   ✓ In this case ADD replaces a binary code.

(b) Address of data is stored in the address pointed to in the instruction.
(c) Address is added to the contents of the Index Register (IR) to give the data address.

2.
(a)
   ✓ Describes machine code/assembly language
   ✓ Languages which use the basic machine operations of the processor

✓ Close to the architecture of the processor
✓ Assembly language has a one-to-one mapping with machine code
✓ Assembly language uses mnemonics/labels.

(b)

✓ Problems are modelled with objects
✓ Objects are defined in a class
✓ Objects contain both the properties/attributes and the methods (needed to manipulate the properties)
✓ Properties can be read or written using methods
✓ Uses inheritance to allow some objects to use the data and methods of a parent class
✓ Mention of data encapsulation
✓ Accept polymorphism/containment/aggregation (although note that containment is not in the syllabus).

(c)

✓ Describes 'what' is to be accomplished
✓ Not 'how' (no algorithm written)
✓ The user states what is to be found/set a goal (query)
✓ Consists of a set of facts and rules
✓ Rules are applied to the data until the goal is reached
✓ Mention of backtracking/instantiation.

(d)

✓ Program describes how to solve the problem in a sequence of steps/algorithm
✓ Lends itself to top-down design/modularisation
✓ Using procedures/functions.

3. (a) The combining together of an object's properties and methods
An object can only read/write a property value using methods of the class
Class contains both properties and the methods to use it
Example: `PayScale` property can only be output using the `getPayScale` method in the `dministrator` class.
(b) Properties and methods of a base class are available to a subclass
Subclass can have properties and methods of its own.

Chapter 22

Progress Check Answers

Progress Check 22.1

PupilNumber, StudentName, Form, Address, YearEntered
(a) PupilNumber
(b) StudentName
    Beacuse we shall frequently want to search the database by student name.

Progress Check 22.2

(a) CourseCode.
(b) Integer (or if you are using a program which supports it – Byte (as a range of 0–255 will be OK).
(c) Address and the course(s) on which they can teach – although this second suggestion presents a problem as some data may need to be stored in a new table).

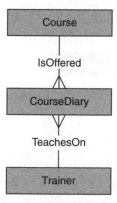

(d) TrainerName (as there will not be too many trainers and it is highly unlikely we shall have two trainers with the same name).
(e) **Note:** It cannot be date (as we have two different courses scheduled for the same date).
    So, it will be a composite key of CourseDate + Course-Code.
(f) One trainer will deliver many CourseDiary sessions.
    One Course is offered many times in the CourseDiary table.
(g) Trainer to link back to the TrainerName attribute in table Trainer.
    CourseCode to link back to CourseCode in table Course.
(h) E-R diagram as shown.

Progress Check 22.3

Four features of DBMS software.
✓ Allows the database design to be created
✓ Stored all the data about the design in its data dictionary
✓ Allows for rapid setting up of queries and reports
✓ If the data design is changed we will not need to change applications program code which already use the database data
✓ Data integrity (validation) is part of the data table designs and so does not need to be programming within the applications programs
✓ Better security of the data, for example, backup of the data is now 'centralised' and the responsibility of the DBA
✓ Supports multi-access to the database
✓ Allows different access rights to be created for different users of the database.

Progress Check 22.4

(a) The list of attributes used for all tables – **YES**
(b) Detail for all attributes; Data type – did it have a secondary index – **YES**
(c) The customer data – **NO**
(d) The results for all queries – **NO**
(e) Query descriptions – **YES**

Progress Check 22.5

1. (a) No – that statement is First Normal Form.
   (b) True.
   (c) True.
   (d) No – if it has a composite primary key we need to look carefully at the non-key attributes.
   (e) True.
       Student(StudentID, StudentName, TutorName, TutorInitials, TutorRoom)
2. (a) True.
   (b) True – i.e. if we know the tutor initials we shall automatically know the tutor name.
   (c) True– i.e. if we know the tutor initials we shall automatically know the tutor room.
   (d) No.
       Student (StudentID, StudentName, TutorInitials)
       Tutor (TutorInitials, TutorName, TutorRoom)
   (e) TutorInitials.
   (f) "One tutor will be responsible for many students".

Answers to Exam-style Questions

1. (a)

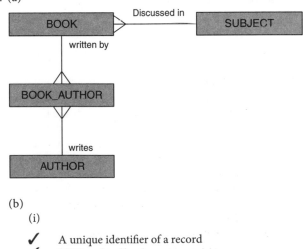

(b)
   (i)
   ✓ A unique identifier of a record
   ✓ ISBN code of book

(ii)
   ✓ A key other than the primary key used to identify records
   ✓ Book publisher

(iii)
   ✓ A primary key in one table that is used as a link to another table
   ✓ SubjectID in book table

2. (i) A table holding information about the database
       Uses a meta-language to describe the design of the data
       Used by developers/managers of the database
       Maps logical database to physical storage.
   (ii) Description of the data structures //
        Description of the tables/attributes/data types
        Defines the structure of relationships / indexing / reports.
   (iii) Language used allow user to access data…
        Change data // add-modify-delete data in the database
        Search for data in the database // design and use queries.

Chapter 23

Progress Check Answers

Progress Check 23.1

(a) Pseudo real-time
(b) Real-time
(c) Real-time
(d) Real-time

Progress Check 23.2

Temperature – Pressure – Force (Air flow or liquid flow) – Light – Motion

Progress Check 23.3

(a) Pressure – when in contact with the opponent Light – to detect the movement/position of the opponent
(b) Actuators will control all movements of the robot – its wheels and various lifting equipment fitted to the robot

Progress Check 23.4

All the movement of the box is controlled by hydraulics which are driven by actuators.

The hydraulic movement is co-ordinated exactly with the action showing on the display screen.

For example a ski-jump at some point will cause movement of the box which convenes to corresponding apparent movement to the customer.

Progress Check 23.5

The modelling of the problem is done entirely by computer software.

Progress Check 23.6

For example, the body can be injected with drugs and the changes to the body recorded.
This is desirable as to actually do this would be dangerous to a actual patient.
Various inputs can be produced and their outputs and effects noted.

Answers to Exam-style Questions

1. (a) A system in which the output is produced quickly enough to affect the next input/current process. A system that reacts fast enough to influence behaviour in the outside world

   (b)
   - ✓ A number of *sensors* stationed around apartment
   - ✓ Temperature/Humidity *sensor* sends temperature/humidity to processor
   - ✓ Use analogue to digital converter to convert the temperature/humidity measurements
   - ✓ Processor decides whether air conditioning system is in operation
   - ✓ Processor compares measured temperature/humidity to required temperature/humidity
   - ✓ If necessary *actuator* is used to adjust settings/turn on cooling/heating/humidifier
   - ✓ Delay before next reading is taken from temperature/humidity sensor//temperature readings are sampled//taking readings is repeated
   - ✓ Sensors on windows to warn if they are open during operation.

   (c) Any suitable real-time or pseudo-real-time application. Examples:
   - ✓ To play a racing game
   - ✓ so that the player can steer the car realistically
   - ✓ Any reservation type system
   - ✓ to prevent double booking.

2.
   (a)
   - ✓ Cost of creating the real thing == Different braking units would need to be built
   - ✓ Time that would be needed to create the real thing == The parameters of the simulated braking system can be changed immediately
   - ✓ Time taken to run the tests == Test time can be greatly reduced
   - ✓ A wide variety of conditions need to be tested == For example, it may be necessary to drive for 100000 miles/at different speeds, this could be simulated
   - ✓ Ability to change conditions immediately == For example, not necessary to transport car to different parts of the world
   - ✓ Extreme case scenarios can be tested == conditions may never occur during real life testing.

   (b)
   Speed
   - ✓ in order to simulate stopping distances
   Weight of car and load
   - ✓ in order to simulate the effects of inertia with different loads
   - ✓ materials used/size of structure used/methods of fixing to car
   - ✓ to try to reduce final cost while still remaining efficient.

   Driving style
   - ✓ gentle braking/hard braking/cornering/reaction time
   Tyres
   - ✓ wear/type of tread/tyre material
   Road surface
   - ✓ roughness/material
   Weather conditions (temperature, wind, precipitation)
   - ✓ in order to replicate different climates…

Chapter 24

Progress Check Answers

Progress Check 24.1

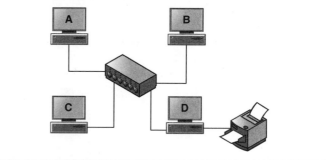

Progress Check 24.2

(a) 3 segments
(b) 2
(c) 168.13.13

Progress Check 24.3

(a) Valid
(b) Invalid (the first byte is a number greater than 255)
(c) Valid (we assume it has been written in binary)

Progress Check 24.4

See the text for the basic definitions.

Answers to Exam-style Questions

1.
   (i)

   ✓ Short distances/Good conductor/Mention of coaxial or twisted pair
   ✓ Used for connecting accounts department computers as they will be on desks and hence cabling is permanent.

   (ii)

   ✓ Allows movement of system around so that user can stay connected to LAN without physical restriction/subject to interception of data
   ✓ Used for connecting computers in warehouses so that they can be moved to area of working.

   (iii)

   ✓ Switch with information about computers on network
   ✓ Used to connect each LAN to internet.

   (iv)

   ✓ Links two LANs/Limits access between the LANs
   ✓ Links the accounts and warehouse LANs while ensuring that confidential accounts details do not become available in the warehouse.

   (v)

   ✓ Alters signal to a form that is suitable for computer/communication medium
   ✓ Used to allow manager separate internet connection via a telephone line.

2.

   ✓ Must safeguard against unauthorised access to the computer system
   ✓ Firewall used to restrict access to known sources

✓ Control access to the network using (accounts/user IDs with) passwords//Procedures in place for authentication
✓ File contents can be encrypted
✓ Procedures in place to protect against malware
✓ All payments/communication can be made through a secure connection
✓ Need to safeguard against bogus websites
✓ Procedures in place for authorisation of resources
✓ Users allocated access rights to various resources// Users have access to certain files/folders only
✓ Files can be password protected/read-only
✓ Users can access the network from certain terminals only/certain times of the day only
✓ Use of digital signatures.

3.
   (a)

   ✓ Networked communication system//Content provided by a web server
   ✓ Probably provided on the Internet
   ✓ Restricted access…
   ✓ to specific members authorised by the health ministry
   ✓ Access is password controlled
   ✓ Content viewed using browser software.

   (b)

   ✓ Limited number of users speeds up access
   ✓ Information being communicated is sensitive/confidential
   ✓ Needs protection from being seen by unauthorised people
   ✓ Information on system will be relevant/easily updated
   ✓ Less information makes it easier to navigate
   ✓ Easier to control who can access the content.

Index

beta testing, 121
    black box testing, 120–121
    white box testing, 121
third normal form (3NF), 205
time-driven simulation, 212
token-ring networks, 39
top-down approach, 54
touch screens, 34, 68
trace table, 122
track index, 23
transaction file, 25
transaction processing, 8
tree terminology, 166–167
tree traversal algorithms, 169
twisted pair cable, 39, 215
two-dimensional array, 19
two's complement, 161

U

Universal Product Code (UPC), 33
universal resource locator (URL), 216
universal serial bus (USB), 40, 214
unwinding, 169

upper bound, 104
user-defined functions, 97
user interface, 72
    required characteristics, 76–77
user interfaces, 9–12
    command line, 11
    form-based interface, 9–10
    graphical user interface (GUI), 10
    menu-driven, 12
    natural language, 11–12
    'WIMP' interface, 10
user manual, 54–55
utility software, 12–13

V

validation checks
    format check, 69, 114
    'from a list' check, 69, 114
    length check, 69, 114
    presence check, 115
    range check, 69, 114
    required entry, 69
    uniqueness check, 69

validation of data, 69, 114–115
variable, 103, 116
    initialising, 117
    scope of, 116
vector graphic program, 64–65
video capture, 68–69, 71
virus checker, 13
visual display unit (VDU), 34
Von Neumann architecture, 154

W

web forms, 67
web servers, 217
White box testing, 121
wide area network (WAN), 38
'WIMP' interface, 10
Windows 7 operating system, 12
wired connection, 214
wireless communication, 216
Word processing software, 5, 63
workgroups, 38
World Wide Web, 217